St. Dunstons in the east
St. Hellen
The Bridge

The Innholders

INNHOLDERS

The Innholders

A History of the Worshipful Company of Innholders

STEPHEN COOTE

Collectors' Books
2002

First published in 2002 by Collectors Books · The Pool House · Kemble Cirencester Gloucestershire · GL7 6AD. ☎ 01285 770239
(An imprint of Dianthus Publishing Limited)

Editorial Direction: Adrian House
Design and production: Christian Brann

ISBN 0-946604-22-3

Illustrations on endpapers: ***a Panorama of London seen across the River Thames from Southwark,*** by C.J. Visscher, 1614
reproduced by courtesy of The Guildhall Library, Corporation of London

Frontispiece: *College Street, looking West towards St. Michael Paternoster,* in 2002.

CONTENTS

ILLUSTRATIONS

Unless otherwise shown, the copyright of these illustrations belongs to The Worshipful Company of Innholders

ACKNOWLEDGEMENTS

I would like to thank the staffs of the Bodleian, Guildhall and London Libraries for their help in gathering information for this book. Stephen Freeth of the Department of Manuscripts of the Guildhall Library kindly read the text and John Fisher and the staff of the Department of Prints and Maps gave generously of their time in tracing records for the illustrations. Copyright illustrations have also been made available by The Royal Collection, The National Portrait Gallery and the Museum of London. Michael O'Sullivan supplied the photographs of the Hall and its treasures.

Many members of the Innholders' Company provided invaluable information and I would like to thank Past-Masters Adrian House and Christian Brann for their care in editing the text, designing the book and researching the illustrations.

September, 2002 Stephen Coote

PREFACE

In 2000 the Court of the Innholders' Company invited Stephen Coote, a historian who has specialised in the 16th and 17th centuries, to write this book with two purposes in mind.

The first was to fill a gap in the Innholders' knowledge of their past. Neither of the previous short histories, published in 1922 and 1962, explored the Livery's roots among the Saxon and medieval guilds, or set its story in the wider context of London, particularly the City and of English inns throughout the ages. As a result many liverymen have never been fully aware of the richness of their heritage or the obligations willingly borne by their predecessors.

The second purpose was to describe the Innholders' remarkable revival in recent years. By 1975 they were sruggling to meet their financial commitments and, in common with many other City Companies, played no part in supporting the trade or craft to which they owed their existence. To restore both their fortunes and their purpose decisive measures were needed and successfully taken.

This informative account of the Livery's colourful history fulfills its double purpose and, in its final pages, sets out the Company's current aspirations – to be worthy of the century ahead and also of the London innkeepers who obtained their first charter nearly five hundred years ago.

September, 2002 *Master and Wardens*

Innholders' Hall
30 College Street
London EC4

TALBOT INN
Tabard now the Talbot Inn, in the High Street, Southwark

Chaucer's Tabard Inn, Southwark, from where his pilgrims set out for Canterbury

PROLOGUE

CHAUCER'S INN

The Canterbury pilgrims – Monasteries and early inns
The Tabard Inn

Let Chaucer set the scene. It is spring around the year 1387 and people from across the length and breadth of England are making their pilgrimage to the shrine of St Thomas à Becket in Canterbury. Many of them have gathered at the Tabard Inn, Southwark. Here, as they will soon discover, they are to be entertained according to the best traditions of English innkeeping.

Among the pilgrims assembled at the Tabard, Chaucer first shows us the courageous but modest Knight who has newly returned from the wars in which he distinguished himself as a shining example of chivalry. At his side is his son, the dashing young Squire, dressed in the height of fashion and skilled in all the arts of the courtly lover. Here too is the demure and ladylike Prioress cuddling her little lap dogs. The Monk and the Friar represent the less seemly side of the medieval Church. They are worldly men, the one passionately given to hunting while the other makes a soft living from those who come to him for confession. The professionals among the pilgrims appear absorbed in their particular interests. The smartly dressed Merchant thinks constantly of money, as does the Doctor of Physic. The unworldly Clerk of Oxford, meek and penniless, is a fountain of scholarship. The vivacious but ageing Wife of Bath is clearly on the lookout for yet another husband. And still there are more: the modest Parson and his humble brother the Ploughman, the skilful if drunken Cook that the five London Guildsmen have brought with them, the ebullient and pleasure loving Franklin or Freeman, the sour-tempered Reeve whose business is to look after a gentleman's estates, and finally those two representatives of the gargoyle side of medieval life – the Summoner and the Pardoner with their repulsive looks and dubious lives. What a marvellously rich and varied cross section of medieval society Chaucer shows us, and how apt it is that they should all meet in a hostelry. What other place could be more sociable, more convivial, more fully human?

Pilgrims such as these, gathering from all parts of the country, would have experienced a wide variety of inns and other places at which to stay during their journeys to London. Many people in medieval English society were on the move and accommodation had to be provided for them. Some might have found shelter for the night in a gentleman's manor house, for the tradition of hospitality to strangers was still very much alive. Chaucer's white bearded Franklin was certainly an enthusiastic advocate of such generosity. Hospitable by nature, he made sure that a passing stranger would always be welcome at his door, and his richly stocked fish ponds, dovecotes and pantry guaranteed that his house veritably 'snowed' with meat and drink.

A large table, groaning with skilfully prepared dishes, stood ready for guests in the great hall of the Franklin's house, for it was the hall that for many centuries had been the focus of hospitality. It was here that the newly arrived guest ate with the lord of the manor at a table placed on a raised platform or dais erected at one end of the room. The retainers of important guests were seated at lower tables ranged along the side walls. The high table would have been covered with fine linen cloths, and careful instructions were issued to butlers to ensure that these valuable items were carefully folded and either kept in a chest or hung from a rod. Indeed, the greater houses required a large number of such servants to officiate at the entertainments provided, the chief steward being responsible for seeing that the servers' livery was neat and clean, while the groom of the hall was in charge of the pages who arranged the elm wood trestle tables and saw to the changing of the rushes that lay strewn on the floor.

Dinner was served at 10 o'clock in the morning. The evening meal began at about five. In the great houses at least guests could enjoy a huge variety of food – fresh and salted fish, all kinds of roast and boiled meat (Chaucer's Franklin seems to have been particularly fond of partridges) along with pies and tarts in plenty, some of them flavoured with the expensive spices that had been introduced from the East by the Crusaders. By the 13th century, wealthier people were acquiring a taste for vegetables, salads and even such exotic dried fruits as raisins, currants, dates and candied orange peel. Often these delicacies were carried in on wooden or pewter serving dishes. Sometimes the guests' plates too were made of pewter, but trenchers of thickly sliced bread were still common.

It was usual for each guest to serve himself with his own knife and then to eat with his fingers and a spoon, tossing the bones and other discarded matter onto the rushes for the dogs - a habit that later came to be considered bad manners. As the mark of a civilised society, manners were highly regarded in the Middle Ages. Chaucer's Prioress was particularly sensitive about them, being careful not to let any of her food fall on her breast or to leave a trace of grease in her cup. Books of manners advised people not to drink with their mouths full, not to blow on food that they found too hot, not to put their elbows on the table, and not to stroke the dogs while the meal was in progress.

When supper and conversation were over, everybody retired to bed. Sometimes there were special rooms set aside for the guests, but in many of the smaller houses visitors would sleep with the master himself in his 'solar' on the first floor. Retainers slept on mattresses spread about the hall.

*

In addition to the hospitality provided by manor houses, monasteries offered accommodation for rich and poor alike. The monks of the Benedictine Order took a major lead in this, building their monasteries to a generally uniform pattern designed to facilitate the entertainment of guests. A large gatehouse gave way to a courtyard on one side of which was the almoner's office while on the other lay the visitors' quarters. The necessary stables, granaries, bake houses and breweries led off the north and south sides of this courtyard. Many Benedictine foundations were also provided with an outer parlour where the monks could receive their visitors. It was not only the Benedictines who provided such hospitality. For the Knights of the Order of St John of Jerusalem the sheltering of travellers was the first of their duties. These men had establishments all over England and were consistently generous to poor travellers in particular, their accounts listing the considerable expenditure they lavished on strangers. The Order was especially generous when it came to entertaining medieval grandees who, nonetheless, so often abused the hospitality they were offered that complaints reached the ears of the king, and Edward I had to issue regulations moderating their behaviour. Edward was nonetheless well aware of the vital social function performed by the Benedictines and the Knights of St John and he tried to make clear that: 'the king intendeth not that the grace of hospitality should be withdrawn from the destitute.'

Eventually, the pressure on religious institutions was acute and it became necessary for the monks to build separate lodging houses for their more prosperous visitors. These they called inns. The word was originally Saxon in origin and meant a chamber or room. Over the course of time it came to acquire two further meanings. First, it was frequently used to describe the London residences of the aristocracy. For example, the town house of the Earls of Warwick was situated in Warwick Lane and came to be known as Warwick Inn. It was clearly an establishment of considerable size, for when Warwick the King-maker came to London in 1458 he was able easily to accommodate 600 of his men there. The usage survives to this day, for Lincoln's Inn and Gray's Inn were once the London mansions of the Earls of Lincoln and the Gray family.

Because of the very large numbers of retainers these great families surrounded themselves with, inns also became synonymous with lodging houses, and for many centuries the Inns of Court were the lodging places of those young men who had come to London to study the law. The provision of food and accommodation was central to all these different types of inn and, to distinguish the true commercial inn from taverns and ale houses, the word will be used here to describe those establishments offering to feed and lodge sojourners and their horses. Similarly, the word 'Innholders' will refer exclusively to members of the Company, while 'innkeeper' refers to those whose business is or was the running of an inn.

As we have seen, the monasteries often took the lead in the building and running of such enterprises. Since they were wealthy and well managed, the monasteries had the considerable capital required to build an inn and, at a time when other forms of urban property speculation would not necessarily provide a reliable investment, they could expect a reasonable return on the money they had laid out. A number of these establishments survive to this day. The beautiful old Star Inn at Alfriston in Sussex, for example, once belonged to nearby Battle Abbey, while the George at Glastonbury was also built by the local monks. The George is a particularly handsome building erected in the second half of the 15th century by Abbot John Selwood whose initials appear prominently on it. The external walls, three storeys high, are built entirely of stone, every inch of which is articulated with finely mullioned windows and carved panels. The building gives one the magnificent sense of prosperity and local pride, while the disposition of the whole suggests its monastic origins.The George is what architectural historians call an inn of the 'gatehouse' type. Just as the Benedictine monasteries were entered by a large central archway and made provision for visitors to the left and right of this, so the main part of the George is distributed along the street to either side of a gateway. Such inns often survive in areas where good building stone is relatively abundant.

In other regions a different form of inn was more common. Frequently timber-framed, the main buildings of the so-called 'courtyard' type lay back from the street and ranged around a galleried yard. A particularly fine example of this is the building once known as the New Inn and still to be seen on the corner of Ship Street and Cornmarket in Oxford. While the George in Glastonbury was an ecclesiastical initiative, the New Inn was a secular speculation. It was built by the wealthy vintner John Gibbes who was five times Mayor of Oxford and owned several other inns across the city. Gibbes probably began work on the building some time in the late 1380's, realising that a large courtyard inn incorporating a number of shops and erected on one of Oxford's main thoroughfares would be a good investment. What finally emerged was an inn built round a long, rectangular courtyard with stone and timber ranges on its north and south sides, and a row of timber-framed shops along Cornmarket to the west. In its medieval heyday, its elaborate gables, bold corner jetty and dragon beam would have marked out the New Inn as a place of comfort and quality among its score of rivals.

The courtyard and the gatehouse inns had a number of features in common. In particular, both made frequent use of internal galleries. The principal purpose of these was to provide independent access to the various upstairs rooms. While in many private houses it was the long-tolerated convention that one room should lead directly to the next, the transitory residents of inns understandably required a greater degree of privacy and security. Many travellers were merchants and would naturally need somewhere to lock up their valuables. Galleries helped to ensure that such people could come and go as they pleased, although the degree of security offered should not be overestimated since many of the rooms in medieval inns were sufficiently large to contain anything up to four beds and could thus accommodate some half-a-dozen people or more. The inn gallery was nonetheless a very long-lived feature and was particularly popular in London.

While little is known about the planning of inns before the late 14th century, it is probable that the earliest inns consisted principally of a large hall with a central, communal fire. By the time that the New Inn at Oxford was being built however the hall had become smaller and less important. This was a general feature of domestic houses as well and was commented on by satirists and others who deplored the relative decline of communal life. What more prosperous people were now requiring was what William Langland, the author of *Piers Ploughman,* described as 'a privy parlour, or a chamber with a chimney'. As this trend developed, so inns began to provide individual rooms furnished with tables, chairs and beds where residents could be served their meals in private. Elsewhere in the inn there would be rooms for the use of non-residents.

It is difficult at this distance of time to determine the precise details of the private accommodation provided, but it seems likely that privies would have been collected together in some comparatively remote part of the building (supplemented perhaps by close-stools in the more important rooms) while portable or hanging lavers, cisterns and stone shoots would have been provided for washing. Many inns also had gardens. These were useful as places where the proprietors could grow herbs, but they were also a pleasant amenity for the guests, and a delightful passage in *The Tale of Beryn* (a continuation of *The Canterbury Tales* by one of Chaucer's many followers) shows those two unlikely fellow travellers, the Prioress and the Wife of Bath, gently idling their time away in one such garden on arriving at their destination. Clearly, lone women felt comparatively safe in these places, and when the Wife and the Prioress have finished their stroll they agree to share a glass of wine in the hostess's parlour. This again was a relatively common practice.

It is clear that by the close of the 14th century such urban inns were becoming comparatively sophisticated establishments, and a small but fascinating quantity of documents allows us to glimpse what guests might have expected from them. Around the year 1415, the writing master William of Kingsmill provided a French conversation manual for his pupils which includes a model dialogue showing six travellers with their three servants and nine horses arriving at what was probably an imaginary Oxford inn. For all that these guests are excited by the news of the English victory at Agincourt, they are exhausted from the dangers of the day's journey during which they have been attacked by robbers. This last was something more than just an exciting little scene put in for the benefit of Kingsmill's pupils. Travelling in medieval England was always an arduous and often a dangerous business. The few roads were invariably in a bad state of repair and in winter were all but impassable. The country was also still densely wooded and the dangerous, muddy tracks that passed for highways often wound through forests infested with robbers. Matters were so bad around St Alban's that the Abbot of the local monastery provided an armed guard for travellers making their way to London. By and large, people rode or walked if they had to journey at all and, like Kingsmill's travellers, often preferred to go about in groups for the sake of safety and companionship.

Once his travellers have arrived at their destination, Kingsmill gives a delightful account of what guests at a medieval inn might find. The ebullient landlord comes out to greet them, asks after the state of their horses, airily remarking he has stabling for a hundred. The tired horses are then led away and provided with straw, hay, horse-bread and oats. The exhausted travellers themselves must next be attended to, and now the hostess of the establishment appears and, after exchanging pleasantries, asks her guests if they would like to go into her hall or up to their chamber. They require her to make a good fire to warm them and then bring bread and ale. Ever the good business woman, she suggests that she send out for exotic wines, but the travellers insist on their first choice and ask what there is for supper. The hostess claims she has every type of cooked bird from swan to starling, along with apples, pears, cheese, eggs and, should the men wish for these things afterwards, 'a good candle and a fair damsel in your bed.'

Kingsmill's hostess is a familiar type and she appears caricatured in a number of medieval carvings and paintings. She is presented as an alluringly naked woman with an elaborate head-dress and carrying a generously proportioned tankard. She is invariably placed with those others of the worldly and the grasping destined for hellfire – usurers, lawyers and the rest. Today perhaps no one can really blame her for wanting to make the maximum from her guests, but profiteering by medieval innkeepers was a widely recognised problem. Complaints about excessive prices eventually reached the ears of Parliament and the king and, in the twenty-third year of the reign of Edward III, the Commons promulgated a statute requiring hostelers to sell food at reasonable prices. The initiative had little effect and, four years later, Parliament had once again to try to put an end to the 'great and outrageous cost of victuals kept up in all the realm by innkeepers and other retailers of victuals, to the . . . detriment of people travelling through the realm.'

For all the hostess's attempts to make her guests part with more money than they really wish to, there are no hard feelings and, after supper, the company sits around drinking and talking before asking the host to make up the bill. This he does by using counters. The guests also arrange that tomorrow morning's breakfast should consist of boar with mustard, beef, mutton and boiled pork. Then, at last, it is time for sleep. The guests are told that their beds have been made up with feather pillows, white sheets, coverlets, blankets and curtains so they can rest untroubled by nightmares. This all sounds very comfortable but it may not have been quite true for English inns were notoriously flea-ridden, and the French conversation manual gives an indication of what many guests might expect. Two rather hard-done-by brothers lament to each other. 'William', says one, 'undress and wash your legs, and then dry them with a cloth, and rub them well for the love of the fleas, that they may not leap on your legs, for there is a peck of them lying in the dust under the rushes .. Hi! The fleas bite me so! and do me great harm, for I have scratched my shoulders until the blood flows!'

*

Let us hope that Chaucer's pilgrims gathered at the Tabard were altogether more comfortably housed. The inn itself was a well-known London establishment, having been built by the Abbot of Hyde in 1307 as a guest house and pilgrim hostelry close to his own palace on Bankside. Southwark was an ideal location since it was situated where the roads from Sussex, Surrey and Hampshire met the Dover Road or Pilgrims' Way. In addition, the area was notoriously free from the jurisdiction of the City and the strict hosting laws that applied there. Indeed, Southwark had a reputation as a raffish and bohemian area, and many innkeepers took advantage of its freedoms to run their businesses there. The poll tax return of 1381 lists some twenty two people involved in the trade, a dozen of whom were located along the High Street. Competition ensured high standards, and Chaucer himself tells us that the rooms and stables at the Tabard were all generously proportioned. This long continued to be the case, and a lease on the Tabard drawn up in 1538 mentions glazed and latticed windows, a drinking bower and two parlours, one of which, after the fashion of the day, was called the Rose. Access to the street was controlled by a 'great gate', and close to this would have been found the inn's splendid sign.

These early inn signs were often elaborately fashioned, for not only was it a legal requirement to display them but they were, of course, an important form of advertising. Often they were suspended from an iron bar attached to the front wall or displayed on a post standing immediately outside. In either case, the most elaborate metal work gave them an added dignity while, in some provincial towns where there was sufficient room, the sign was suspended from a sort of triumphal arch spanning the road. So much pride was invested in these signs, and so closely were they associated with the inn itself that, when a disreputable innkeeper lost his licence, his humiliation was symbolised by the pulling down of his sign.

There was no fear of this happening while Chaucer's Host was in charge of the Tabard. Harry Bayley is a glorious character, the archetypal innkeeper. The nomenclature of his trade was already old by his day. The earliest use of the word 'host' dates from 1254. The more common form 'hosteler' was already in use by 1204, while the frequently used term 'herbergeour' can be found as early as 1184, denoting the provider of a 'herberge' or shelter. Harbingers were the officers who preceded the sovereign and the greater nobility in order to secure them a lodging or 'herberge'. The first use of the word 'innholder' comes from a while later and apparently dates from 1394.

All of this suggests that long tradition and experience lay behind Harry Bayley's expertise, but Chaucer makes it clear that he was also a man by temperament perfectly suited to his trade. The sheer ebullience of Harry's character makes him a natural leader, but he is far from being irksomely overbearing. Chaucer describes him as seemly, shrewd, well-mannered and manly. Harry Bayley is also an excellent business man. He makes all of his guests, even the most retiring, feel welcome, and a fine supper is served without the least difficulty. Here, we feel, is a first-class establishment.

Such qualities have made Harry Bayley a prosperous man and he walks through London with a confidence that wholly becomes him. This was indeed the case, for if the Host of the Tabard was one of Chaucer's most convincing and enduringly recognisable characters, he was also an historical figure, just as the Tabard was a real inn. The records allow us to know quite a lot about him. He was clearly a man held in considerable regard for he had been chosen in 1376-7, and again in a 1378-9, to represent Southwark in the parliaments that were called in those years. In a Subsidy Roll for 1380-81 he is described as an 'ostler', while in 1392, and again the following year, he was appointed a special coroner at two murder enquiries. Such a coroner had to be a selected 'of the most lawful and wisest knights, who can, may, and will best attend upon that office'.

A short walk from the Tabard brought Harry Bailey to the south bank of the Thames which was spanned by one of the engineering wonders of the medieval world: London Bridge. With its nineteen arches rising from massive piers, the bridge was the mightiest stone building of its kind to have been erected since Roman times. Crowded on either side with houses and shops, the bridge led across to the City on the north bank. It was an essential part of the City's defences, as were the Roman walls pierced with seven gateways. At the eastern end, the walls terminated with the forbidding bulk of the Tower of London. Upstream from the bridge lay the busy quays : Dowgate, Broken Wharf and Queenhithe. Higher up still, as far as Westminster, the north bank of the Thames was lined by the fabulous palaces of the nobility.

Meanwhile, above the warren of narrow, dirty and bustling streets of the City, the towers and spires of a hundred churches reached to the sky only to be dominated by the massive bulk of Old St Paul's. Built close to the booths and warehouses of Cheapside market, the cathedral was obliged to perform a double service as both a temple of prayer and a place where Londoners conducted their never-ceasing business. Here were hucksters hawking their wares, businessmen shaking hands over deals, and licensed journeymen of the all-important guilds anxiously offering their services for hire. London – busy, self-confident and thrusting – was a natural focus of trade, and people from all over the country and abroad were inevitably attracted to the City and required inns for their lodging places. In such an atmosphere as this the London innkeepers flourished.

Chapter 1

FOUNDATIONS

54BC – 1399AD

Roman London – the Saxons – the Normans – Guilds and patron saints

Medieval London was, in origin, a Roman city. Harry Bayley may have heard of Caesar's expedition to Britain in 54 BC but it is improbable that he knew about the invasion launched by the Emperor Claudius in 43 AD. Then, 40,000 legionaries assailed the native Celts and, within a decade, established a flourishing outpost of empire.

London, or the Romans' Londinium, was ideally situated as a base for such activity, and as the communications centre for their colony. A pontoon bridge linked the two banks of the Thames here, at a point some fifty yards to the east of the modern London Bridge, as close to the sea as was feasible. The estuary below it flowed out into the North Sea, opposite the mouth of that artery of western trade, the Rhine, which connected some of the other great trading cities of the Roman empire. London thus became a natural focus for the empire's sea-borne trade, and a network of highways soon connected it to key Roman settlements across the country. As a result, the city gradually became, in the words of the Roman historian Tacitus: 'filled with traders and a celebrated centre of commerce'.

Such traders, travelling to and from London, necessarily required accommodation during their journeys and a small but interesting quantity of information survives to reveal what the very earliest English inns or *diversoria* were like. That they could be elaborate affairs is suggested by excavations at Silchester, a Roman town just South of modern Reading where the roads from Cirencester, Exeter, Dorchester and Winchester all converged. The model for the inn at Silchester appears to have been the traditional Roman villa. Like them, it was built around a pair of courtyards. The first of these opened off the road, and the weary traveller would immediately have been confronted by the dining room that lay opposite the main entrance block. The other two sides of this first courtyard were occupied by the sleeping quarters and the kitchen respectively. The fires that fuelled the kitchen also served to heat that typically Roman necessity, a series of bathrooms in which a traveller could relax, tone his muscles and clean himself after a hard day's journey. With this done, he could then idle some of his time away in the second courtyard which was an enclosed garden surrounded by a colonnaded walkway. A good meal, accompanied perhaps by locally grown wine, might then be followed by a game of chess, the chequered board of which often served as an inn sign to attract travellers on the long roads.

All of these principal roads led to London, and it was against the prosperous capital that Boudicca – despoiled of her lands and humiliated by her Roman overlords - launched her terrible anger in 60 AD. She razed the metropolis to the ground. Such was the commercial importance of London however that the capital was swiftly rebuilt. The new London became a major city honoured with imperial rank and graced not only by a new bridge, harbour and extensive waterfront buildings, but by an amphitheatre, public baths, a forum, and what was probably the provincial governor's Palace, erected on the site now occupied by Cannon Street Station.

By the time of the Emperor Hadrian's visit in 122 AD, London had also become a considerable industrial centre. Much of this work centred on the valley of the Walbrook. This originally sizeable stream was Roman London's main fresh water supply but it is now entirely covered over. Excavations conducted in 1989, when an extensive refurbishment of the Company's Hall was taking place, revealed in the area now housing the lift some demolition debris and refuse deposited in late Roman times, in order to raise and stabilise the Walbrook's eastern bank. In addition, a small wooden drain, one plank in depth, was also uncovered. This probably served to draw off excess moisture from the surrounding waterlogged area and so prepare the ground for use. The present 17th century Hall of the Innholders Company thus has its foundations on an historic site. The south wall stands over the foundations of the Roman quay along the then north bank of the Thames, while the west wall, at right angles, stands on the east bank of the Walbrook, where it flowed into the Thames.

For all the evident signs of London's prosperity and civilisation, the outbreak of a disastrous fire a few years after the Emperor Hadrian's visit marked the slow but progressive decline of London from its Roman heyday. The city's status as a major focus of trade within the province and with the empire at large began to decline, and there was a drastic reduction in the capital's population, perhaps due to plague. That London nonetheless remained of great strategic importance is suggested by the building of its immense defensive wall somewhere between 190 and 225 AD. Constructed principally of Kentish ragstone, the wall was two miles in length, nine feet thick and twenty one feet high. So massive a structure profoundly influenced the future layout of the metropolis and helped shape its political and military importance. Above all, encircling a site of 330 acres, the wall defined the boundaries of the City of London and thus the nature and scope of its civic and administrative institutions.

This influence can be felt up to the present time but, during the second and third centuries, all was far from well within London's wall. Accelerating decline was symbolised by physical deterioration. The Roman forum, the basilica and the governor's palace were all demolished. The embankments of the Walbrook stream collapsed. Disorder and decay in the empire at large led to the disintegration of London itself and, in 296, the Emperor Constantius (father of Constantine the Great) was obliged to reinforce the city against mounting barbarian threats. But London was not proof against this menace and, in a gesture of political despair, Roman troops were withdrawn in 410.

*

The increasingly victorious Saxon invaders had no sophisticated sense of civic life, and it would be nearly five bleak centuries before military, political and commercial initiatives brought London back to prosperous life as what the Venerable Bede, in the 8th century, called 'the mart of many nations'. Very little is known about the intervening centuries until Alfred the Great regained the City for law and order in 886, rebuilt its walls and organised its citizens into an effective fighting force. Later Scandinavian threats ensured that this citizen militia was kept in constant readiness, entailing an organisational system which divided the city into wards, each of them administered by an elder or Alderman who was responsible for ensuring military preparedness. These fighting forces were sufficiently effective to ensure that when, in 1016, King Cnut became the monarch of all England, Londoners could 'welcome' him into their city rather than abjectly surrender to him. They were obliged to pay their new ruler a vast sum in tribute, but it was the energetic young Cnut who now fostered the development of London so that it finally and permanently replaced Winchester as the nation's capital.

Saxon London meanwhile began evolving its own distinctive administrative institutions. In addition to ward meetings, the entire body of London's citizens met three times a year at the so-called folkmoot, later known as the Great Assembly. Here they would be informed of royal decisions by the king's 'portreeve' who was also responsible for tolls and the daily administration of justice, and whose office may have been the origin of the Sheriffs who emerged more fully later on. Similarly, the increasingly powerful Aldermen of the City wards were responsible not only for defence but for the collection of taxes. They also presided over the local court or wardmoot. Finally, there was a bench of the principal local citizens called the Court of Husting which managed general administrative and legal business under the supervision of royal officials known as 'stallers'.

In addition to such institutions as these, the citizens of Saxon London also associated for various defensive, religious, charitable and trading purposes, and herein lies the origin of the guilds. The laws of Alfred the Great refer to bands of people known collectively as *gegildan,* and if the precise terms on which they came together are no longer clear it is evident from the ways in which the laws were framed that members of these early guilds recognised mutual responsibilities that were legally enforceable. Often such associations had important civic functions. For example, the so-called *cnihtengild* was originally a group of thirteen military men who appear to have taken on responsibility for defending the eastern side of the City of London from Scandinavian invaders. The association seems to have attracted people of influence and to have included a significant measure of religious practice amongst its aims. Such a mixture of piety, privilege and responsibility became increasingly characteristic of these organisations and many ancient Saxon customs would later characterise the functioning of the more familiar trade guilds, such as the Innholders, who regulated the City's business.

Saxon London was thus a strong, thriving and well organised city, and one far too important to be arbitrarily crushed by William the Conqueror after the Battle of Hastings.

*

William I recognised that he needed to woo and support London, and early in his reign he granted it a charter guaranteeing its privileges and promising that he himself would not 'suffer that any man offer you any wrong'. It is clear that the thriving capital city soon developed a self-conscious civic pride and, in 1183, the monastic writer William Fitz-Stephen declared with pardonable exaggeration that London was 'happy in the healthiness of its air, in the Christian religion, in the strength of its defences, the nature of its site, the honour of its citizens, the modesty of its matrons', adding that it was also 'pleasant in sports' and 'fruitful of noble men'. The only disadvantages under which the capital laboured, as far as Fitz-Stephen could see, were 'the immoderate drinking of fools and the frequency of fires'.

The self-confident citizens of Norman London were aiming at a considerable degree of autonomy, and this was enhanced in 1191 when, in return for their loyalty to the king, the City was granted the status of a 'commune'. Such a form of self-government was relatively familiar on the mainland of Europe where, often in response to some crisis, the townsfolk drew together in sworn associations devoted to their common good. This usually resulted in the creation of a new municipal magistrate: the Mayor. London followed this pattern, the first Lord Mayor of London being Henry FitzAlwin, a senior Alderman appointed in 1192 to a post he held for nineteen years.

The twenty five Aldermen from among whose number FitzAlwin was chosen were now emerging as the principal force in the City's public life, their Court coming into full dominance during the 13th century when 'five and twenty of the more discreet men of the City were sworn to take counsel on behalf of the City, together with the Mayor'. As magistrates, they were men to be held in the gravest respect and indeed remain such for, to this day, all Aldermen are Justices of Peace who sit in judgement in the Mansion House and appoint the Magistrates' Clerks there. Dressed on ceremonial occasions in their scarlet robes (as now) and on other days wearing a distinctively cut hood, they were to be addressed as 'gracious', 'wise', or 'worshipful'. Once elected, the Aldermen could only be removed from office by the Lord Mayor acting in concert with the king. In these days, before the formation of the Court of Common Council, the Aldermen were, to all intents and purposes, a self-perpetuating oligarchy who neither individually nor collectively owed any responsibility to the ordinary people they governed. However, they appear to have exercised their magisterial role with considerable discretion and care for the well-being of the civic community, including the regulation of the city's craftsmen and tradesmen.

*

Certainly, the Aldermen kept a watchful eye on the City's innkeepers who, as early as 1327, had joined together in a trade association known as the Hostelers and Haymongers, the body from which the present day

Innholders were eventually to derive. Along with the Crown, the Aldermen were determined to see that these men were upright people and that some degree of control was exercised over their customers.

It was a point of law that nobody could keep a hostel within the City limits save those 'who are Freemen of the City, or who can produce a good character from the place whence they have come'. Being a Freeman of London was a privilege of the utmost importance and one that eventually became the almost exclusive right of the guilds to confirm. Freedom of the City showed a man to be a person of standing, somebody who was trustworthy and competent, somebody the City authorities believed could be relied upon to fulfil his public duties and who, in return, could be granted the privilege of buying and selling goods within the City limits and exercising a range of political rights there. In particular, it was agreed that the Freemen of the wards should have the right to elect two men who could make ordinances for the whole community. From these elected officials the Court of Common Council would gradually emerge and very slowly acquire those legal, administrative and financial powers which, over the centuries, would allow this body to supersede the Court of Aldermen as the City's main instrument of government.

Confining the keeping of a hostelry to men of standing like Freemen was long to be an important theme in the history of London innkeeping. So too was the altogether more difficult matter of keeping a check on those who used London's inns, and it was early decreed that a search was to be made 'by the Aldermen and two of the best men of their ward touching those who keep hostels and those residing in them . . . that they may know who and of what kind or condition they may be'. The Aldermen were also concerned that where strangers and drink met together there might be violence and they required 'that hostellers warn their guests to lay aside their arms on entering their hostels'. It was later considered necessary to repeat this order for there were those among the innkeeping fraternity in London who refused to acknowledge the ruling with quite the degree of respect it deserved. In the late 14th century, for example, Adam Grymmesby 'was committed to prison for not warning his lodger to leave his knife indoors, for which neglect the knife was confiscated, and when the said Adam was asked to redeem it, he refused, and showed contempt for the Mayor's summons to appear, saying he would come next day'. The innkeepers of medieval London could be an independent-minded lot, and some of them were not above sailing on the windy side of the law.

For example, they infringed the monopoly of the Bakers and betrayed city regulations when they took to baking bread in their own premises and attempting to sell it to their guests at one halfpenny per loaf, whereas four such loaves are really not worth a penny'. The Aldermen consequently decreed that the City bakers alone had the right to sell bread and that this should have the correct assize mark. And when the innkeepers slipped across to Southwark to buy cheap horse food, prices for hay were fixed at no more than twopence a horse for a night and a day while, for a bushel of oats, the City's innkeepers were 'to gain sixpence and no more'.

London innkeeping could at times therefore appear something of a national scandal. Certainly it was thought so at court, for when Edward III summoned a session of Parliament in the hope of raising money for his interminable French wars, the Lord Mayor and Aldermen issued a proclamation declaring that a great number of the Lords and Commons would be staying in London for as long as the session lasted and that they did not wish such people to be 'subjected to outrageous demands for the price of victuals'. A list of acceptable prices was drawn up.

The authorities further insisted that innkeepers were not to keep their businesses open after 10 o'clock at night. Finally, innkeepers also had special responsibilities when there were scares of a French invasion or civic disorder. The Aldermen were required to 'keep the names of hostelers in their wards, and cause each inhabitant to swear that he will be ready with his harness [i.e. armour] to maintain the peace, if affray arise'.

*

There was a further dimension to the values and customs binding these early innkeepers which derived from two institutions embedded in the very heart of medieval life: the parish and trade guilds, both of which had developed from the Saxon *gegildan.*

There were more than 150 parish guilds spread across the capital and these provided the opportunity for their members to enhance their piety and charitable interests. Each focused around the cultivation of a particular saint or devotional practice, and was actively concerned with the accumulation of property and funds which could be devoted to the upkeep and beautification of its place of worship or to the gift of alms to members who had fallen on hard times. These activities required a considerable amount of administration, and regular quarterly meetings were held to transact the necessary business. Again, just as the rules of the *gegildan* had been enforceable at law, so those of the parish guilds were underwritten by the church courts.

In much the same way the trade guilds, whose responsibility was the regulation of a particular craft, also took advantage of their status as religious fraternities to give charitable support of their members. There was the 'Fraternity of the Blessed Mary the Virgin, of the Mystery of Drapers', for example. There was also 'the Guild . . . of the Skinners of London, to the Honour of God, and the Precious Body of our Lord Jesus Christ'. Later the first charter granted to the innkeepers described them as 'a certain fraternity or guild to the honour of Saint Julian'.

*

The veneration of the saints was a central aspect of medieval religious life. Their stories were commemorated in the annual cycle of the liturgy and they were richly the subjects of art. Walls and elaborately painted rood screens portrayed saints' lives, their exultations and despairs. Protected in elaborately carved niches or standing in proud, polychromed glory on brackets in naves and chancels, statues of the saints were loved in the Middle Ages as perhaps never before. Over fifty days of the working year were set aside for their adoration, and people were expected to fast on the eve of a saint's day and then to attend matins, mass and evensong on the anniversary itself.

For parish and trade guilds alike, the feast day of their patron saint was the high-point of the communal year. It began with 'the whole company of the fellowship' going in solemn procession to their church where mass would be celebrated before their special altar and benefactors would be commemorated. This was an imposing occasion, an expression at one and the same time of the worldly power and magnificence of the guild and of its spirituality. Here, above all, was a visible manifestation of that sense of fraternity, of lives lived and regulated for the common good, which underlay the very existence of the guilds. That the patron saint's day was regarded as an occasion of the greatest importance is suggested by the fact that those who failed to attend without a good reason would be fined for their apparent disregard.

Then, after mass, the company would return to whatever hall it owned or rented and the secular business of the day would begin. First, an official would read out the ordinances or rules of the guild, a process which in some cases could take a considerable time. This would be followed by the election of that year's officers, the approval of any new ordinances that might be considered necessary, and perhaps the airing of controversial issues. After this, the day would be concluded by the rank-and-file members of the company being offered refreshments while the senior figures would go off to dine, content in the knowledge that they had honoured both their fellowship and the patron saint who protected and inspired it.

To the people of the middle ages the saints were above all examples of the grace, love and redemption that should flourish between heaven and earth in a Christian society. St Julian, the patron saint of the Innholders, fitted this last category exactly. Scholars now believe that the St Julian of medieval legend was not a historical figure but a composite character fashioned to conform with a taste for melodrama, pathos and the miraculous. France in particular was early concerned in his creation, and windows in

The carved statuette of St. Julian in the reception room of the Innholders' Hall

the cathedrals of Chartres and Rouen witness to his popularity there as, for this country, does the beguilingly naive versification of *The South English Legendary.*

The hero of the legend begins as the amiable young son of devoted parents who likes nothing more than to spend his time hunting. One day, deep in a forest, he corners a stag which, apparently on the point of death, turns to Julian and miraculously and terrifyingly prophesies that he will kill both his parents. In the vain effort to avoid so terrible a fate, Julian flees far away, serves with great distinction under a foreign prince, and eventually marries. His loving parents in the meantime have wholly given over their lives to finding their son and in time come to the place where Julian is living.

A hideous series of misunderstandings now leads Julian to believe that his wife has betrayed him and then to the long-prophesied murder of his parents. In the agony of accidental crime revealed, Julian devotes the rest of his life to severe penitence and conspicuous charity. He sets up a hospital or inn close to where travellers must ford a dangerous river. For many years he labours in humble-hearted poverty until, one bitterly cold night, he hears a leper calling out to him and goes to his aid. Julian takes the suffering man to his inn and there, as he is ministering to his wants, the stranger is suddenly transformed into an angel who tells Julian that Christ has now received his penance. Julian himself soon afterwards dies and is received into the heavenly company of the blessed, while the memory of his merit is perpetuated on earth under the title of St Julian the Hospitaller. The legend, turning as it does around the spiritual rewards to be gained from the care of strangers, is ideally suited to the trade of innkeeping, and suggests that charity is altogether more important than profit in the enriching of human life.

The story of St Julian reminded medieval London innkeepers of their duties towards the living, but their guild was also concerned with what they conceived as their responsibilities towards the dead. Just as the parish guilds made extensive provision for the funerals of their departed brethren, so too did the trade guilds. Death was a very public event in the Middle Ages. The mournful tolling of the funeral bell alerted the neighbourhood to an imminent passing and there were well known rites and rituals when it came to laying out the body, watching over it, carrying it to church and placing it before the altar in preparation for the celebration of the Office of the Dead. Guilds would participate in all these ceremonies, but the responsibilities of the living did not end there.

Only the truly virtuous, those wholly purged of every trace of sin, might hope to be admitted immediately into the bliss of heaven. A deathbed confession could save a parting soul from the eternal agonies of Hell, but the great mass of ordinarily erring mortals could expect to spend an unspecified time atoning for their sins amid the pains of Purgatory. The living imagined a strong sense of community with these suffering souls for they were 'your late acquaintance, kindred, spouses, companions, play fellows, and friends.' To fail to pray for them was an act of the greatest cruelty and a denial of one of the principal reasons why people gathered together in guilds in the first place. Hence the emphasis placed by the guilds on the fraternity of their dead. Many people would leave money in their wills so that priests could be hired to offer prayers for the well-being of their souls, and sometimes this money was administered by the guild the deceased had belonged to.

*

It is clear from this evidence that medieval guilds recognised the responsibility to tend for their members' body and soul, but how was it that trade guilds like that of the innkeepers also acquired a quite extraordinary degree of control over not only their members' working lives but also their political rights? Something of the origins of this process can be found in the increasing responsibilities of the early folkmoots. These citizen meetings were held three times a year – at Michaelmas, Christmas and Midsummer – and any Londoner who failed to attend three times in succession incurred a hefty fine payable to the king. In addition to hearing royal commands from the Sheriffs and organising such necessities as fire protection, the folkmoots were also acquiring various legal functions, including the elementary regulation of trade.

As the quantity of business increased so the king's representative at the folkmoots started to meet with each trade separately. The Bakers and Fishmongers were particularly involved in this process, the first holding four annual meetings or courts to settle matters arising from their business, while the Fishmongers held two such sessions. Eventually these courts began to meet weekly and to secure for themselves a number of the functions usually exercised by a court of public law. Meanwhile, other groups such as the Weavers acquired the power to regulate their trade through the granting of a royal charter. This set an important precedent and, by the close of the 14th century, a number of leading London trades had followed the Weavers' example and were incorporated under royal charter. These chartered guilds included the Goldsmiths, the Merchant Taylors, the Skinners and the Mercers.

The guilds thus acquired exclusive control over who conducted business in the City and they insisted that only native born Londoners – people who had the freedom of the City which they alone could grant – should practise a trade there. Freemen were given their status by their identification with their guild, and legal documents named the craft to which a man belonged. Membership of a guild thus became evidence that he was not one of the *inferiores,* but a figure of probity, one of the *bons gens.* Such a man had given proof that he had a sound reputation and was capable of earning his own livelihood. If he had spent the years of his adolescence as an apprentice to a citizen then his master's sponsorship was sufficient for his receiving the freedom. This could also be acquired by patrimony, that is through his family. Lastly, if a man was seeking the freedom by redemption (that is, by purchase) then six solid citizens had to stand surety for him. In addition, the would-be Freeman also had to give assurances of his political rectitude by taking an oath of loyalty to the king and the City government.

Armed with such powers as these, the guilds were now becoming an established force in London life and their corporate power and pride was greatly enhanced by their being given the right to search the premises of their members for examples of defective workmanship and illicit practices, both of which they could punish in their own courts. The Wardens of the Goldsmiths' Company were empowered by Edward III, for example, to visit the shops of the craftsmen of their guild to test the quality of the gold and silver used by rubbing it on a touchstone. Anything made out of materials of less than adequate quality was to be forfeited to the king. Such a rule clearly provided that the work of members of the guild should be of a high standard and that its reputation should be founded on recognised levels of quality and skill.

But the Wardens' aims were also protectionist. For example, no goldsmith was to take on an apprentice without the assent of the Wardens of the guild. In other words, no craftsman was to grow so big that his business threatened his brethrens' share of the market. It was also a commonplace of medieval economic thinking that, as far as possible, everything should be produced in the local area by local people and, to this end, the Goldsmiths acquired the right of veto over any foreign (i.e. non-native) practitioner of the craft working in the City or seeking admission to its freedom. What they sought, in other words, was a monopoly, and this can be seen particularly clearly in the case of the founding fathers of the Innholders' Company, that association of London's Hostelers and Haymongers dating from at least 1327.

It was in that year, and in order to protect their trade, that these men petitioned the Lord Mayor and the Aldermen for legal help in stamping out competition from 'foreigners'. The words of the earliest document concerning the Innholders' origins are worth quoting. It was the Hostelers and Haymongers' case that:

> whereas they used to buy hay to serve our Lord the King [Edward III] and the great people of the land and the common folks coming and repairing to the same city, there now come foreign folks, and bring the hay in ships to divers quays in the City, and whereas they were wont to sell their hay

> upon the water and not elsewhere they now stow away in houses, gardens, and other places, just as though they were free of the City, and also that foreign folk who bring their hay by land in carts ought to sell their hay by the whole cartload or by trusses, and that before the hour of noon; they now bring their carts laden with dozens of small boteles [bundles] powdered with dust and other refuse, and sell it for halfpennies and farthings, and stay to sell it at their own will.

The Hostelers and Haymongers prayed for redress 'as the foreigners will be in better plight than those that are denizens and free of the City, and are charged towards rating the same'. The petition was favourably received and inspectors were appointed to prevent 'foreigners' intruding from outside London or abroad. This idea of protecting their trade and profits will be a constant theme in the early history of the Innholders' Company.

*

The greater guilds were not only fiercely and sometimes violently competitive with each other but were occasionally confronted by threats of an altogether more dangerous nature. On 13 June, 1381, the City faced the threat of the Peasants' Revolt.

This was a time of bitter disaffection across the whole of South East England. The terrible contagion known as the Black Death had swept across it resulting in the deaths of thousands. For a generation, there was a shortage of labour so serious that the burdens and restraints of the old feudal ties grew intolerable. Hatred between landlords and tenants became so bitter that confrontation was inevitable, and the working people of London joined the rebels' cause. When disaffected and angry peasants from Kent and Essex streamed into London and swarmed through the City, pandemonium ensued. Palaces were looted, Richard II was obliged to take refuge in the Tower, and nearly three dozen Flemish merchants were murdered, along with more than a hundred leading citizens including the Treasurer and the Archbishop of Canterbury. At a critical moment King Richard – at the time a boy of merely fourteen – rode out to mollify a contingent of rebels under their leader Wat Tyler at Smithfield. But Wat Tyler became so aggressive that the Lord Mayor, William Walworth, fatally stabbed him and the King succeeded in dispersing his followers. The worst of the violence seemed over but resentment was far from dead.

In October 1381 the enigmatic and machiavellian John of Northampton succeeded Walworth as Lord Mayor. He held the position for two years, ensuring a continuing support partly by a careful use of his influence at court, partly by appealing to the still smouldering popular resentment that had led to the Peasants' Revolt, and partly by the use of armed retainers. This so worried the leading men of the City that, in the election of 1383, they ensured that Northampton was ousted in favour of the more conservative Nicholas Brembre, a member of the Grocers' Company. With the enthusiastic support of the greater merchants, Brembre saw that power and influence were returned to the Aldermen who were also members of the greater guilds. The government of the City was thus once again in the hands of 'men qualified by means and understanding' rather than those of the lesser crafts. That alliance between the guild magnates and the forces of law and order which was to characterise London for the next three centuries was now being formed.

Among the groups that Brembre and his colleagues were determined to bring to heel were the London innkeepers whose premises – public places where men and alcohol came together – could easily be seen as conducive to disorder. The City's hostelries had always been supervised with a careful eye and now (especially since one of the leaders of the Peasants' Revolt had set up his headquarters in the White Hart in Southwark) Brembre and the Court of Aldermen decided to clamp down on them all. An incomplete list of the capital's inns made in 1384 lists some 197 of these establishments, to whom Brembre's officers rehearsed their familiar objections. Delivering their judgement in medieval French, they declared:

> Whereas larcenies and divers ill deeds are commonly perpetrated more openly, notoriously and frequently in this present than in past times in the City of London, its suburbs and neighbourhood, which would not have been possible if the thieves and evildoers had not been maintained and harboured by persons dwelling in the City and suburbs and residing with innkeepers, who cared little what kind of men they received, to the great damage of the citizens of the City and of those repairing there and to the great disgrace and scandal of the same, and in order to prevent such a damage and scandal, it was agreed by Sir Nicholas Brembre, Mayor, and the Aldermen that all innkeepers within the liberty [i.e. the City] should be sworn to harbour no one longer than a day and a night, unless they were willing to answer for them and their acts, or to receive to their tables any strangers called travaillyngmen [i.e. wayfarers] or others, unless they had good and sufficient surety from them for their good and loyal behaviour, under penalty of answering for their actions and paying £100 to the Chamber for the use of the commonalty, if they were convicted of offending in either of the two above-mentioned points, and further that the said innkeepers should be sworn to inform the Mayor if they had knowledge of any innkeeper or others harbouring men of ill fame or persons suspected of larceny.

There was probably an element of overstatement in all of this, but London inns were far from being free of crime, and hostelers paid dearly when it could be proved that they had fallen short of the standards expected of them.

However, profound change was taking place across the country at large, and in London the City fathers were no longer minded to tolerate the shortcomings and increasingly arbitrary behaviour of Richard II and Brembre. They therefore sided with those magnates who supported

Henry of Lancaster in the war that led to Richard's deposition and the accession of Lancaster himself as Henry IV. After his victory the leaders of London, the City's chief guildsmen, willingly accepted the newly victorious Henry as their king. For the next 250 years the City would largely be guided in the ways of wealth and stability by such an alliance between the liveries and the Crown. In such a world as this the Innholders would flourish.

* * *

Chapter 2

THE FIRST CHARTER

1399 – 1530

The first Liveries – the composition of a Livery –
the regulation of inns
Henry VIII grants the Innholders a charter

The Aldermen of the late middle ages were all too painfully aware that any failure to preserve the highest standards of law and order would result in royal displeasure and the consequent loss of the City's liberties. In the attempt to erase memories of Northampton and Brembre's controversial periods of influence the citizens of London were forbidden for the honour of God and the good of the realm openly to discuss their political opinions, and those caught doing so were subject to a year's imprisonment in Newgate. Gradually, the silenced populace came to accept these conditions and even to welcome them. To such 15th century commentators on London's political life as John Carpenter (whose charitable bequest helped fund the new City of London School in 1837) experiment was a deeply dangerous and divisive folly to be avoided at all costs. The old ways were the best ways and the great men had the greatest wisdom. It was essential, Carpenter believed, to present a strong and united face to the potentially hostile Crown and it seemed best to him at least that those who dissented from the City authorities should be disenfranchised along with their heirs forever. Quiet acceptance of things as they were was the surest means of preserving a prosperous security.

A similar hardening of attitudes and a similar acceptance of hierarchy can be seen among the guilds. They too recognised that it was ever more necessary to present themselves as embodiments of the utmost respectability, organisations in which the great, the good and the prosperous were firmly in control. To this end, the 15th century saw many of the guilds dividing their membership into those who were entitled to wear an official livery in the company colours and those who were not. The liveried members of the guild were those able to pay the dues that were charged and it was these wealthier and more successful men who increasingly tended to have an option on the guild's offices. It became their practice to withdraw into quarterly meetings to discuss the company's affairs away from the presence of their lesser brethren. They also had extensive political privileges. In particular, they and the members of the Court of Common Council eventually acquired the sole right to elect the Lord Mayor, one of the sheriffs and later the City's Members of Parliament.

The wearing of a livery by these men was no mere ornamental matter. This was a flamboyant age and the dress of all sorts and conditions of people reflected their status. Magnates moved through their palaces to the tinkling of the little bells sewn on their hoods and sleeves; samite, silk and velvet were often chosen and frequently encrusted with gold thread. The best robes of even the lesser merchants were always furred and Chaucer's Merchant (for all he was in debt) went on his pilgrimage in an expensive fur hat. Similarly, the five guildsmen on the pilgrimage proudly disport themselves in new clothes, girdles and pouches, and carry little knives expensively capped with silver rather than the more commonplace brass.

Such conspicuous display was apt to cause problems for the authorities. Elaborate sumptuary legislation was therefore introduced in 1363 in an effort to control the situation. Only the very wealthiest were permitted to wear ermine, silk was allowed to the greater merchants, while cheaper materials were to be worn by lesser citizens. Such regulations were highly impractical and needed frequently to be revised. Nonetheless, they indicate a way of thinking that preoccupied medieval minds and suggest how the wearing of a livery by the senior members of a guild was the outward sign of a profoundly important social difference, especially on great occasions such as funerals and the annual feasts.

The livery clothing was generally made under the direction of the

Master and Wardens and was bought by the members at cost price. It consisted of two parts: the gown and the hood. Occasionally a distinction was made between those who could wear only the hood and those who could wear the whole suit, but this was not an invariable rule. At the beginning of the 15th century a full suit cost about 15s or 16s, while the hood on its own cost some 2s 6d. Such liveries were almost invariably of two colours, and it is probable that the colours eventually chosen by the Innholders were blue and white. The liveries made a fine show, and the London historian John Stow had particularly fond memories of the liverymen's hoods and described how they were worn by these figures: 'the roundlets upon their heads, the skirts to hang behind them at their necks to keep them warm, the tippet to lie on their shoulder or to wind about their necks'. Such pageantry made a lasting impression.

*

A wide range of responsibilities fell to these liveried members of the company. The guild's reputation for high quality and honest dealing lay in their hands and they were responsible for searching members' premises and detecting faulty goods and sharp practices. In addition to this they were in charge of the distribution of alms and the advance of loans to members who required them. The administration of chantries and charitable foundations similarly fell under their remit. Finally, it was the duty of the liverymen to summon contentious brethren before them and arbitrate in any disputes that may have arisen or to discipline those who had infringed the rules. Punishments could be severe, particularly when the offence concerned the dignity of the guild and its senior members. One fifteenth-century goldsmith was obliged to abase himself on his knees in front of the whole Company merely for having criticised the Wardens' severity in expelling one of his fellows.

The precedent for liverymen acting together as a court in this way was well-established. Such a body was to be known in time as a Court of

Assistants, and by the close of the 15th century the formation of such committees was becoming general practice. The Court of Assistants had the nature of a self-perpetuating oligarchy. It was made up of Wardens and retired Masters who were co-opted for life and who named both their successors and those Freemen who were to be appointed to the livery and who would, in the fulness of time, follow them. Their duties were exacting and only men who were comfortably established in their businesses could afford the time and considerable expense incurred. Even they were sometimes reluctant, although the burden of the work was to some degree lightened by the employment of paid minor officials. While some of the Greater Companies were employing a Clerk by the close of the 14th century, most of the lesser companies did not find the need for such an official for another century and a half and relied instead on their Beadle.

This indispensable functionary kept a list of members; summoned them to meetings, feasts and funerals; collected the quarterly fees; distributed alms and attended the searches made by the Wardens of members' premises. When a particular company was of a sufficient standing to acquire a hall, the beadle became its caretaker and tended its garden while his equally indispensable wife washed the linen. The couple received a modest salary, but there were also perks. The beadle of the Pewterers' Company, for example, was admitted to the Master's dinner and there was allowed a boiled capon or cock, half a goose, half a pike, half a pie, half a custard, a rabbit, a dish of sturgeon, two casts of bread and a gallon of drink. This was a generous recognition of the work of the man who was the necessary link between the liverymen, the Freemen who were self-employed, and further Freemen, the yeomanry, who worked for others.

The membership of the yeomanry was highly diverse, just as its origins were colourful. It had begun at the beginning of the 15th century as a prohibited organisation made up of disaffected journeymen, or those members of a company who had graduated from being apprentices but were unable to open their own businesses and so had to work as wage-labourers. Gradually, as the century passed, the yeomanry was transformed into a legitimate if subordinate branch of the livery company. It continued to be made up from journeymen along with those who, for whatever reason, had never succeeded in setting themselves up independently: artisans, pieceworkers, and hired servants. The degree of separation between the liverymen and the yeomanry varied from company to company, but was always evident. Sometimes the yeomanry shared in the religious observances of the livery and sometimes they formed themselves into a separate fraternity. Often they managed their own finances and had their own accounts. Some even had separate officers, although these last frequently had to be approved by the liverymen before they could be appointed. By the end of the 15th century virtually every company had a yeomanry.

Finally, there were the Apprentices. Although the evidence is scanty and far from reliable it seems that a considerable number of apprentices were drawn from outside the City itself. Immigrants to London frequently took the name of the place from whence they had come and this suggests that by the early years of the 14th century the capital was drawing on the entire kingdom for labour. Not only did the London apprentices represent most parts of England, they also came from most of its social groupings except the very poor and the higher nobility; a considerable proportion belonged to families already engaged in the trades they wished to learn. The length of an apprenticeship varied from guild to guild, but terms of between seven and ten years were common and since many guilds refused to admit boys under the age of sixteen such people would be well into adulthood by the time they had completed their apprenticeship.

Teaching was not free and, before enrolling an apprentice, a master would try to extract a premium from the boy's family which supposedly covered board and lodging, along with his instruction. Some of the guilds tried to fix the rate of these premiums, but the more realistic practice of a sliding scale adjusted to the means of the boy's family seems to have been common. The general practice was for a master to take no more than two or three apprentices, and then only if he were able to support them. Because apprenticeship to a master usually led to the granting of the freedom of the City it was important that a register of apprenticed boys be kept in the Chamber of the Guildhall to avoid future complications, a record that was apparently begun in the year 1274-5.

It was generally recognised that an apprentice was being prepared not only for the mastership of his craft but also for participation in the City government, and to this end he was carefully reared in habits of deference. His relationship to his master was fundamentally filial and he was also encouraged to regard senior members of the livery with the utmost respect, the Grocers making the apprentices in their Company swear to hold 'all the clothing of the fellowship in due reverence'. Cheeky and recalcitrant boys were inevitably subjected to corporal punishment which, in some indentures, takes on more of the appearance of a master's duty than a right. Severe curbs were also put on these growing boys' sexual behaviour, along with the other temptations they might be subject to. For example, an apprentice was not to gamble or go to taverns except on his master's business If all these rules were strictly adhered to then many apprentices passed a rather joyless youth, but at least they received the chance of a career.

*

During the 15th century frequent petitions were sent to Parliament urging that the most stringent measures should be taken to regulate the keeping of inns and eventually, in 1439, a hosting statute was passed.

Its regulations were initially introduced for a term of eight years. They were extremely difficult to enforce and in 1446 were one of the principal concerns that the innkeepers of London had when they went in a deputation to the authorities. 'Came good men of the Mistery of Hostelers into the Chamber of the Guildhall, before John Olney, the Mayor and Aldermen, and presented a petition', reads the entry in the Letter Book for 12 December, 1446. It was a historic moment in the history of the Company, for this is the first occasion on which we can see it acting in a corporate manner to advance its own interests and weave itself firmly into the systems that regulated City life. The deputation was in a serious mood. Its members were determined to show that they could keep their own houses in order and that they were men of sufficient gravity to be given the powers to do so. By recognising and accepting the part they had to play in ensuring the moral and social orderliness of the City, the Hostelers also hoped they would secure that monopoly control over their trade which was the principal aim of every guild.

The preamble to their petition presents an image of London pululating with wasters, petty criminals and foreigners. Such people, harbouring with those who were not free of the City, who did not pay their taxes and whose hostels (some of which were clearly brothels) were ashamed to advertise themselves with a proper sign, 'did great mischief and hurt'. Something needed to be done, and the first request of the men of the Mistery of Hostelers was that the Wardens of the craft should have the right to search all common hostelries for guests of evil reputation who, along with their hosts, they would bring before the City authorities for due punishment.

The innkeepers then asked that it be made a legal requirement that anybody running an inn should advertise the fact by having an 'open sign' clearly displayed outside his premises. In addition to this, the innkeeper himself was to be a person 'knowen of good name and good fame by the Wardens and other persons' of the craft. The Wardens took it upon themselves to regulate this last requirement conscientiously, petitioning the authorities for the powers to insist that all innkeepers in the City report 'foreign' guests to the Lord Mayor within twenty-four hours, specifying at the same time the reasons for an alien's residing in London. Failure to comply with this regulation would result in a hefty fine. The erring hosteler would have to pay 6s. 8d for a first offence, double this if he were caught out again, and 20s if he was so foolish as to break the rule for a third time. A familiar social problem was to be solved in this way, but it was also a useful source of revenue for the guild itself since it was entitled to half the sums so raised, the remainder going to the City coffers.

It was not only the managers of London's inns that the Wardens wished to control however. They were also concerned with the staff and they requested that no innkeeper was to employ as an ostler anyone who had previously been a servant to another innkeeper, in case that servant had been 'vicious or untrue' to his former master or any of the guests who had stayed with him. In other words, a servant who had been sacked for bad conduct would never again work in a City inn. The last of the Hostelers' requests was that all members of the guild should be obliged to be obedient to its Wardens and present themselves whenever summoned. Any member failing to appear was to be fined a sum to the value of a pound of wax, half of which was to be paid to the Guildhall coffers and half to the mystery.

The terms of the petition were willingly granted, and the Mistery of Hostelers was now a company vested with the powers of self-regulation enjoyed by the other London guilds. The innkeepers could now proudly play their part in the pageantry that was so conspicuous an element of City life throughout the Christian and municipal year.

The most glorious and all-inclusive celebrations were the Midsummer Marches. Everybody turned out for these, and the guilds were happy to pay between them for 500 of the 700 torches which illuminated the procession. Bonfires were also lit in the streets. Thousands of night lights were hung along the greater thoroughfares, all of the houses were garlanded with greenery and flowers, while a vast procession of some 2000 marchers passed by.

*

These public celebrations are evidence that 15th century London largely avoided the horrors of the Wars of the Roses which were raging in the north of the country. Nonetheless, for all the sense of community and civic pride the occasions expressed this was a deeply hierarchical age, in which social distinctions were very important and reflected in the daily life of the guilds. Because of this, in 1473, the leading innkeepers took another petition to the Court of Aldermen. The term 'hostelers' no longer suited them. It was a label more appropriate to their servants and, in order to preserve the necessary lines of demarcation, they petitioned the authorities 'praying that they might be called innholders, and in no wise 'hostelers'.'

The petition was granted and, by 1483, when they sought once again to have the rights of their Mistery or Craft reconfirmed, the word Innholders was the accepted term. Pursuing their rights and duties, they insisted for example that 'no person within the City and its liberties shall lodge people or horses in private or petty hostelries but that all such people and horses should be lodged in open inns having signs hanging in the open streets, and lanes or places'. In addition, no 'botell' or bundle of hay was to weigh more than five pounds troy weight. Finally, it was asserted 'that the Wardens have the power to search and execute the ordinances and to search all inns and hostelries'. Such were the powers and duties of the liveried members of the Innholders.

The City records confirm that, by 1501, some sixteen senior members of the company were entitled to wear the livery, but there was still one further and vitally important stage for them to negotiate before they could come into the full flowering of their independence: incorporation under royal charter. For many years this had been a somewhat exceptional privilege, but in the reign of Henry VI (1422-61)most of the greater guilds received royal charters. Once incorporation in this form had become the norm among the leading companies the rest naturally aspired to follow suit. The independence thus granted by the king was a matter of grave concern to the city authorities who believed that under the cover of their charters the guilds would seek to fix prices and unfairly manipulate other matters to their own advantage. Nonetheless, the tide was running in their favour and, with the accession of Edward IV, it picked up pace. This was maintained during the able and prosperous rule of Henry

VII, the first of the Tudors, whose accession in 1485 brought the Wars of the Roses to a welcome end. Early in 1509 the Innholders applied to him for a charter, but a few weeks later he died.

Under his son, Henry VIII, the country began to experience an unfamiliar sense of well-being. The handsome young king was immediately popular. Gifted, self-confident and enterprising, his characteristics were soon apparent among his subjects and reflected in the prosperity of the country and its capital.

The Innholders were among the guilds who were quick to perceive and take advantage of the new climate, again applying for a charter. But incorporation was a slow and expensive business. Legal advice and searches were costly, and the more modest companies were obliged to institute a special levy on their members to cover them, but the advantages it bought were worthwhile. The Innholders therefore pressed their claim with the new king and, in 1514, they were successful.

*

The charter is a proud and lovely document, beautifully illuminated with naturalistic Tudor roses, achievements of arms and an elaborate initial letter under which sits a still young, svelte and Catholic Henry VIII rather than the obese tyrant immortalised by Holbein. Before him kneel four liverymen of the Company: the current Master, Roger Barker, and the Wardens John Cannon, John Wakefeld and William Gatte. The document they are about to receive is itself drawn up in legal Latin and, having expressed 'the sincere devotion which we bare and have towards Saint Julian', the king grants the kneeling men the right to establish 'a certain fraternity or guild'. Both men and women are entitled to be members and they are given permission to site their guild anywhere within the liberty of the City that they deem appropriate. Precisely who should be admitted as 'brothers and sisters' is a matter for the guild itself to decide.

The next clause of the document states that: 'the brothers and sisters of that fraternity or guild – thus set up, created, made, founded, and established – and their successors should have power for ever to elect, ordain, and successively appoint, each year from among themselves, one Master and three Wardens for governing and supervising the said fraternity and also for having rule and custody of all the lands, tenements, rents, possessions, goods and chattels which thereafter will happen to be acquired, given, conceded or assigned to the same fraternity or guild'. Not only are the Innholders by this an independent and self-governing body with powers to remove erring Masters and Wardens, they also have the right of a corporation to hold property inalienably and impersonally – in the technical phrase in mortmain. Such holdings would, in time, provide the Company with an income and a fair measure of prosperity. In addition they were allowed rights of assembly so that they could discuss their business. Their senior members were also granted the privilege of wearing the livery. Their power to enforce their regulations, including the search of premises, was also reaffirmed.

The symbol of this newly achieved corporate status was the Company seal and, armed with the rights it implied, the Master and Wardens of the Innholders (who were to be 'persons practised and qualified in the law') had the power to represent the guild as a corporate entity in the courts. It is also probable that by now they occupied a hall on the site of the present one.

The constitutional and legal position of the guild was transformed. Prior to this its rights to hold courts and to levy quarterage fees, and its powers of search, were dependent on the approval of the Lord Mayor, the Aldermen or the City authorities. At the same time the whole elaborate mechanism of its meetings, livery, subscriptions and charitable functions belonged to it through its status as a religious fraternity, sanctioned by the Church courts.

Incorporation under Royal Charter changed and simplified all this. The Company retained all its powers and privileges but henceforth it enjoyed them independently of both the Municipal and Church authorities. Thus, in the closing years of the Middle Ages, the Innholders achieved maturity as a livery company apparently existing safely and in perpetuity under a royal charter which at once assured their independence and their right to an income.

By 1520 the Company could look on its achievements with justifiable satisfaction. It was a thriving body of considerable strength and prestige, qualities that would become increasingly important as the active and virile young Henry VIII precipitated a series of changes that would profoundly and irrevocably change the course of English life.

* * *

The Family of Henry VIII,
(ca. 1545, artist unknown)
The Royal Collection © 2002, Her Majesty Queen Elizabeth II

The Charter of Henry VIII, 1514

Chapter 3

TUDOR LONDON

1530 – 1603

The Reformation – Elizabethan London – the Innholders take shape
Innholders' Hall

The religious reformation initiated by Henry VIII, the change from Catholicism to Protestantism, struck at the core of the medieval guilds, altering their modes of piety, charity and social responsibility. In particular, devout Protestants believed that the cult of the saints and the doctrine of praying for souls in Purgatory (both of them once fundamental to the guilds' spiritual life) were aberrations foisted on credulous congregations by a corrupt church. They used the law to change matters and eventually 'no candles, tapers, or images of wax' were to be set before any devotional image such as that of St. Julian. There were to be no prayers for those suffering in a non-existent Purgatory, and money left to pay priests to pray for the souls of the dead was forfeited to the Crown which was now head of the church in England. Hence the Innholders' declaration to the authorities of the sum of £42 left to them by one John Gefford for the saying of masses for his soul.

Deprived of their traditional religious pieties, the guilds would have to rethink their role. The reformers taught that those who exercised power over the community did so with the blessing of God. It was their responsibility to maintain political and ecclesiastical order, promote common tranquillity and, where necessary, oblige people through punishments and incentives to adapt their conduct to human society. A concept of the 'godly magistrate' was gradually being created, and the liverymen of the London guilds accepted this with alacrity, thereby helping to secure the grip of the newly protestant Tudor regime over the often turbulent City.

For reform was not introduced into the nation's capital gently. Medieval London was a Catholic city. The ecclesiastical palaces of the princes of the church lined the north bank of the river between Blackfriars and Westminster like the beads on a rosary. The City's innumerable churches were lavishly encrusted with shrines and effigies, with painted walls and richly coloured stained glass. Elaborate vestments, sumptuous furniture and massive stores of plate completed the inventory. Now all this wealth was suddenly redistributed with rough and greedy hands. Altars, images and screens were torn down and burnt. Twenty three medieval religious foundations (many of them of great beauty) were razed to the ground or otherwise pillaged. Asset stripping and sacrilege became the order of the day, and marvellous properties passed rapidly from the impoverished crown to courtiers and timeservers rapacious for social position and the chance of increasing their fortunes.

The process was at once terrible and invigorating for the immense windfall that derived so suddenly from the dissolution of the monasteries fuelled a London property boom and an extraordinary expansion of its manufactures. Despite this marvellous expansion however (or perhaps because of it) London was very far from being a safe place in which to live. Plague and other epidemics ensured a high death rate, and a total of some 5,000 migrants a year was necessary if the capital were to sustain its phenomenal rate of growth. Young men came from every part of the country, some hoping to make their fortunes, others more realistically aspiring to no more than a modest living. Very gradually the majority of Londoners moved to the suburbs and thus beyond the immediate control of the guilds and other City authorities but, for the moment, the greater part of the population – rich and poor, apprentices and masters, the successful and the merely hopeful – lived cheek by jowl in that dark maze of noisy, often smelly, courtyards and alleyways which made up what were now the twenty six wards of the City.

Alarmed by the potential for unrest, the Privy Council noted 'the great number of dissolute, loose and insolent people' living there. But if London was vibrant and occasionally violent it was neither anarchic nor forever teetering on the edge of social crisis as were many of the great cities on the continent. This was in large part due to the fact that the city, like the rest of the nation (despite the ardent Protestantism of Henry VIII's son Edward VI and the

Catholic fanaticism of his daughter 'Bloody' Mary), escaped the worst of the religious turmoil which for decades agonised so much of northern Europe. The leading officials of the City – the Aldermen and the liverymen especially – wisely built on this stable foundation, by teaching that the reformed congregations of the prosperous capital were people specially chosen by God, and nothing so clearly illustrated God's Providence to his elect than the accession of Mary's sister, the protestant Queen Elizabeth.

*

The loyalty of Londoners to Elizabeth and all that she represented was perfectly symbolised by the great celebration which the City and its livery companies organised for Elizabeth's coronation. Here, indeed, was a display of all that English protestantism represented.

It was ordered that, at the City's cost, the processional route should be lined with fine pageants 'and rich cloths of arras silver and gold'. The command was taken up with enthusiasm and the result was spectacular. The queen, accompanied by a thousand horsemen, rode in an open litter trimmed to the ground with gold brocade. All around her were lavish expressions of loyalty. In the words of the Venetian ambassador: 'the houses on the way were all decorated; there being on both sides of the street from Blackfriars to St. Paul's, wooden barricades, on which the merchants and artisans of every trade leant in long black gowns lined with hoods of red and black cloth ... with all their ensigns, banners, and standards, which were innumerable, and made a very fine show'. At the lower end of Cornhill, a triple arch stretched across the street and showed a child representing the queen sitting on 'the seat of worthy governance'. Among the allegorical figures around her, Pure Religion stamped on Catholic Ignorance and Superstition. Elsewhere, Elizabeth was represented as Deborah, 'the judge and restorer of the house of Israel' which, as everyone knew, symbolised Protestant England. At the climax of the ceremony the queen was presented with an English Bible, and 'as soon as she had received the book, [she] kissed it, and with both her hands held up the same, and so laid it upon her breast, with great thanks to the City therefore'. Amid the acclamations of the liverymen, Crown and City were at one in their assertion of the virtues of godly protestant rule.

The influence and prestige of 16th and early 17th century livery companies such as the Innholders was very considerable. For all that the Aldermen (and, increasingly, the Common Council) had more power, the guilds were key institutions in the City precisely because they controlled access to the freedom and hence to the political, legal and economic privileges that went with this. In addition, they were fundamental to the organisation of business life and the relief of their poorer colleagues. Bonds between members of the livery companies continued to be reinforced by a lavish round of feasting and other convivial occasions while their hierarchical structure emphasised the patterns of rank and deference which people then saw as fundamental to a stable and well-ordered society.

The livery companies were also vital to the administration of the City as a whole. For example, it was they who were responsible for disseminating the all-important precepts of the Lord Mayor and thus ensuring that the majority of people were aware of what the Aldermen had decided for them. These decisions might range from efforts to control morality and public behaviour to handling the altogether more desperate crises which from time to time afflicted the City. In 1582, for example, the companies received a precept warning their members not to 'suffer any of their servants, apprentices, journeymen, or children to repair or go unto any plays, prizes, or interludes' within the City or its environs.

Many of these entertainments were held in The Belle Sauvage, a huge and popular venue well known for wrestling matches, cockfighting, a dancing school and above all, plays. These last were of the utmost cultural importance. In 1574, Queen Elizabeth began to licence groups of players and soon there were six companies of actors based in London. They made such a living as they could from the money paid by the 'groundlings' who stood in the yards of the inns where they performed;

the receipts from the wealthier members of the audience, who crammed the galleries, went to the innkeeper.

When James Burbage built the first London theatre in 1576 he substantially followed this architectural arrangement. It was the combination of the big platform stage, the absence of a curtain, and the need to make language and gesture clear to the large and often noisy audiences crammed into the inn yards, which helped determine the fluid action and rhetorical glory of Shakespeare's drama. This long continued to be the case, and as many as half a dozen London inns were used for theatrical performances after Burbage had built the first permanent stage. These included The Bell and The Cross Keys in what is now Gracechurch Street, as well as The Belle Sauvage on Ludgate Hill. Shakespeare's company used the latter during its 1594 season when *A Midsummer Night's Dream* and possibly *Romeo and Juliet* and *The Merchant of Venice* were among the new works on offer.

The City's protestant authorities were thoroughly censorious about the whole business and frequently tried to curb it. They were gravely concerned about what they called 'evil practices of incontinencey in great inns', and painted a lurid picture of turbulent crowds, affrays and quarrels. The plays themselves they considered to be immoral, being full of 'unchaste, uncomely and unshamefast speeches' which, on Sundays and holidays especially, lured people away from church and encouraged them to squander their money if this had not already been stolen by pickpockets.

Alcohol was often apt to overheat the already excited minds and imaginations of the audiences, while the existence of 'chambers and secret places adjoining to their open stages and galleries' were invitations to all manner of vices including the 'inveigling and alluring of maids, specially orphans and good citizens' children under age, to privy and unmeet contracts'. As if all that were not bad enough, there was also the fact that 'sundry slaughters and maimings have happened by ruins of scaffolds, frames and stages, and by engines, weapons, and powder [i.e. gunpowder] used in plays'. It was even said that the devil himself made an appearance

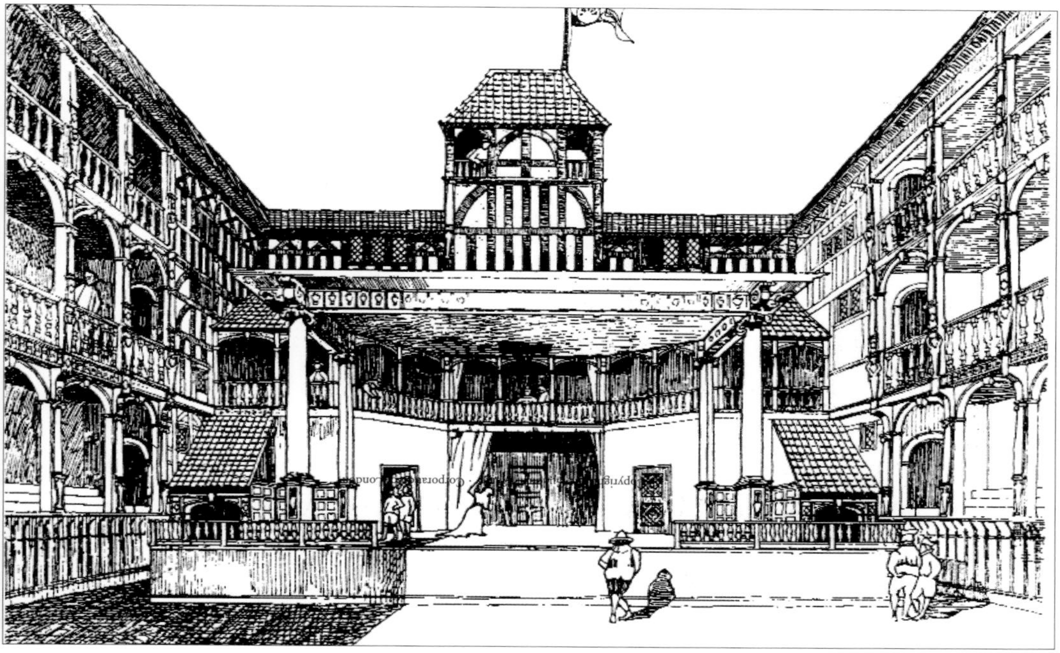

The Fortune Theatre, at the George Inn, Southwark and, (below) Shakespeare's Globe Theatre, Southwark (Visscher, 1616)

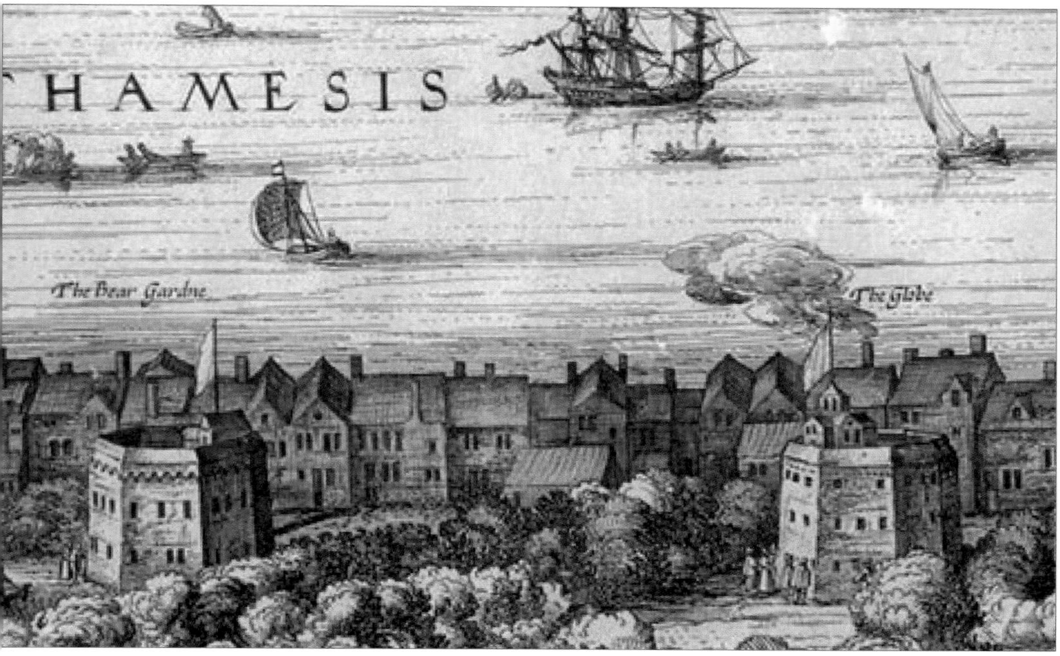

Later scholars believe that the captions for the Globe on the right and the Bear Baiting House on the left were accidentally reversed

during a performance of Marlowe's *Doctor Faustus* at the Belle Sauvage. All in all, attending performances of some of the world's greatest drama was considered a peril to body and soul alike, and the Privy Council eventually stepped in and demanded that theatrical venues be licensed. As a result, the City's inns had largely passed out of use as theatres by the end of the century.

In the spring of 1594 a particularly virulent epidemic of the plague attacked the City and the desperate Lord Mayor demanded that every Freeman should 'yield a third part of every of their clear gains towards the doing or furnishing of a house or hospital now in hand for persons who shall be visited by the plague'. It was the livery companies who collected this levy.

Again, it was the livery companies who were responsible for raising men and money for the defence and policing of the City. To this end they stored and supplied quantities of armour and weapons, including the complicated arquebuses introduced during the time of Henry VIII. Issues of law and order on the London streets were always a problem in a capital lacking a sizeable or efficient police force, and here the guilds showed their mettle. The Innholders already had a long and honourable tradition of participating in such activities. As early as 1518 they had supplied six of the 204 archers who had attended on the Lord Mayor when trouble was expected on the vigils of St John and St Peter. The number of men so marshalled is particularly impressive when it is considered that altogether larger companies such as the Fishmongers and Merchant Taylors only provided eight men each.

Keeping the City adequately fed was another major consideration. As early as the 1570s the livery companies had played an important part in setting up and administering permanent grain reserves for London. These were stored at the City granaries in Southwark where there were ten public ovens in which loaves could be baked and afterwards supplied at cheap rates to poorer citizens. Again, the Innholders were periodically required to provide money to buy coal so that this too should be available to poorer citizens at advantageous rates. Finally, in a city regularly plagued by fire, the Innholders were expected to provide '12 buckets, 2 ladders, 2 hooks, 2 pickaxes, 2 shovels and 2 spades' to fight this ever-present menace. Liverymen were expected to contribute to such expenses personally, the Court deciding how much each should contribute – revealing how the companies were made directly responsible for assessing and collecting some of the taxes in London.

Such social provision was an important part of the role of these 'godly magistrates' who also recognised their immediate duty to their members who fell on hard times, including their widows and orphans. Those permanently disabled usually received an annual pension or weekly dole, drawn from the company's regular income or from bequests for the relief of the poor.

*

The day to day administration of the Innholders' civil responsibilities was in the hands of its Court, that elite group of liverymen which invariably included all those who had served at least one term as a Warden. The Master presided over the Court of Wardens and Assistants. It was the duty of these officers, and of the Renter Warden especially, to have charge of the 'sums of money, jewels, plate or other things' that were the Company's property. This was a comparatively onerous charge and one requiring the utmost scrupulousness. It appears that the Renter Warden held all the Company's money in his personal possession, paying the accounts that had been approved by the Court, and giving sureties that he would hand the balance to his successor when his term of duty had expired. An annual audit of the Company's finances was an obvious necessity, and the Court usually appointed some twelve to fourteen of their number to deal with this matter, a quorum of four usually being thought sufficient to examine the expenses in detail. The annual audit was then followed by one of the Company's great annual feasts: the Renter Warden's dinner.

But the duties of the Court of Assistants did not end here. It usually met once or twice a week to deliberate on lesser matters, and the proceedings were formal and grave. The Clerk recorded the hearings, while the beadle acted as marshal and usher. Disputes could be presented to the Court either in the form of a written deposition or by word of mouth. When the Assistants had heard the evidence, they judged the issue and then awarded compensation or meted out punishment. An enormous range of cases was presented to them, and for many Londoners the Court of Assistants of their guild was their court of first instance, arbitrating in conflicts arising from trade and settling a wide range of civil disputes and quasi-criminal offences.

The powers of the Court were wide-ranging since it was within its remit to handle all cases where the defendant was a member of the company, regardless of the status of the plaintiff. After a time the Aldermen who had originally seen this as a threat began to welcome the practice. In a city with a rapidly expanding population, routine legal work proliferated and the Aldermen were glad to have their burden eased by competent men in positions of authority. A precept of 1579 encouraged the companies to extend the work of their Courts in order to save time, expense and pressure on the Guildhall.

Since members of a chartered Livery swore not to refer their differences to a civil court, it fell to their own to reconcile their contentions. Usually they tried reason and persuasion, but the Court of the Clothworkers sent four of their members to prison for having left a local inn without settling what they owed. The fact that members of a Livery Court had spent lifetimes in their craft gave weight to their decisions since they were familiar with every trick of the trade.

In such ways as these the Court of the Company was making the Innholders into a successful and useful London guild possessed of its own hall, rental properties and plate. But what of the lesser members of the Company? What were the roles and aspirations of those Freemen who had not and might never aspire to the liveryman's gown? As in most companies, there were three divisions of these people: the Householders, the Journeymen and the Apprentices.

The householders of the company were those who had paid a fee and were permitted to run their own businesses. If not ambitious they had gone through a long period of training in their craft which they knew well and practised daily. Their advice on technical matters was valuable and regularly sought. They also possessed a certain, if relatively small, amount of wealth necessary to their businesses and to pay their entry fees. To become a householder was a rite of passage to professional advantage.

Many journeymen might aspire to the status of householder, but for the time being they were people who had passed through their apprenticeship and gained the freedom of the City but were not allowed to set up businesses of their own. Instead, they were obliged to work as day labourers in the establishments of their superiors. Numerically they could make up a large percentage of a company, but in many ways theirs was a thankless lot: their rates of pay were set, and the people for whom they worked were carefully listed, and they were obliged by their oaths to conform to very strict codes designed to prevent them from squandering their masters' time.

The London Apprentices possessed a complex web of rights and responsibilities. The terms of their indentures required them not only to serve faithfully but also 'not commit fornication nor contract matrimony, refrain from gambling and keep away from taverns and playhouses'.

In return for his apprentice's good behaviour, a master was required to teach him the skills of his trade, 'finding unto his said apprentice meat, drink, apparel, lodging and all other necessaries, according to the custom of the City of London'. Masters failing to honour the terms of an apprenticeship could be brought before their Court of Assistants while, when a young man had finally completed his time of training, it was his master's responsibility to pay his fees for becoming a Freeman, while custom also dictated that he should provide him with money or goods to help him start his career.

*

By 1522, the Court of Assistants of the Innholders could adjudicate such matters in the Company's own Hall, for a reference in a valuation of Londoners' lands and goods for that year assesses the movables contained there as being worth £22. The building was almost certainly that mentioned by Stow when he briefly wrote of Elbow Lane and described how 'in this Elbow Lane is the Innholders' Hall and other fair houses; this lane runneth west and suddenly turneth south into Thames Street, and therefore all that that bending is called Elbow Lane'. This 'bending' was the junction of College Street and what is now Little College Lane.

It is possible to conjecture what some of the Hall's general features may have been like. By the time Stow was writing in 1598 he could make mention of some forty six company halls. The earliest of these were usually private houses built around a courtyard and bequeathed by their owners to their companies. The basic form of such properties continued to be employed, for they all had a large hall which was essential for ceremonies, meetings and convivial occasions. It is probable that, like the Pewterers whose hall was being furnished at roughly the same time, the members of the Innholders' Company were obliged to pay benevolences to help with the costs. Wealthier individuals perhaps offered to glaze a window while others gave the necessary tables, joint stools, iron spits and silver spoons.

Among the greatest of the treasures belonging to the Innholders is its collection of silver St Julian spoons. These are similar in form to the more familiar apostles spoons, the crowning figure in this case being the guild's patron saint who is portrayed in old age – the charitable hospitaler of pious legend. An inventory of 1636 states that the Company possessed 'two dozen and five St Julian spoons', all of which probably followed the common form of having octagonal stems, the front and reverse being wider than the sides. The earliest of these lovely spoons bears a London hallmark and a date letter for 1539. Like most of the others it is engraved with its donor's name, in this case John Coop. Over the course of time the Company was to acquire more such spoons and now possesses a fine collection of them.

Facilities for the preparation of feasts were necessary in all the early company halls including, it may be supposed, that of the Innholders. The first hall owned by the Goldsmiths for example had a kitchen, a pantry, and a buttery. In addition, it also had two smaller chambers. These were the more private rooms where the liverymen could retire to dine apart from the lesser members of the company.

Large numbers of members and their guests feasted in the company halls and the liverymen were required to find from their own pockets any costs in excess of the allowance granted to them by their courts. In William Harrison's *Description of Britain* (1577) he describes the ethos of Elizabethan guild feasts:

> It is a world to see what great provision is made of all manner of delicate meats from every quarter of the country, wherein besides that they are often comparable herein to the nobility of the land, they will seldom regard anything that the butcher usually killeth, but reject the same as not worthy to come in place. In such cases also jellies of all colours and, mixed with a variety in the representation of sundry flowers, herbs, trees, forms of beasts, fish, fowls, and fruits, and thereunto marchpane wrought with no small curiosity, to parts of the divers hues, and sundry denominations, conserves of old fruits, foreign and homebred, suckets, codinacs, marmalades, marchpane, sugar-bread, ginger-bread, florentines, wild-fowls, venison all sorts . . .

To match such victuals an ever-growing collection of plate now beautified the Master Innholder's table. As one of the Company's most valuable assets the plate was, at times of extreme financial difficulty, liable to be melted down or sold, but much survived and an inventory of 1636 records how the Company owned five gilt cups or goblets, twenty five St Julian spoons, a gilt tankard, a large silver tankard, a set of a dozen salts, another large salt, two further silver-gilt salts and 'one great gilt salt'. Of the five goblets listed, one - the Gwalter Cup -remains to this day in the Company's possession. It is a fine piece of Elizabethan craftsmanship, a baluster stem rising from a richly decorated base to support a cone-shaped bowl decorated with raised and moulded bands between which appear the arms of the Company. Engraved around its rim is the inscription: 'Though I be gon remember me for as I am so you shall bee The Gifte of Grace Gwalter in Remembrance of her Deceased husband John Gwalter The 27th daye of February 1599'.

Of all the surviving early pieces the most magnificent by far is the famous Anne Sweete salt of 1614. Standing nearly sixteen inches high and fashioned entirely out of silver-gilt, the salt represents the work of the Jacobean craftsman at its finest. The cylindrical body rises from a base standing on three claws and half-balls; the moulding at the top and bottom of this is stamped with a geometrical pattern; set into the top is a shallow well for the salt. From its rim four scroll brackets rise with airy elegance to support an inverted bowl. From this four more brackets rise to a circlet bearing a third set of brackets which support a slim pyramidal steeple, surmounted by a perfectly proportioned finial. The Anne Sweete salt achieves a near perfect balance between the solid and the fantastic, the earthbound and the soaring, the exuberant and the classical. It is the Company's greatest treasure among its plate.

All this suggests that by the time of Queen Elizabeth's death in 1603 the Innholders flourished in a flourishing London, which had ceased to be a minor conurbation much on a level with Prague, Seville or Cologne, and was now one of the Europe's five chief centres of population. Dynasties of great international businessmen had started to appear, and the City slowly prepared for its role as a centre of world finance. Luxury trades such as those of the goldsmiths, mercers and furriers clustered around the central thoroughfares like Cheapside; brewers, millers and dyers who needed access to water gravitated naturally to the river; while the City's indispensable and thriving innkeepers were to be found everywhere, and along Fleet Street especially. From their hall, beside the Walbrook and close to the Thames, their company administered their prosperous trade in a booming city.

* * *

'The Gifte of Grace Gwalter in Remembrance of her Deceased husband John Gwalter The 27th daye of February 1599'

The Anne Sweete Steeple Salt, 1614

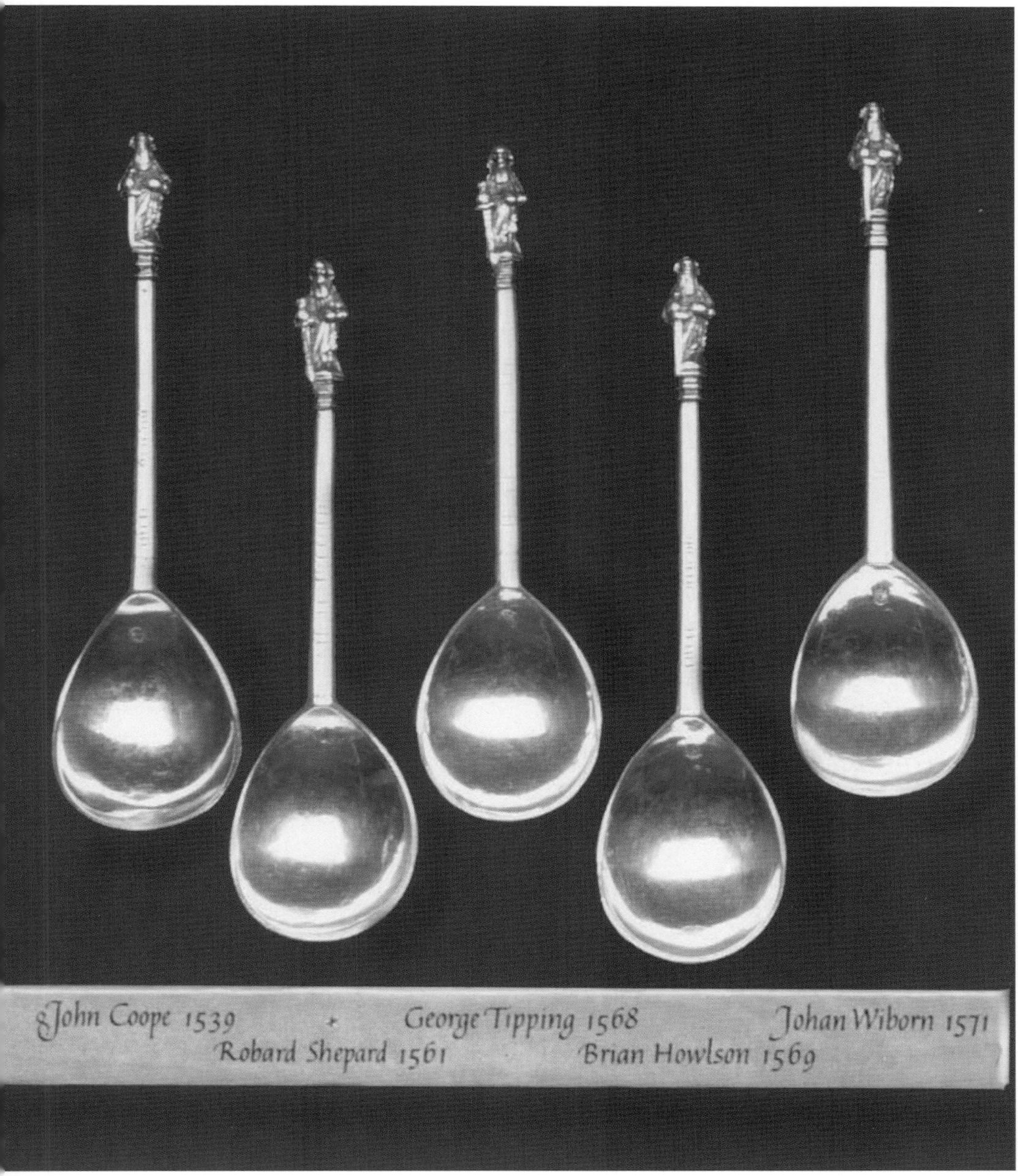

The five oldest St. Julian Spoons in the Company's possession

Chapter 4

MONARCHY AND COMMONWEALTH

1603 - 1660

Country inns – London inns - innholding regulations
London's new problems – the Innholders' problems – the nemesis of Charles I
the Commonwealth.

James I and the House of Stuart who succeeded Elizabeth, were to have more effect for good and ill on the Innholders than any other royal dynasty. However their early decades were deceptively calm.

By now inns and innkeepers were closely interwoven with life in the nation's cities, towns, villages, and at regular staging posts along its roads. Though not uncritical of them, the topographical writer William Harrison believed that our inns were still 'far better than the best that I have heard of in any foreign country'. 'Innkeepers abroad tried to exert a 'lordly authority' over their customers, whereas inns in the provinces of England especially vied with each other to provide the best entertainment. 'And it is a world to see how each owner of them contendeth with others for goodliness of entertainment of their guests, as about fineness and change of linen, furniture of bedding, beauty of rooms, service at the table, costliness of plate, strength of drink, variety of wines, and well using of horses'. All the same, he wrote censoriously of the continuing magnificence of their signs. Some of these cost £30 or £40 which was 'a mere vanity' in Harrison's opinion, but he recognised the need 'to give some outward token of the innkeeper's wealth... to procure good guests to the frequenting of their houses'.

The inveterate 17th century traveller Fynes Moryson described the hospitable reception guests could expect. 'As soon as a passenger comes to an inn the servants run to him, and one takes his horse, and walks him till he be cold, then rubs him and gives him meal'. After that, another servant would show the guest to his room where he would kindle the fire while yet another pulled off his boots and polished them. Once the guest had settled in, the host and hostess would make themselves known. 'If he will eat with the host, or at a common table with others, his meal will cost him sixpence, or in some places but fourpence; yet this course is less honourable and not used by gentlemen'. Such a person preferred to eat privately in his room and could reasonably expect to order whatever food he wished and to be entertained with polite attention. 'When he sits down at table, the host or hostess will accompany him, or if they have many guests will at least visit him, taking it for courtesy to be bid sit down'. While such a guest was eating (and especially if he were accompanied by friends) he would be entertained by musicians. Delightfully, the same musicians would wake him in the morning. Moryson was very proud of the hospitality provided. 'A man cannot more freely command in his own house than he may do in his inn', he declared, adding how 'at parting, if he give some few pence to the chamberlain and ostler, they wish him a happy journey'.

By now many people travelling about the country were using the system of posting houses set up by the Crown which paid rural innkeepers a small salary for keeping fresh horses ready for the royal couriers. Such inns often declared their presence by having a painted sign of a horn hanging outside. There was great competition among landlords for becoming a postmaster, less for the fee that was offered than because they thereby gained extra custom. Travellers using the system were required to pay twopence a mile and also to hire a guide at a charge of four pence a stage. The guide would carry the passenger's luggage and blow his horn three times in a mile as they cantered through the countryside.

Other travellers preferred to make their journey by means of the growing body of carriers. Perhaps the best known of these men was Tobias Hobson, a Cambridge innkeeper who inherited a cart and eight horses from his father with which he transported people and goods across East Anglia. Later Hobson expanded and ran a second service between his Cambridge premises and The Bell on London's Bishopsgate Street

Within. These early carriages were extremely slow and uncomfortable, having no springs, a rudimentary covering and just sufficient space to cram in some two dozen passengers. It was not for his carriages however that Hobson was principally known but for the fact that anyone wishing to hire a horse from him was obliged to take the one standing nearest to the stable door. There was sense in this since it meant that each of Hobson's horses was equally used, but the practice soon gave rise to the phrase 'Hobson's choice'.

Many of these provincial inns were not simply convenient resting places, lavishly decorated, but local business centres as well. The White Hart at Aylesbury, demolished in the 19th century, was a particularly fine example. The façade of the building overlooked the market square. It had three floors, each jutting out over the one below and covered with a profusion of carving which terminated in three splendid gables. A huge gate on massive fluted columns gave access to a spacious yard, half of which was defined by an open but roofed gallery onto which the bedrooms opened. There were, in addition, large rooms on either side of the main entrance. Business deals were negotiated in the so-called 'Change' room. Customs, excise and other duties were collected in the 'Crown'. Ecclesiastical rents and taxes were collected in the 'Mitre', while the 'Fountain' room appears to have been the bar. Ample provision was also made for feeding and entertaining the inn's innumerable guests. The kitchen range lined one end of the yard, there was a bowling green in the garden and, beyond this, an ancient orchard where cows, pigs and lame horses wandered between the fruit trees and mulberry bushes or drank at the shallow stew pond where eels and freshwater fish were kept in readiness. The great stable block could hold fifty horses, feed being kept in the lofts above, while harness rooms and lodgings for ostlers and postboys filled the remainder of a site which, in all, covered some six acres.

*

As England became increasingly prosperous it became the fashion for the greater part of the gentry to winter in London, and the luxury trades in particular waxed fat on their presence. The early Stuart kings, James I and his son Charles I, looked on with distaste and when, in 1632, some 250 peers, baronets, knights and gentlemen refused to obey Charles's proclamation ordering them home they were summoned before the Court of the Star Chamber and prosecuted. This had little effect. The capital's economy now had to adapt itself to a huge influx of rural landowners and their families.

In order to accommodate them new luxury inns clustered around such areas as Holborn, Smithfield and Bishopsgate, and while ladies such as the Duchess of Newcastle might divert themselves by going to the theatre or being driven in their coaches around Hyde Park, their menfolk met together in their favourite inns to drink, discuss business, or criticise the actions of the government. Some have argued that the origins of English club life lie in such informal gatherings.

There was also a considerable expansion of inn building around Aldgate at this time, and The Crown in Aldgate High Street might serve as an example. Large portions of Aldgate Street itself had once belonged to Holy Trinity Priory, and the fact that there was a policy of selling off parcels of land while continuing to charge small annual payments for them, which were recorded, makes it possible to reconstruct the history of an inn now wholly obliterated by Aldgate underground station.

In 1581 the building had been purchased by William Couch, Innholder. Couch died in 1583 and was buried under a stone with a brass inscription in the next door church of St Botolph. However his widow took the business over (a common practice at the time) and a survey made by Ralph Treswell in 1610 shows the inn very much as the couple must have known it. The principal rooms lay towards the street. There was a hall lit by fourteen panes of glass, a wainscoted parlour and other rooms for drinking and socialising. The Crown also had two courtyards separated by an inner gatehouse beyond which lay the ample stable accommodation. This would always have been busy with what William Harrison described as 'certain hostlers [ostlers] or hired servants, appointed at the charges of the goodman of the house, who in hope of extraordinary reward all deal very diligently after an outward appearance in this their action and calling'. The stable yard of The Crown in its turn gave onto the great garden of what had once been the priory.

Such inns were vulnerable to theft, a hazard which appears to have been common all over the country. Harrison wrote that if a guest 'lose aught while he abideth in the inn, the host is bound by a general custom to restore the damage, so that there is no greater security anywhere for travellers than in the greatest inns of England'. This boast was perhaps slightly disingenuous since Harrison was perfectly well aware that when a traveller arrived at an inn the ostlers often slyly felt his luggage to see if there might be anything valuable in it, a process sometimes repeated by other servants when they put his luggage in his room. Some inns were widely regarded as being in league with highwaymen and other sinister figures responsible for 'the utter undoing of many an honest yeoman as he journeyeth on his way'. Harrison here echoes complaints voiced two centuries earlier by Chaucer's Parson.

*

The Privy Council, the City authorities and the Innholders each devised regulations intended to protect the safety, security and well-being of anyone using an inn. Their scope was remarkable.

To ensure that inns maintained civilised standards a broadsheet was published, 'meet to be fixed upon the wall of every chamber', describing precisely how an innkeeper should behave. Innkeepers were told that 'it must not be accounted a small matter to afford house room, lodging, rest and food to the comfort of God's children'. A regulation which sounded equally devout, but which was also pragmatic, concerned the observance of fast days when fish only was to be eaten, especially in Lent. Year after year the Privy Council issued proclamations banning the eating of meat during this time, placing innkeepers under a £100 bond not to prepare it – the practical purpose being to protect the fishing industry and thus the availability of mariners in time of war. However, officers found many innholders in the Farringdon ward openly flouting the law, while at the famous Bell Savage in Ludgate Hill searchers found two pieces of beef boiling in a pot over the fire. In the nearby Red Lion Peter Potter, innholder, had a tray full of neats' feet ready dressed and a calf's chaldron' bubbling away, and Alexander Langford, of The Rose near Smithfield, was busily preparing a chine of pork. When accused of a similar misdemeanour Shakespeare's Mistress Quickly roundly declared: 'All vict'lers do so. What's a joint of mutton or two in a whole Lent?'

By far the greatest portrayal of inns as the home of human weakness and crime is offered by Shakespeare in the two parts of *Henry IV*. It is a part of the rich and sometimes troubling humanity of Shakespeare's genius that much of the education of Prince Hal, the future Henry V, takes place at a succession of English inns. As Hal allows himself to be inveigled into the farcical plot of the robbers robbed, so he has his insight into the foibles and fecklessness of his less respectable compatriots, those vivid fragments of all too erring humanity, some of whom he will eventually weld into the army he leads to victory at Agincourt. Chief among them is, of course, Falstaff that fat, cowardly, comic and ultimately pathetic figure, who personifies the chaotic and earthbound energies of inns at their most exuberant.

Who can forget the hostess Mistress Quickly's picture of Falstaff swearing on his goblet to marry her, when he was 'sitting in my Dolphin chamber at the round table by a sea-coal fire', at the very moment when the butcher's wife came in to ask for a drop of vinegar because she had just come by a good dish of prawns? Here is the very stuff of evanescent life matchlessly caught in its emotional and physical detail. And it is just this detail - precise, observed and trustworthy - that gives these scenes their credibility.

This really is a world where a dishonest landlord will put powdered limestone into a glass of sack to make it dry and sparkling, a world where Falstaff will order anchovies with his drink to provoke a greater thirst, a world where men denied a chamber pot will urinate in the chimney corner and thereby hugely increase the number of resident fleas. We even hear the slang. They call drinking deep 'dyeing scarlet'; and when you breathe in your watering, they cry 'Hem!' and bid you 'Play it off'.

It is in this situation, as Hal himself reflects, that he has 'sounded the very base-string of humility.' He gets involved in the life of dishonest inn servants and footpads which, as Harrison and Shakespeare's audience knew, was no mere literary fiction. It is a world of anarchy, absurdity and lawlessness that is at once humanly valuable and morally all but worthless. At times it is almost surreal, as when Hal, the most powerful young man in England, meets the young apprentice innkeeper Francis who, chafing at the terms of his indenture, has a fair claim to be its most feeble. It is also a world of cruelty and ultimately of the deepest pathos. It is a measure of the price of great power that when Hal becomes king he is forced to reject Falstaff with a coldness that kills the old man.

In *Henry V,* Mistress Quickly describes Falstaff's death at her inn with words that are among the most moving that Shakespeare ever wrote. He 'parted ev'n just between twelve and one, ev'n at the turning o' the tide: for after I saw him fumble with the sheets and play with flowers and smile upon his fingers' ends, I knew there was but one way; for his nose was as sharp as a pen, and a' babbled of green fields'.

Shakespeare not only provided the definitive picture of contemporary inn life, he was also a shrewd businessman and in March, 1613, he joined with the wealthy landlord of The Mitre in purchasing the Blackfriars' Gatehouse. Inns such as The Mitre were now becoming increasingly necessary to London life as, from the early 17th century, the capital developed into a centre for conspicuous consumption.

*

In the first half of the 17th century the expansion of London – its suburbs especially – became a major problem and an issue which was to have a long-term and profound effect on the livery companies, including the Innholders themselves. The rise in the capital's population was prodigious. Between 1550 and 1660 it rose from some 75,000 to close on 140,000. Many of these people were the rootless poor attracted yearly in their thousands by London's ever increasing prosperity and the hope of wages which were fifty per cent higher than in other parts of the country.

Newcomers crowded into the suburbs, especially those to the east and the north. By about 1630, the combined population of the northern suburbs equalled that of the City itself, and those in charge feared not just the rise in numbers but the proliferation of crime, disease and social discontent in areas over which they had no official control. The worried Aldermen wrote to the Privy Council pointing out that the rapid growth of the capital's population 'would prove of dangerous consequence, not only to this great metropolis, but likewise to the nation in general if not timely remedied'.

Elizabeth had responded to this approaching threat with a proclamation forbidding all new building within three miles of the gates of London and also prohibiting the subdivision of existing houses and the letting of rooms to lodgers. Her successors now issued similar proclamations and continued to do so throughout the century, but all to no avail. The forces promoting expansion were irresistible.

The Aldermen were particularly concerned to defend the City's business. It was patently clear to them that if people freely followed their trades in the surrounding areas, where the livery companies had no effective control, then the City's unique position as a protected market would be fatally undermined. In 1632 they therefore wrote again to the Privy Council describing the parlous state into which London was falling - the influx of beggars; the contamination and even destruction of the water supply; the constant risk of plague.

Above all, there was a genuine threat to the adequate supervision of trade as exercised by the guilds. The Aldermen gravely lamented how 'the freedom of London which is heretofore of very great esteem is grown to be of little worth, by reason of the extraordinary enlargement of the suburbs, where greater numbers of traders and handicraftsmen do enjoy, without charge, equal benefit with the Freemen and citizens of London'.

In response the Privy Council sensibly suggested that the City Corporation absorb these areas into their control, but the City fathers had no wish to do so. They wanted to protect their own interests by having some measure of authority over the troublesome suburbs, but they drew back from being solely responsible for the maintenance of law and order there, and from the enormous burden of poor relief this would involve. As a result, for the next two centuries, the ever-expanding London suburbs were left largely to their own devices. In consequence, livery companies such as the Innholders were obliged to watch their control over their trades slowly but inexorably weakened.

*

Apart from the menace of unregulated craftsmen and traders in the new suburbs, the Innholders and other livery companies now found their monopolies were being challenged within the City itself. Since the last years of Elizabeth's reign lawyers had been at work in a series of cases under Common Law to undermine their ancient prerogatives and increasingly resented restrictive practices.

In 1599, for example, the confiscation and forfeiture of goods made during the Wardens' searches had been declared illegal while, in the same year, the ordinances which most companies had drawn up to regulate their trades were declared valid 'only so far as they are consonant to law and reason'. A few years later judgement was given to the effect that any person who had served a seven year apprenticeship to one trade might 'well and lawfully relinquish that trade and exercise any other trade at his will and pleasure', doing so without joining the appropriate livery company. Then, in 1616, two provincial cases established the precedent for challenging companies' rights to compel those not free to enrol under their aegis. The guilds fought back, but their medieval monopolies were increasingly under attack.

In two cases, however, on specific points of law, the Innholders vigorously defended their rights. In 1617 the Master, John Sweete, was obliged to fight a legal challenge to the Company's ownership of two tenements with their attached shops in Coleman Street. These had been left to the Company in the will of Thomas Baylie and the Company had purchased the various leases to which these buildings were subject. However when a descendant of the original owner tried to recover possession of the properties through a Chancery suit, the attempt failed and the case was dismissed.

Ten years later, on 15 November, 1627, 'Edward Lycorise, Master of the Company of Innholders of London, Thomas Browne, Henry Barnard, and William Lether, Wardens of the same Company', had to petition Sir Thomas Coventry, Keeper of the Great Seal of England, in the matter of a disputed annuity to be paid to the poor of the Company. The case was that when a certain Arthur Ranescraft, 'citizen and innholder of London' and proprietor of the Bell in Friday Street, had drawn up his will he had determined that provision should be made for an annuity of ten shillings which the Company could use to support its less fortunate members. The annuity was to be paid from the continuing turnover of Ranescraft's business and was to be distributed 'whole and entire' by the Company in their hall on St Bartholomew's Day.

When Ranescraft died his business passed to his son who sold it to a certain John Edwards, the price being a favourable one because of the continuing charge of the annuity. Paying ten shillings a year to the Innholders irked the new proprietor who was determined to get out of his responsibility. He therefore 'suppressed' Ranescraft's will, alleged he had bought the business from another owner and claimed he had never 'received any notice of the said annuity'. How the case was resolved is unknown.

That the company remained prosperous and powerful, despite its problems, is suggested by the Innholders' growing collection of plate. There remain with the Company to this day four Elizabethan Julian spoons, six made during the reign of James I (including the generously proportioned John Faucett spoon) and a single example from the time of Charles I. In addition to these are the two massive, plain but handsome silver-gilt salts presented, as their inscriptions proudly record, by John Waterworth in 1626. The more elegant Reeve salt, over six inches high, dates from 1639.

Another indication of esteem is reflected in the fact that in 1634 the livery sought to have reconfirmed its grant of arms. The livery were seeking a recognised symbol of their status, what the grant of arms itself calls: 'fit ensigns of honour assigned unto them to use at all times upon occasion as well as to the worship of themselves as in honour of this noble City of London wherein they reside'.

Particularly impressive in the elegant parchment eventually presented to the Innholders by Sir Richard St George, Clarenceux King of Arms, is the aptness of its symbolism. The cross of St Julian on the chief or upper third of the shield is a clear reference to the Company's original patron saint, while the three golden sheaves of corn represent the abundance and health that good hospitality necessarily provides. The golden star of sixteen points is surely a reference to the star shining over the inn at Bethlehem. The suggestion of charity and well-being is further developed by the Latin motto *Hinc spes affulget* ('Hope shines here') which, in its turn, appears related to an earlier biblical motto of the Company that appears in certain manuscripts: 'Come, ye blessed, when I was harbourless ye lodged Me'. Even at this moment of worldly glory the innkeeper's trade was not wholly divorced from Christian ideals.

*

Waterwortt Salts, 1626

Reeve Salt, 1637

The Grant of Arms by Sir Richard St. George, Clarenceux King of Arms
17 December, 1634

...all and Singular aswell

...ellmen and Gentlemen as well to whom these presents shall come to...
...George knt Clarencieux King of Armes of the East west and south partes...
...from the river of Trent Southward sendeth greeting Know ye that wheras
...the renewing the vertuous acts of worthy persons have ben commended to...
...monuments and remembrances of their good deserts amongst wch the...
...ensignes of signes and tokens called armes wch are evident demonstrations
...and dewly distributed according to the quallety and deserts of the persons
...to the intent that such as have done commendable service to their Prince
...warr or peace or otherwise by their laudable and courageous enterprises
...degree or provinces for augmentacon of their estate & honor greatly
...[illegible] And wheras the corporacon of the art or mistery of
...inholders of the citty of London are incorporated by the name of Master and
...ens & Masters and are made a body politique and are to have perpetuall succession
...art & may be owner of there said corporacon with a comon seale [illegible]
...and [illegible] And for that they find it needfull for them as other corporations
...aswell to the upholding of themselves as in honor of the noble citty of London
...the Grett Master Andrew Davies and Thomas Eccleston the wardens & William Sym...
...ayne such Armes & Creast with supporters as they and their successors may [illegible]
...and have thought fitt to assigne unto them these Armes Crest and Supporters
...on a cheife Argent a St Julians cross sable and for there Crest a starr
...rgent as more plainely appeareth depicted in the margent The which
...tify and confirme unto the aforenamed Master & Wardens of the sayd
...ssors as aforesayd may at all tymes and upon all occasions use & beare the
...greater in generall and not otherwise In witnes whereof I have hereunto
...the [illegible] yeare of the raigne of our soveraigne Lord [illegible]

R. St George Clarenceux
King of Armes

Their charters, the grant of their arms, their halls, properties and gleaming plate ensured that the liveries – including the Innholders – fell under the rapacious eyes of the constantly impoverished and autocratic early Stuart kings. The extravagance of the scholarly and foolish James I with his belief in the divine rights of kings, and the continental wars of his son Charles I ensured that this was so. Between 1604 and 1626, these two monarchs negotiated through the Privy Council six loans via the Corporation of the City who, in turn, assessed the livery companies for the contributions they were to make.

In such ways as these London was gradually being transformed into a major centre for raising capital, but the Crown was so arbitrary and so unreliable in financial matters that, by 1639, its credit was at its nadir and armed conflict was becoming inevitable. Nevertheless, for a time London remained loyal to the king and in 1641 the Innholders resolved to meet their share of the levy imposed on the companies by the City authorities.

The matter was decided by the Court of Assistants: Henry Worthington presided as Master; Richard Reeve, William Lakins and Henry Tooley were present as Wardens; while Messrs Lycorise, Meare, Walter, Lether, Playsted, Glazebrooke, Smyth, Ro [...], Sanderson and Tilsey were the Assistants. Their mood must have been serious for the Company was required to raise the considerable figure of £600, 'being part of the sum of £100,000, agreed to be lent by several companies of this City to the honourable Houses of Parliament'. In the event, the entire amount was lent personally by Mr Glazebrooke in return for the 8 per cent interest which Parliament had promised as the figure they would pay on all moneys lent. Mr Glazebrooke was generous and even altruistic, for historically the prospects of repayment were unreliable at best.

For a time the patriarchal hands of the City fathers preserved stability in the capital but forces of a new and frightening hostility to the king were at work. An ever-increasing number of evangelical Protestants looked with fear and loathing at the Roman Catholics gathered around the royal family and Queen Henrietta Maria, who was French, in particular. Their hatreds were then made the more bitter by the imperious methods chosen by Charles and Archbishop Laud to impose the beauties of High Church Anglicanism on the radically Protestant capital. Puritan preachers whipped up their congregations with increasingly passionate sermons, and encouraged public fasts and prayers. Throughout the difficult months the City authorities hoped to avoid anarchy at all costs, but the voices of anger at the King's refusal to consult Parliament and to take account of his subjects' deepest feelings became ever more raucous, driving Charles to desperate duplicity, betrayals and folly. At last Parliament found itself in a position where compromise with the monarch was no longer possible.

On 4 January, 1642, the King, determined to assert his authority, marched into the House of Commons and resolved to arrest the five leading members of the opposition. They escaped into the City which gladly hid them in Coleman Street (where, as we have seen, the Innholders had property) while Charles processed to the Guildhall, surrounded by hostile crowds demanding that Parliament's privileges should be recognised. Perhaps only the presence of the still loyal livery companies provided Charles with brief comfort. Among their number was a representative of the Innholders, Peter Walker, who was paid four shillings 'for carrying arms to the Guildhall... when the king came through London'. But such forlorn displays of support were insufficient and Charles' nerve broke.

Fatally, he fled his capital and left it to the radicals - Parliamentarian and Protestant - who seized control of the militia, curtailed the power of the Aldermen, and then saw the royalist Lord Mayor impeached, imprisoned and replaced with one of their own kind. London was preparing for war.

During the Civil War the Innholders played their part in the defence of the City. Company records show the Court agreeing 'that for the speedy raising of money to buy threescore quarters of wheat... it is ordered that the Assistants shall lend 40s, Liverymen 30s, Yeomanry 20s' London, newly surrounded with vast defensive earthworks, was now a parliamentary city and the engine of the eventual parliamentary triumph. The financial cost was high indeed and, once again, the livery companies were obliged to help meet the costs. This is almost certainly why, at a meeting of the Court of Assistants of the Innholders held on 30 May, 1643, it was decided 'in consideration of the urgent need of money for the payment of debts and interest by the Company, they have ordered that some of the plate to the value of £100 be sold, but not without the consent of the Assistants, livery, and yeomanry'.

Eleven substantial items, including a great covered goblet weighing just under sixty four ounces, were requisitioned along with twenty six gilt headed spoons. This was still not enough, and a dozen more spoons and a quantity of 'white plate' had to be added to achieve a final painful total of £100. 2s. But even now the parliamentary need for money remained clamorous. £50,000 was called for and, once again, the livery companies were expected to provide. A slight note of desperation enters the Innholders' minute book for 22 August, 1643, when it was decided to 'take up on the common seal of Mr John Taylor £300, or any other that will lend the same' for six months at 7 per cent. Such worry was far from being unprecedented. The London livery companies paid dearly for backing the parliamentary cause. None of the individuals who so handsomely contributed to these levies (and who were also paying high levels of direct taxation) ever had their loans repaid.

Meanwhile the great national drama of the Civil War moved to its crisis. After four years of fighting concluded in the capture of Charles, Cromwell reluctantly decided on his trial, and assented to the king's execution on the scaffold outside the Banqueting Hall in Whitehall. The event shocked the nation. In Europe, too, people looked on with the gravest concern as one of the great families of their time was replaced by a Commonwealth, and eventually by the stern, puritanical Protectorate of Cromwell himself.

*

In Cromwellian London, despite the dourness of the abolition of Christmas and enforced sabbatarianism, the Innholders continued their traditions of hospitality, albeit under somewhat straitened circumstances. The first surviving account books from early in the second half of the 17th century show that the Innholders were careful in the ordering of their feasts. For example, they did not employ a regular cook but preferred to hire an outside caterer called James Ellis to prepare, at a cost of 13s. 4d. a quarter, the small number of dinners the Company hosted. Ellis also supplied the food he was to cook and would certainly have needed an assistant to help prepare it.

Special care was taken of the cutlery and linen. The latter was precious and the Court 'ordered that the linen shall remain in the chest' after it had been washed, and that the Renter Warden was to keep the key. A little later they decided to see 'whether [the] tablecloths will serve; if not, new ones be bought, and holland cloths and napkins for ordinary use'. The problem was solved in part at least by Nicholas Cooke, a prosperous liveryman and at one time its Master who, in addition to presenting the Innholders with a silver-gilt cup, also donated 'a green cloth carpet with a green silk fringe for the Master's table in the hall'.

Feasts were expensive, and it was now ordered that no man save the Master should bring any guest into the Company's Hall for its quarter day feasts, 'upon penalty of 5s'. Those wishing to bring guests to the Renter Warden's and Steward's feasts were liable to a sum of twice that amount; even the Renter Wardens and the Stewards themselves could only invite guests on the understanding that 'they must provide a table for them by themselves'. Nevertheless the necessary decencies were recognised, and the Court ruled that the widows of Innholders who had bequeathed £10 or more to the guild, in money or plate, 'shall be invited to the Hall when the Company's wives come to any feast'.

Gradually the depredations on the Innholders' collection of plate were made good, and a number of interesting pieces survive from the Commonwealth period. In 1657 the Court made it compulsory for all those aspiring to membership to present the guild with a Julian spoon, along with a pair of gloves and an entrance fine of 17s. 6d. Early account books show that this order was regularly complied with and, in the following year, one Peter Hals presented the Company with a particularly fine example of a Julian spoon that has an elongated and elegant handle. The Company then ordered four more Julian spoons in 1660, while six more of the same type and inscribed with their givers' names were donated by members of the Company between 1660 and 1661.

This was unusual since comparatively little silverware was produced at this time but, in addition to the handsome Charlett tankard, the Company also possesses three excellent standing cups from this date. These include the magisterial Osborne cup of 1658 and two earlier examples, both from 1654, presented by Nicholas Cooke and Thomas Hinde. Cooke, as we have seen, was a prosperous and important member of the Company. He was Master some time before 1641 and would show his continuing devotion and generosity twenty five years later. Hinde, too, was a devoted Company man and in his will left a yearly rent-charge of £5 out of his business, The Spur in Southwark, to be distributed among needy Innholders.

This last suggests that, despite its financial straits, the Company was still vigorously and efficiently exercising its functions as a guild. Despite the bewildering succession of constitutional experiments at Westminster and the fact that the City of London itself was periodically in the grip of some of the most radical factions in the land, the Great Rebellion did not upset the fundamental structures of the City's administration, including the livery companies. The old institutional oligarchies survived and, for all the great defensive earthworks that had been raised around outer London, no attempt was made to establish a unitary authority for the whole metropolis.

In such an atmosphere, the Court of Assistants of the Innholders' Company could adapt their familiar procedures to solve current problems. The fire-scorched minute book of 1642 – the Company's earliest continuous record – shows Innholders not only ensuring that their grip

Charlett Tankard, 1654

Osborne Cup, 1658

Cooke Cup, 1654

Hinde Cup, 1654

The Innholder's Rare Commonwealth Silver

over their trade remained firm but also fulfilling their public and civic duties. For example coal was bought for distribution among the poor; when the aged Beadle, Mr Somner, was no longer able to execute his office, he was given a pension of £8 a year; and funerals of members were dutifully attended. However there were still funds left over for dinners with the Lord Mayor, and various improvements to the Hall, such as instructions that the chimney piece in the parlour 'be new beautified, and an iron back and a table be bought'.

The Court also fought for the Company's business interests. In November 1654, and again in April 1657, voices were raised suggesting that London innkeepers should be obliged to take out licences. This was fiercely and successfully resisted, while the Company also made repeated and strenuous efforts to ensure that retired Cromwellian soldiers wishing to become innkeepers should be required to join the Company and pay proper fees, despite a new law which allowed them 'to use any trade'. The Innholders sought the advice of the Court of Common Council as to whether they could enforce this regulation. Clearly they were told that they could, since many would-be landlords were 'summoned to appear' before the Court of Assistants where they were sternly informed that they must either take up the freedom or face being sued. All, apparently, submitted.

But beneath this appearance of orderliness and efficiency, profound unrest was developing in the nation at large. The constant shifts and turns taken by the Parliamentarians to reconcile their religious, egalitarian and foreign policy aims with stable government proved painful, divisive and in the end unacceptable. Their radical experiment was failing, and after Cromwell's death in 1658 there were no natural leaders to continue it. A return to the supposed securities of hereditary monarchical rule appeared, to an increasing number of people, the only and necessary alternative. By 1660 the Innholders, along with the greater part of the country, were ready to welcome the return of the late king's son as Charles II. For the moment, at least, it seemed that it would be business as before.

Chapter 5

THE CHARTER OF CHARLES II

1660 - 1664

The Restoration and the City – The Innholders reinforced by an Act of Common Council –The charter of 1663 – Applying the new charter – The Charter of Inspeximus, 1664

The Innholders joined enthusiastically in the mood of national rejoicing which broke out with the return of Charles II from exile in 1660. A vast and lavish procession through London was planned and led by the king himself: a tall, saturnine, pleasure-loving man of high intelligence and the deepest guile. Charles entered the City via Blackheath and his seven hour procession made its way to Whitehall along streets that were strewn with flowers and hung with tapestries. Trumpets blared, cannons roared and the public fountains ran with wine. Here was the monarchy triumphant, and the livery companies added to the sense of occasion by appearing at their most magnificent.

A body of some 600 liverymen attended the Lord Mayor when he offered the king the City's loyal address and that they should be mounted on horseback, dressed in black velvet coats, wear gold chains, and be accompanied by footmen apparelled in the liveries of their companies and carrying their company banners.

The Innholders spared no expense in their efforts to display their loyalty. They were determined that the livery should appear at its most prestigious and the Court 'ordered that every person that rides sends his footmen to Innholders' Hall on Tuesday morning by ten of the clock May 22nd to have measure taken for their liveries trim'd with white and blue ribbons and mixed grey serge. King's colours in the hat and every footman a short truncheon of white fur tipped with blue at each end'. In addition to this, it was ordered that the Company's flag should be 'new beautified' and that it should be carried in the procession by Mr Langhorne.

Members of the different livery companies were invited to a 'sumptuous collation' provided in a 'very magnificent tent' erected on St George's Fields in Southwark.

The Company held a feast on the day before the king's coronation when, during the evening, Charles rode in sovereign splendour from the Tower of London through the City to Westminster. The procession the following morning was again a sumptuous affair. Charles wore a suit of cloth-of-gold ornamented with the jewelled star of the Order of the Garter. The horse of state was gorgeously caparisoned with a saddle worked with gold, pearls and a splendid ruby. A further 12,000 jewels decorated the stirrups. Along the processional route magnificent triumphal arches predicted a glorious future for the nation. Allegorical panels showed Monarchy supported by Loyalty, while Rebellion and Confusion were routed. A second arch showed the benefits that would flow from peace. In particular, it extolled the virtues of the country's mighty navy and the enormous wealth that commerce would bring as Britain gained the mastery of world trade. This last was far from being an empty promise since, in the next fifty years, the country would establish itself as one of the great maritime and commercial powers in the West.

Nonetheless, despite the confidence and the opulence of the coronation celebrations, there were strains under the surface which would eventually prove of the utmost importance to the development of parliamentary democracy and hence to the nation's future.

The Innholders would be closely and painfully involved in these events but, in the meantime, they had more immediate concerns. The Civil War had left them in straightened circumstances and a range of legal judgements had begun seriously to threaten the guilds' monopoly powers. They could no longer be absolutely sure of their ability to enforce membership on those not free who were practising their trade. Nor could they necessarily compel men who had served an apprenticeship under one guild to transfer to a more appropriate one when those men decided to change their occupations. In addition, the guilds' ancient powers of seizing goods

KING CHARLES II.
triumphal Entry into the
City of London at his
Restoration.

during the search of business premises were in dispute, and it was now doubtful precisely how far their prescriptive ordinances could be enforced at law. But many of the London guilds, including the Innholders, were determined not to take matters lying down. Their income and prestige – even, in the long-term, their survival – were at stake.

There were widespread complaints from many livery companies that their rights were being flouted, and even the once prosperous Goldsmiths confessed that they had been well-nigh ruined by the encroachment of alien craftsmen who were firmly resolved to promote the cause of free trade – the day of the independent capitalist, the unfettered entrepreneur, was dawning. Such men chafed at the restrictions placed on them by the guilds, and sometimes even offered violence and 'very abusive words' when Wardens came to inspect their premises.

The wavering policies of the Court of Common Council provided only fitful support to the beleaguered Innholders. On occasions the Corporation was temporarily convinced that the answer to economic competition did not lie in enforcing restrictive practices on inns in the ever-expanding London suburbs. Instead, they thought they should try and lure them back into the City with offers of relaxing the stringent terms on which the freedom was granted. More often, however, the Court of Common Council was inclined towards regulation and believed that rigid control was the best means of ensuring prosperity. It was in this mood that they passed an Act prohibiting the use of inns as unlicensed shops.

The Innholders were naturally in sympathy with such a line and were determined to enforce their authority by petitioning for new powers under a new royal charter. No doubt, like the Goldsmiths, they realised that royal pleasure was likely to incline to them, 'it now being a favourable time wherein the King's Majesty upon all occasions is willing to grant the citizens of London anything that can in reason be desired and that he may lawfully grant'.

*

Charles II
by an artist in the studio of John Michael Wright (ca. 1660-1665)

Along with a number of other companies, the Innholders sought to reinforce their ancient privileges and, in particular, to extend the area over which they could exercise their control. They would not allow inns to proliferate across the London suburbs without making a strenuous effort to have some authority over them.

The Company therefore appointed a committee of its most active members to pursue the matter. This committee consisted of 'Alderman Cooke, Master; and Wardens, Mr Tooley, Mr. Osborne, Mr. Pennington; Mr. Jenkinson, Mr. James Davyes, Mr. Malcher, Mr. Bennett, Mr. Moorhouse, Mr. Penner'. They decided on a two-pronged approach. First they would approach the City authorities and seek their recognition of the Company's right to supervise all those working in the innkeeping trade across the City and its Liberties. (These last were those formerly monastic precincts such as Whitefriars and the Charterhouse that were normally immune from outside interference and were, as a result, pockets of poverty and lawlessness). Then, with their powers assured, the committee of the Innholders would approach the king and seek a fresh charter which would not only define the Company's rights, privileges and forms of operation in far greater detail than before but would also considerably extend its area of authority.

Accordingly, on 23 May, 1663, the committee went before the Court of Common Council at the Guildhall and secured from them an Act which stipulated that: 'all and singular persons, of whatever society they were then or would be thereafter in future, using the art, mistery or occupation of innholder or holding, keeping or occupying any common inn, small lodging-house or common stable (called livery-stables, in English) within our City of London or the Liberties of the same, thenceforth should be transferred from the society of which they were then free or would be free to the Society of Innholders and it should be admitted into the same and be sworn'. The Act also provided that the Innholders should have the right to monitor all employees of the innkeeping business across both the City and its liberties. Those running London's inns were required to present all of those working for them at the Innholders' Hall 'in order that there their name and names might be registered and they might take the oath as appointed to be taken by the ancient ordinances of the said society by all servants, stable-men (called ostlers, in English) butlers of ale and drink (called tapsters, in English) and chamberlains'.

As it was essential that all those concerned should be informed of the Act, the Innholders' Court ordered that 600 copies of the newly reinforced regulations should be printed. This was a very considerable number and clearly suggests that it was not only respectable Freemen of other companies working as innkeepers who were to be informed. The Beadle was also to post the notices in more dubious establishments which the Company had undertaken to supervise. The Innholders thus sought not only absolute control over London innkeeping but also to enhance its income from the fees payable by all those required to swear its oaths.

The oath sworn by innkeepers joining the Company is of particular interest for a number of reasons. First comes the necessary declaration of loyalty to the Crown and the Company:

> You shall be true and faithful to our Sovereign Lord the King that now is and to his Heirs and Successors, Kings and Queens of England. You shall be obedient lawfully to the Master and Wardens of this Society for the time being in all such things as concern the good government of the said Society.

To ensure that this bond of loyalty between master and man did not appear to condone them both conniving in crime the oath goes on:

> And if your Master with whom would you serve shall use any subtlety or crafty demeanour in his weights, hostelry, lodging or double hostelries contrary to the Orders of this Society, you shall at the request of the Master and Wardens of this Society for the time being utter and show the same unto them.

One of the Company's principal concerns appears to have been the prevention of theft and violent crime in the City's licensed premises.

Hence the following obligation laid upon those who worked in them:

> And moreover if you have knowledge and intelligence of any felons, murderers or other suspicious persons resorting to your Master's house or to the houses of any other of the said Society, you shall with all diligence disclose and show the same unto your own Master or else unto the Master and Wardens of the Society of Innholders for the time being. You shall not wittingly nor willingly receive, harbour or cherish a thief, robber or other suspicious persons. You shall not be of counsel with any thief, robber or other suspicious persons. You shall not be of counsel with any thief, robber or other persons for the setting of any robbery or doing of any violence, theft or fraud to any person nor shall know the like intended by any, without disclosing the same either to your own Master with whom you serve or to the Master and Wardens for the time being of [the] Innholders to the intent it may be discovered by some magistrate. So help you God.

It is important to remember in this context that London still had no police force. The watchmen of each of the parishes were supposed to keep a weather-eye open for suspicious characters and it was the duty of the parish constables to apprehend criminals with the help of such honest citizens as would come to their assistance; but the constables were inefficient at best. They were the lowest officeholders in the whole hierarchy of local authority officials and were appointed by the vicar and church wardens of the parishes for a fixed term and at a very low rate of remuneration. Most busy men no doubt hoped that they could avoid the duty, but it was incumbent upon them to accept if they were nominated, and it is easy to imagine how many were dilatory. The City Liberties therefore remained rife with crime, and the Innholders' strongest suit in the effort to obtain a new and more potent royal charter lay precisely in the strenuous efforts they could and would take to control this social menace.

*

As so often, the Innholders reconstructed themselves on the basis of their traditions. After dissolving, for legal purposes, the original charter of 1514, the Charter granted to the Livery by Charles II on 21 December, 1663, is largely concerned with reconstituting the Company as a perpetual corporation, with the full range of ancient rights and privileges conventionally granted to guilds now greatly elaborated.

The charter paints a vivid picture of a London underworld pulsating with disorder, violence and organised crime. This, it suggests, was largely because a great number of 'inns, small lodging-houses and livery-stables' were kept in the City and surrounding areas by men who were not members of the Innholders' Company and therefore not constrained by its ordinances. The charter describes a mêlée of traitors and seditious people frequenting such houses of ill repute where 'their horses are concealed and robberies and unlawful things are devised'. The new charter states that the king out of 'our royal rights and . . . kingly supremacy' was determined to re-establish the Company on a firm legal basis to prevent such things.

This was entirely in keeping with Restoration ideas about the nature of the monarch's powers, or what was then termed the royal prerogative. Charles was no mere constitutional king, a state figurehead. His all but miraculous return to the country in 1660 had shown to the greater part of the people at least that, in defiance of the republican ideas advocated by the supporters of the Commonwealth, royal power rested on divinely planned foundations and permeated every aspect of society. It was entirely right that on his own authority, the king should reconstitute the Innholders as an instrument of law and order. He was the source and origin of every legitimate enterprise in the country; he alone had the right to create the peers who were the country's perpetual legislators; he, too, could alone grant the charters by which he enfranchised boroughs and corporations such as the Innholders whose temporary legislators (the Court of Assistants) promulgated their rules and regulations with his authority.

All the Company's rights under its original charter were confirmed and the members of the Court were required to swear their oaths of office before the Attorney General, the Solicitor General or one of the Masters of Chancery. Thus constituted, the Assistants then had the right and duty, in the presence of the Master, to administer the oaths of the lesser members of the Company – the apprentices, ostlers, tapsters and chamberlains – who were all to be, to the best of the Livery's knowledge, persons of upright character.

The Clerk was to be a man of unimpeachable loyalty among whose duties were to record the decisions of the Court without fear or favour, and keep their records private. For these duties Gregory Peake, who was to hold office 'during the term of his natural life', was paid 'the yearly salary or fee of £14 . . and all other fees, profits, commodities, and things whatsoever to the same office in anywise appertaining . . ., according to the custom and usage of the Clerks of other Societies and Companies of the City of London'.

The Beadle, John Aspinall, was to be paid £2 a quarter day for summoning before the Court of Assistants such persons as they commanded, and to do so 'without sparing of any person for affection, lucre, gain, hatred or malice'.

Under the terms of the charter the king once more granted the Court of Assistants powers of 'supervision, search, examination, guidance and correction of all and singular persons' keeping inns within the area of their authority. In order to exercise these provisions, the Master and Wardens of the Innholders were given 'power to enter any stable or stables, dwelling-house or dwelling-houses or any other buildings whatsoever' maintained by such people, and to do so whenever they saw fit. In support of this the charter gave the Court the right to call on 'all mayors, justices, bailiffs,

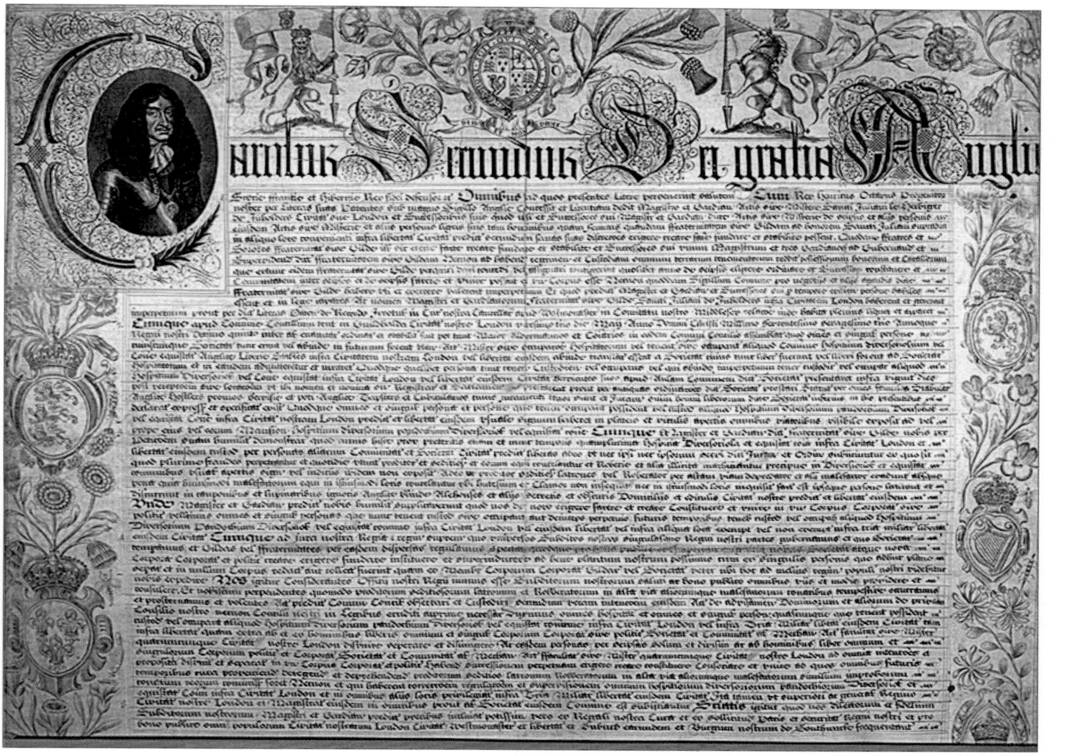

The Charter of Charles II , 1663 (above) and that of James II ,1685 (below)

constables and all other officers, ministers and subjects whomsoever, that they should give assistance, help and succour'.

Dishonest dealings with weights and measures were one thing, however an altogether more serious reason for the wide-ranging powers vested in the Innholders was the maintenance of law and order in Charles' capital, and the charter makes this explicit. But London was no longer conceived as being simply the City; it now included the inhabitants of 'Westminster and the liberties and suburbs of the same, and . . . those frequenting, hastening into and thronging our borough of Southwark and all other places within three miles of the liberties of the City'.

In other words, the area covered by the Innholders' remit was to be considerably extended to take in areas hitherto less organized and unused to centralised authority. The Innholders were charged with the duty of 'taking action against, detecting and discovering the criminal schemes of factions, seditious persons, thieves, highway robbers and other evildoers'.

*

In order to achieve this a radical remodelling of the Company's membership was required, a fresh and altogether sharper focus on the business of innkeeping itself. This was not done without some unprecedented moves and a consequent measure of acrimony. For example, just before the election of Robert Whitborne to the mastership in 1663 the powerful figure of John Knott took his place on the Court for the first time. Knott, who had been a member of the Company since at least 1654, was a considerable presence in the world of London innkeeping. He was the proprietor of the Three Cups in Bread Street which, from the time that John Stow made his survey of the City more than half a century earlier, was 'wholly inhabited by rich merchants, and divers fair inns be there'. Clearly, there were those on the Court who saw Knott as the right man for new times; others were less sure and were clearly aggrieved when his name was given precedence over men of longer standing. Matters came to a head, and an appeal to the Court of Aldermen was mooted, but the matter was resolved internally, though without precedent. Knott was given advanced seniority and, on 20 September, 1664, was sworn in as Master. Significantly, in the same month, another thrusting London innkeeper, Robert Briscoe, took his place on the Court and, the following year, was elected Master.

Forced change at the top of the Company was mirrored in changes lower down when the requirements of the new charter were applied more resolutely than those of the old one: some thirty-nine named persons 'now holding, keeping or occupying inns, lodging-houses, alehouses, small lodging-houses and livery-stables' were 'separated and put asunder' from whatever companies they had previously belonged to and were reconstituted as 'one body corporate and politic', or the newly revised Company of Innholders. Given the intense loyalty a company inspired, such transfers were a potentially contentious requirement, and not all were straightforward or entirely amicable.

A man called Holtam, for example, declined to comply and the Court resolved that he should be summoned before them and that 'if he then refuse to be sworn to the ordinances of the Company that he be sued'. A surly Holtam duly appeared but was sufficiently aggrieved to return only a dusty answer. Similarly, innkeepers who were free of companies higher on the list, such as the Merchant Taylors and the Barber Surgeons, were reluctant to comply with the Act and the Innholders' Court resolved that these two companies be 'warned' about this. To this end it was agreed that 'some of the old Masters... go with the Master and Wardens to the Lord Mayor Elect Sir Thomas Bludworth about the said translations'.

*

It was, of course, essential that no one should be able to raise substantial legal objections to the new ordinances of the Company, and steps were taken to ensure that this was indeed so. As the charter itself recognised, the ordinances could only be enforced at law if they were confirmed as being 'in accordance with a certain Act of Parliament made the twenty fifth day of January in the nineteenth year [of the reign] of Henry VII, lately King of England'. This Act laid down that no guild could make any ordinances that touched the king's prerogative or adversely affected the profit of the king's subjects, and that these were matters to be decided by the Lord Chancellor, the Lord Treasurer, and the Chief Justices. Accordingly, the ordinances of the Innholders Company were now submitted to the Lord Chancellor, the Lord Treasurer, the Chief Justice of King's Bench and the Chief Justice of the Court of Common Pleas. This was an anxious moment, until a favourable verdict was received on 13 June, 1664.

The judgement was actually delivered in a supplementary Charter of *Inspeximus* of 8 July, 1664, which set out how the main charter should be applied and gives a fascinating insight into the detailed workings of the Company. In particular it shows how discipline and cohesion were maintained and how, at the same time, the Company's income was maintained by its elaborate system of fees and fines.

These were levied on virtually every aspect of the Company's activities and were particularly steep for senior members of the livery. The Master and Upper Warden, for example, were required to pay 'forty shillings a piece' for their elevation and, along with the Middle Warden were expected to pay a further forty shillings when they left office. No man could easily evade election to the Livery if he was eligible. A severe and unpopular ordinance of the Company made it mandatory for 'any person that is a member and free of the said Society who hath an estate in monies, goods or stock of the value of £200 or more of his own proper goods, money or stock, his just and due debts deducted, to take the livery or clothing of the said Society upon him and to pay his fine at his coming upon the clothing – £10 to the Master and Wardens of the said Society to the use of the same Society'. Those declining the livery could be fined up to £5 a

Two membranes from Charles II's Charter of Inspeximus, *with their beautifully illuminated borders, which had been concealed and preserved behind the uppermost parchment, until they were discovered in 1996, when all the Company's Charters were restored at the Guildhall Library*

year. All in all, members could pay dearly for their status and privileges, but also for refusing them.

Nor were lesser members of the Company able to evade a range of charges. Admission to the freedom was subject to a fee not exceeding £3. Quarterage fees were charged at two shillings a quarter and a fine of five shillings was levied for non-payment. Those taking on apprentices were required to pay five shillings for each of them, and even hired menials were required to find from their pittances a shilling for the Company and sixpence for the Clerk.

Failure to participate in the Company's public business was a fineable offence, while failure to comply when the Court of Assistants ordered a search was subject to a penalty of twenty shillings. In addition, a whole range of fines was levied on those who were found to be in default of the Company's ordinances for the conduct of business. Adamant refusal to pay such a fine could incur summary justice. The Beadle (presumably with the help of some unmentioned strongmen) was to arrive by daylight at the offender's premises and, if payment were not immediately made, to seize such goods and chattels as he considered equalled the sum involved.

In such ways the Worshipful Company of Innholders sought to re-establish its authority and income. It did so with the authority of the King and the City fathers. Everything that the laws of man could do to back them had been done, but nothing could now protect them from the two acts of God.

* * *

Chapter 6

THE YEARS OF PERIL

1665-1702

The Plague – The Great Fire – a new Hall
Battles with Charles II – The charter of 1685
Battles with James II – The new world of William and Mary

There had been many outbreaks of the plague during the century but the most terrible of them was first noticed in London during May 1665. Forty three people died during that month but, as the summer came on, the toll mounted horrifyingly. Nearly 600 people died during June while, in the following month, deaths were being counted in their thousands. The agony reached its crisis in September when 30,000 people fell to the disease. Suffering was appalling and, because there were no adequate hospitals, the sick were left in their houses. The poor were the most cruelly affected because, living in crowded tenements and filthy basements, the presence of one victim could bring certain death to as many as half a dozen families. So many fatalities caused immense logistical problems, for there were too few graveyards, and too little quicklime to pick clean the carcasses tipped from the dead carts into hastily dug, shallow pits, around which crows and ravens circled in the certain expectation of a feast.

If the human suffering was ghastly, the effect on trade was disastrous. The City became a waste land. Grass grew in the once busy streets where there was hardly a cart or a coach to be seen, save for the few country wagons that brought meagre but necessary supplies of beans and peas, hay and straw, to sustain the lives of men and beasts. The consequences for the City's inns were particularly severe since, far from welcoming a great influx of visitors, they watched an exodus fleeing the capital as fast as it could. In that vivid recreation of London's agony, Daniel Defoe's *A Journal of the Plague Year*, the author provides a searing if perhaps apocryphal story to illustrate the sort of horrors faced daily by London's innkeepers.

Defoe tells how a man who had been confined to his house because of the plague escaped and made his way towards Islington. Desperate for a place to lay his head, he knocked on the doors first of the Angel and then of the White Horse. The landlords of both establishments refused him entrance. When he reached rural Islington, still relatively free from contagion and determined to preserve its well-being, the now desperate man realised that his only hope lay in lying. He therefore knocked on the door of the Pied Bull and asserted he was free from contamination. The wary landlord gave him a bed in a garret room and the exhausted guest asked one of the servants to 'bring him a pint of warm ale to comfort him and help him sleep'.

The servant forgot, and only remembered the next morning when he went to call the visitor in the garret. On opening the door, his horror was immediate. The solitary guest had died during the night and his corpse lay with its 'eyes open in a most frightful posture'. Nor did the ghastliness end there, for now there was infection in Islington and, Defoe reports, the plague soon spread to the neighbouring houses.

The City authorities faced the catastrophe with the utmost fortitude, and Defoe paid tribute to them when he described how the Lord Mayor and the sheriffs were continually in the streets and constantly exposed themselves to danger. The Lord Mayor, determined at one and the same time to do his duty and preserve his health, had a glass cabinet constructed in which he could preside over the distribution of charity, the maintenance of food supplies, the combating of petty crime and efforts to ensure that profiteers did not wax rich on the disaster.

The expense of maintaining the bare necessities of life in a moribund city were nonetheless considerable. It is estimated that, in all, the plague killed 90,000 people in the London area. As so often the Court of Aldermen looked to the livery companies for resources to fight the crisis. They forbade all public feasts and common dinners in every hall and then declared that, because of the hardship caused by 'the utter cessation of trade', one third of the money usually lavished upon such occasions was to be given to a common fund for the relief of hardship.

John Knott, the Master of the Innholders, newly elected because of his

LORD HAVE MERCY UPON US.

This is the humble Petition of *England* unto Almighty God, meekely imploring his Divine bounty for the ceſſation of this Mortality of Peſtilence now raigning amongſt us: VVith a lamentable Liſt of Deaths Triumphs in the weekly Burials of the City of LONDON, and the Pariſhes adjacent to the ſame.

1625	total	PL
March 17	161	4
March 24	226	8
March 31	243	11
April 7	239	10
April 14	256	24
April 21	230	25
April 28	305	26
May 5	292	30
May 12	332	45
May 19	379	71
May 26	401	78
June 2	395	69
June 9	434	91
June 16	510	165
June 23	640	239
June 30	942	390
July 7	1222	593
July 14	1781	1004
July 21	2850	1819
July 28	3583	2471
Auguſt 4	4517	3659
Auguſt 11	4855	4115
Auguſt 18	5203	4463
Auguſt 25	4841	4218
Septem. 1	3897	3344
Septem. 8	3157	2550
Septem. 15	2143	1672
Septem. 22	1994	1551
Septem. 29	1236	852
Octob. 6	813	538
Octob. 13	815	511
Octob. 20	651	331
Octob. 27	375	134
Novem. 3	357	89
Nov. 10	319	91
Nov. 17	274	48
Nov. 24	231	27
Decem. 1	290	15
Decem. 8	181	15
Decem. 15	168	6
Decem. 22	157	1

The totall of the Burials this whole year, 54082
Of the Plague, 35428

A Prayer fit to be uſed in this time of ſickneſſe or mortality.

Lord moſt juſt, and Father moſt mercifull, thou it is that reneweſt thy Plagues againſt Man when he offendeth thee: thy vengeance from heaven is both ſudden and fearefull toward the rebellious and diſobedient children: thou for one fin in King David, *deſtroyedſt with the loathſome diſeaſe of the Peſtilence many thouſands of his people: caft thine eyes of mercy upon us, O thou preſerver of men, which languifh now in this land, and in this houſe with the like diſeaſe and fickneſſe. Now, deare God, hath not* David *onely offended thee, in truſting to his ſtrength, and numbring of his people: but even each congregation; and every houſhold hath one way or other provoked thee to plague thy diſobedient people; and now that we ſee thy plagues appearing, to the piercing and parting of our bodies and foules aſunder: Lord, we ſtand amazed in our mindes, heartily fighing with groanes at fight of our fins. Now we conſider, we have ſinned grievouſly, we have done amiſſe, we have dealt wickedly, we have lived ungodly, we have ſwerved from the way of thruth, without any godly feare or remorfe of confcience: thy great benefit of Peace, and rare bleſsinge of long proſperity, under ſo good and gracious a Governor, have brought to too many of us, to ſuch ſecurity and contempt of Religion, that altogether forgetting to be thankfull, we have abufed thy benefits as faſt as they came and that with a churliſh kinde of impiety: the thoughts of our hearts, the words of our mouthes and the works of our hands are vain, carnall, and devilliſh: yeah, our fervice to thee oftentimes but meare abomination: ſo farre (alas) wandered from the path of thy commandements. As thou didft finde with the Iſraelites wickednes in* Gilgal, *ſin in* Bethel, *and iniquity in* Berthabas *ſo in every Church, in every Court, nay, in every concourfe or aſſembly amongſt us, thou beholdeſt how the fleſh hath overgrown the Spirit and how reaſon is over-ruled with affections; fo many labour in theſe our dayes under the diſplayed enſighn of ſatan, that very few deare Father are found ſetled in the dutifull form of upright and ſpirituall obedience, which thou requireſt. We confeffe, thou mighteſt juſtly therefore foreſake us, as we have foreſaken thee; and not onely proceed to ſting the head-Cities, and whole body of this land, with fundry plagues and grievous difeafes; but for our manifold ſins and iniquities, which we daily commit, thou mightſt juſtly and worthily condemne us, man after man, to eternall death, all conſiences being ſo guilty; that they already condemne themſelves. Yet who is he (O mercifull Lord) that can meaſure thy goodneſſe, who by thy word doeſt oftentimes bring ſinners to beliefe, repentance, and ſalvation? though it be not thy pleaſure (good Lord) to viſit the wicked innocent, but rather to viſt their iniquities, yet have we this comfort, that thy mercy to the humble ever reſts unmeaſerable and unmovable:.Be intreated therefore to pitty this land, and the infected people thereof, that we may all ſay, The Lord liveth for ever, worthy of praiſe, becauſe he hath been mercifull unto ſinners.* Amen

Printed at London for *Thomas Lambert* at the ſigne of the Horſ-ſhoo in Smithfield

From a contemporary broadsheet showing the number of burials of plague victims in 1625 compared with all mortalities, together with a woodcut and a suitable prayer.

conspicuous abilities, was faced with an unprecedented challenge. A glance at their ledgers reminded every innkeeper of the parlous state of trade, a worry reinforced by the sinister silence in the once turbulent and deafening streets. There were no longer, in the words of one commentator, any 'prancing horses, no rattling coaches, no calling in customers, nor offering wares; no London cries sounding in the ears'. The conviviality of the Innholders' Company Hall was mute and, on 27 June, 1665, an insufficient number of Assistants attended a meeting called for that day.

Conscientious members of the Court, realising that business must be conducted even in such times as these, finally made their way to a second meeting called for 8 July and resolved that the Company's plate – its greatest moveable asset – should remain in the chest until a further decision about its safe keeping could be made at the Quarter day meeting, three days later. They then decided that the Master should take personal responsibility for these precious pieces of silver and silver-gilt. Consequently, the plate was taken out of the chest and was replaced there by the linen, while the goblets, salts and spoons were taken to Knott's inn – The Three Cups in plague-ravaged Bread Street. There the Master could continuously keep an eye on their treasure.

*

By October 1665 the plague was in retreat, but now a catastrophe of altogether greater magnitude overtook London in general and the Innholders in particular. As is well known, the Great Fire of London broke out during the early hours of Sunday 2 September, 1666, at the premises of one Thomas Farrinor, a baker whose shop was situated in Pudding Lane, a narrow and dingy little passageway close to London Bridge. Farrinor had failed adequately to extinguish his oven, and the building in which he lived and worked caught fire. At first it seemed that this was merely one of the innumerable small conflagrations that were the bane of London life. However, across from Farrinor's bakery stood the

Star Inn where hay and other highly combustible materials were stored in the yard and outbuildings. Flying sparks set light to these and soon the inn itself was ablaze. The wind then drove the flames in the direction of other buildings made tinder dry after a long, hot summer.

The Lord Mayor, Sir Thomas Bludworth, was roused from his bed and grumpily dismissed the oncoming tragedy by declaring. 'Pish! A woman might piss it out!' This unfortunate comment belied the fact that the flames were now roaring hungrily towards Thames Street and the mass of highly flammable material stored on the wharfs there. London Bridge also lay in their path and was soon ablaze, as was Fishmonger's Hall, the first of forty four company halls eventually destroyed in the conflagration. Even now the overcautious Bludworth refused to pull down buildings to make firebreaks, worried as he was by the costs and legal implications of doing so. Consequently, a disaster of major proportions became increasingly certain.

Samuel Pepys reported how he saw great flakes of fire carried high into the air and then fall on distant buildings that were instantly consumed. For all that the king and his brother, James Duke of York, laboured heroically to fight the conflagration, the magnitude of the catastrophe was becoming evident and, as their City burned, so the minds of the helpless populace became inflamed with prejudice. It seemed to many Protestants that such a holocaust could only be the work of their most bitter enemies - the Roman Catholics of over-mighty France.

Pandemonium gripped the City and Samuel Pepys described in his Diary the scenes of chaos: 'everybody endeavouring to remove their goods, and flinging them into the river, or bringing them into lighters that lay off, poor people staying in their houses as long as till the very fire touched them, and then running into boats, or clambering from one pair of stairs by the waterside to another'. Taking a boat along the Thames himself, the better to see the disaster, Pepys described how he saw the flames devour the Old Swan inn, attack Dyers' Hall and then sweep on with merciless speed towards the Steelyard. As the north bank of the

Thames burned, so rumours circulated that 4000 French papists were in arms and eager to assist the destruction. In truth, it was the wind that spread the flames towards the courts and alleyways winding up the hill from Thames Street.

As evening fell, Pepys described a fire that was 'a most horrid, malicious, bloody flame, not like the fine flame of an ordinary fire'. And now, as night came on, that hostile flame penetrated Dowgate and so laid waste the Innholders Hall that only the very large hardwood beams supporting the floor still survive in a partly charred state.

Such desperate precautions as could be taken were put into effect. It seems probable that the Company's linen, plate and charters – its moveable wealth and the testimonies of its authority – were taken to the premises of the current Master, Robert Briscoe, at The Ram in Smithfield. There they narrowly escaped destruction, for the Great Fire stopped some 200 yards short of Briscoe's establishment. His was one of fifty-six London inns to survive the Great Fire.

Many were less fortunate. The Three Cups and Knott's additional properties in Bread Street were completely destroyed. Among other famous London inns also razed to the ground were The Mermaid, The Mitre, The Boar's Head which Shakespeare's Falstaff had made famous, and The Belle Sauvage, where some of Shakespeare's other plays had been performed. The sense of desolation among the Innholders was surely profound, as was the financial hardship of many. About 80,000 Londoners had been left homeless; businesses had been destroyed and the focus of the Company's pride and prestige was in ruins, as were the properties that secured its rental income.

*

Lesser men might have given up in sheer despondency, but in fact the livery companies were at the forefront of the revival of London, and the Innholders were among the most energetic. Like their peers, they were

The GREAT FIRE of LONDON in the Year 1666.

The Great Fire of London: St. Paul's from Ludgate Hill (Jan Griffier, 1646-1718)
Citizens sheltering under arches of London Bridge (P.J. de Louthenbourg ca. 1799)

fully aware of the fact that their continued existence depended on the unbroken ability to supervise their craft or trade, so recently strengthened by their new charter. If they let their authority lapse then it might never be recovered. They must set an example to the homeless around them and their hall would rise from its ashes as a symbol of what could be achieved.

The Master therefore convened a meeting of the Court on 2 October, 1666. Raising money was the first necessity and, in these days before insurance policies, the Company resorted to a number of expedients. The first was maximising the income that they could derive under the terms of their new charter. For all the damage wrought by the Great Fire, innkeeping in London was far from obliterated. In addition to the fifty-six inns within the City itself which had survived - and the further forty-six that were soon to be rebuilt - there were many outside the traditional boundaries, in such areas as Southwark especially, which could be required to contribute to the rebuilding of the Hall.

The Court further resolved that it would collect any rents it might legitimately claim and also obtain such income as it could from the sites of its now ravaged rental properties. Conflicts would be settled by Common Law judges sitting unpaid at Fire Courts set up for this purpose, their judgements being reached on the basis of common sense rather than according to law. As a consequence of such arrangements it was agreed, at a meeting of the Assistants on 6 November, 1666, that a long lease on two houses in Coleman Street should be granted to Mr Alderman Cooke (one of the wealthiest and most prestigious members of the Company) on the condition that he would rebuild them. A short while afterwards Mr Cooke's son and namesake was granted a sixty-year lease on these Coleman Street properties at his father's request in return for an initial peppercorn rent for the first year followed by an annual payment of £10. That the Cookes were a highly regarded dynasty among the Company's membership is clear not only from the fact that Mr Alderman Cooke had presented the Innholders with the magnificent cup that bears his name but also from items among the accounts which suggest that the

Master and his committee made several expensive journeys by coach to visit this prestigious figure at his home in Greenwich.

Others also made arrangements with the Company to help secure both its future and their own. Another tenant in Coleman Street, a certain Mrs Barnes, suggested that she might be encouraged to rebuild her property if she and the Court could agree terms. This they did, the Court consenting to give Mrs Barnes a lease on her property for sixty years at an annual rental of £20. Other tenants were less resilient or less able to afford the expenses involved in extensive rebuilding, and Mr Spooner – another Coleman Street tenant – agreed with the Company that he would surrender the lease of the house next to the Hall in consideration of the arrears of his rent being waived.

The Company faced financial difficulties all the same. The Crown had made repeated calls on the City institutions for money to help pay for its wars against the Dutch and, as a result of such expenses, the Innholders were indebted by bonds to Mr Mather, Mr Ecclestone, and Mr Henley for £100. Now, with the loss of so much of their rental income, the security for any Company loan was impaired and, as a result, it was ordered that some of the pewter and the plate should be handed over to its creditors as security. The need for ready cash was urgent and, in April 1667, the Court ordered that 'the plate, pewter, and linen belonging to the Company shall be sold by the Master and Wardens of the Company about a fortnight after the feast of Easter now next ensuing'. Fortunately, this decision was carried out only in part if at all.

In the meantime, other less drastic measures provided the Company with an immediate income. For example, the Court approached the wealthier members and raised loans of between £60 and £150 from them 'upon the Company's seal', while the Company also successfully negotiated with the City Corporation for the repayment of the considerable sum of £583 8s. 6d lent to the king under their auspices.

It is a tribute to the Innholders' regard for their charitable responsibilities that, despite these financial difficulties, they continued to look after those even less fortunate. For example, at a meeting of the Court of Assistants held at the Ram on 2 April, 1667, it was ordered that the needs of the poor of Newington Butts should be attended to. As a result, £5 was set aside to provide such people with stockings, and a further sum of £5 was then drawn from moneys left to the Company under the terms of the will of Mr William Hinde to see that these people were adequately shod. With such duties attended to the Company could then direct its energies to its own resurrection.

*

On 10 September, 1667, a draft plan for a new Hall was ordered, and a fortnight later the Master and Wardens were directed to view the site and report back. Later it was required 'that the Company's ground where their Hall stood shall be cleared and the foundation laid and the first story raised with what convenient speed may be, and the Master and Wardens are to take care of this business and to advise with such of the Assistants from time to time as can most conveniently . . .'

For all that Sir Christopher Wren and others had proposed far-reaching and ambitious plans for the rebuilding of London, practical problems with the existing boundaries and landlords rendered these dreams impossible of fulfilment. Instead, the Rebuilding Act of 1667 required that the old building lines should be observed except in such areas of the City where the original roads had been so narrow that widening was highly desirable. Surveyors set about staking out the City (those caught tampering with their measurements were to be severely punished) and eventually they marked out the boundaries of the Innholders' Hall. The frontage along Elbow Lane North (now known as College Street) was some forty feet long, while that along Elbow Lane West (now Little College Lane) was some ten feet longer. As the carefully drawn up regulations required, the slight angle halfway along the site was duly preserved. The boundaries to the south, meanwhile, was some fifty-six feet in length, while that to

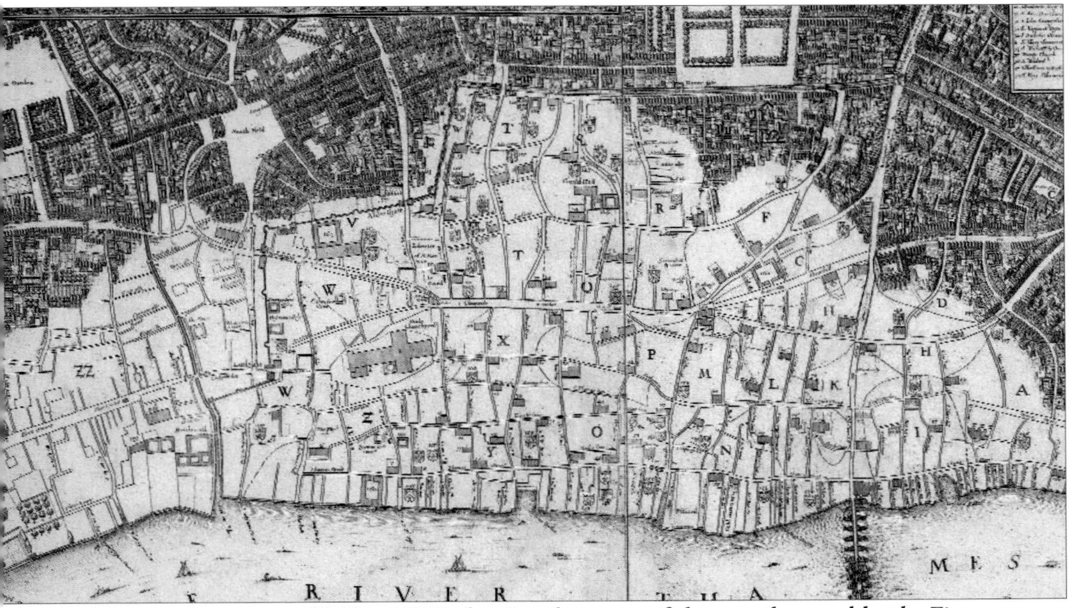

A contemporary map (Hollar, 1666) showing the extent of the area destroyed by the Fire

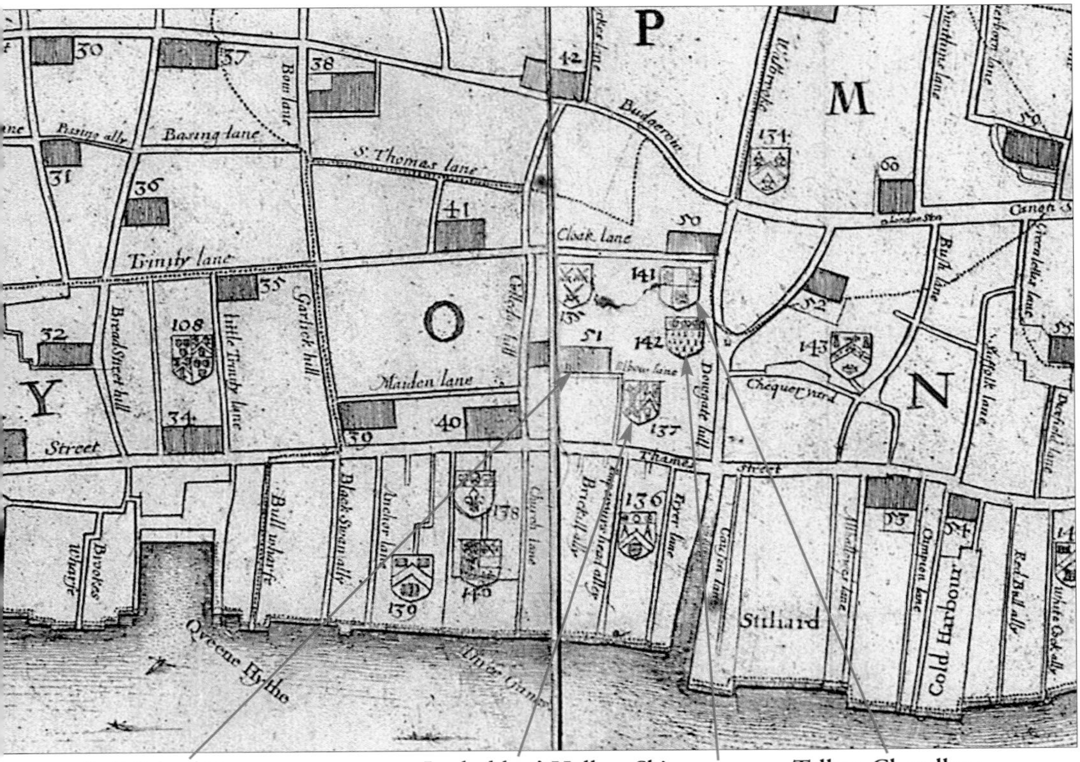

An enlargement of the Hollar Map marking the site of the Innholders' Hall in Elbow Lane, St. Michael's Church and the halls of the Skinners and Tallow Chandlers

the east was about a foot shorter. The same method was applied to the halls of the Skinners and Tallow Chandlers, which were both within 100 yards of the Innholders on Dowgate Hill

With the site staked out, rebuilding could go ahead and, on 16 April, 1668, it was noted 'that the Master and Wardens, with some of the Assistants, are desired to take advice with some able workmen for the most convenient way of building for the commodiousness of the Hall with the least charge to the Company'. It seemed that, in common with many of the lesser companies such as the Painter-Stainers, the Innholders resolved that they would rebuild their Hall not with the help of an expensive architect but by means of a committee of the liverymen working in conjunction with a number of master craftsmen.

Work at first went ahead speedily. By midsummer 1668 the ground had been cleared at a cost of £18.1.0. and the surveyor had done his work. Over the next three years the building slowly rose, the bricklayer, a certain Mr Lem (or Lemm) receiving £500 for his labours, while Mr Darby the carpenter received £344. Other unnamed craftsmen – the joiner, plasterer, plumber, mason, smith, glazier and painter – received sums ranging from £66.8.0. to £11.10.0. As the completion date neared gratuities were handed out to speed the process. The final cost of the building was £1,211.8.10., of which £231 was subscribed by members of the Company.

The Hall has subsequently been much remodelled but a significant proportion of the original fabric survives, along with a 17th century plan. The original entrance door, now disused, may still be seen and is a dignified and pretty feature of the exterior, with its swan-necked broken pediment and thick, garlanded volutes up the sides. The finest remaining feature of the 1671 hall however is to be seen inside the building. Very little domestic plasterwork from the Restoration period survives in London, but Innholders' Hall can boast that the ceiling of the Old Court Room is a fine and rare example of work by a craftsman familiar with the traditions of Jones and Webb. It consists of a central oval molding of fruit and

The Old Court Room with the spandrels from the four corners of its 1670 ceiling

flowers while, in the spandrels, are scrolled shields, one of which bears the date 1670, while the other three display the City's red cross of St. George, the arms of the Company, and those of the sovereign, Charles II. Only the Drapers' Hall retains a similar ceiling complete and *in situ,* but that of the Innholders is of greater interest insofar as it has survived unaltered. The ceiling is perfectly complemented by the plain contemporary wainscoting and the small 17th century fireplace.

By 1671 the Company was ready to resume its activities in this pleasant, dignified but unpretentious building. An inventory of the contents made the year before includes one 'great chair', presumably for the use of the Master at meetings, along with two dozen rush-seated chairs; three 'Spanish tables'; two fire dogs for the parlour; two 'long green carpets' and a further little green carpet which may have been used to cover the Master's table. There were also an ebony gavel for the use of the Master when presiding at meetings, a large Bible on which members of the Company would have sworn their oaths and, rather delightfully, three garlands which were probably made of silver and were worn on official occasions by the Master and the Wardens; these items have all disappeared.

However the Company still possesses a quantity of fine silver made during the time of the later Stuart kings. Of particular interest is the Pennington tankard, a magnificent piece some six inches high and made in 1661. In form it is somewhat similar to the tankard presented to the Company some years earlier by Thomas Charlett, save that its base is lighter in design. The Pennnington tankard has a fine, well tapered handle with a particularly sturdy thumb-knob and is ornamented with a well-wrought engraving of the Innholders' coat of arms. This silver would, of course, have been used or displayed during feasts.

From 1681 Company banquets would have been enlivened by musicians playing from the gallery which was added in the summer of that year at a cost of £38. 1.0.

*

From their new Hall the Company could once more maintain a watchful eye on the business of London innkeeping. Despite the devastation of the Great Fire, the trade remained extremely profitable. Many innholders even issued redeemable tokens in their own names to circumvent the chronic shortage of small change. Today these are collectors' items.

London inns now began to offer a range of services in addition to board, accommodation and stabling for horses. A unique example was the Pea Hen opposite Somerset House where one Mr Mayhew appears to have set up an establishment that functioned as an intelligence bureau. A rare advertisement for the services he offered has been preserved in the Bodleian Library and it appears that Mayhew kept a register of people going abroad, partly with the purpose of tracing fugitive husbands and partly to keep an eye on such undesirables as Roman Catholics, Nonconformists, and runaway servants, seamen and soldiers. Mayhew also seems to have worked as an early estate agent since he had a register of lands and goods for sale. In addition to this, he claimed to provide information about where 'artists of all sciences' could be found, along with reports of new books, curiosities and metropolitan news.

Many London inns profited greatly from the rapidly expanding coach business. Services from London to York and from London to Chester had been established just prior to the Restoration and, by 1660, there were coaches running from the capital to Durham and Newcastle, to Preston, Lancaster and Kendal, as well as to Exeter and Plymouth. Business expanded rapidly over the next twenty years, by which time 119 public coaches were running services to most of the greater towns and cities in the country. The Oxford to London coach was a pioneer in this respect, leaving from an inn close by All Souls College at six in the morning and arriving at the Saracen's Head on Snow Hill at seven in the evening. The fare was initially twelve shillings, but such was the popularity of the route that this was quickly reduced to ten.

As so often, it was the enterprising managers of the Belle Sauvage on Ludgate Hill who took the most conspicuous initiatives. Destroyed in the

Great Fire, it was speedily rebuilt and, by 1667, was offering a service by 'Flying Machine' to Bath. The advertising material prepared for the service still survives and offers an interesting insight into what travellers might have expected:

> All those desirous to pass from London to Bath, or any other place on their road, let them repair to the Belle Sauvage on Ludgate Hill in London, and the White Lion at Bath, at both which places they may be received in a stagecoach every Monday, Wednesday and Friday, which perform the whole journey in three days (if God permit), and sets forth at five o'clock in the morning. Passengers to pay £1 5s. each, who are allowed to carry fourteen pounds weight – for all above to pay three halfpence per pound.

The roads on which such intrepid travellers set forth were almost universally appalling. Each parish in the country was supposed to maintain those portions of the high roads that ran through them but disputes and sheer laziness ensured that this essential public service was very rarely carried out. If pressed, parishioners would sometimes grudgingly offer money to pay labourers to fill up the ruts with whatever material was available. Hard, surfaced roads were unknown before the latter part of the 18th century; in summer potholes could easily overturn a coach while in winter the ruts and holes, filled with water, snow or ice, could become impassable for weeks at a time.

There were other hazards to coach travel in these times, as the intrepid late 17th century traveller, Celia Fiennes, once discovered on her way to Whitchurch. Two rough looking men, swathed in great coats and carrying pistols, suddenly galloped down from the overhanging woods. They dogged her for many miles, one of them riding in front of her while the other kept up the rear. They constantly jostled her horse and tried to separate her from her servants. It was intimidating, 'but the Providence of

God so ordered it that there were sufficient men working in the adjoining fields, and enough people following the same road to Whitchurch where it was market day, to discourage the two villains who eventually if reluctantly rode off'.

Celia Fiennes was lucky. Highway robbery was far from unknown, and innkeepers in remote areas were too often complicit in it. Lives of highwaymen became popular reading, and tell stories such as one of a dishonest landlord who would ride out to accost passing travellers whom he would inveigle into his inn without letting them know that he was the proprietor. As he and the travellers grew ever more sociable, the drink flowed ever more freely. By the morning they had been defrauded of considerable sums of money .

*

It was precisely in the effort to reduce robbery and violence that Charles II had granted the Innholders their new charter in 1664. However, as the reign progressed the King began to have second thoughts about some of the powers he had granted to the City's Livery Companies.

The causes for discontent between him and the people of his capital were many. They rose to a head when it grew increasingly evident that Charles himself, having no legitimate children, would be succeeded by his brother, James Duke of York, who became a Catholic in 1672. A deep fear of Catholicism was now endemic in the country. The majority of people believed that Catholic kings and Catholic churchmen stood for absolutism in government and superstition in religion. It was widely held that the papists were responsible for the Great Fire, and an inscription on the Monument (later removed) asserted that this was indeed the case.

As protection against a Catholic coup Parliament passed the Test Act in 1673. The historical importance of this piece of legislation, forced on Charles II by a zealously Anglican and nationalistic House of Commons, can hardly be overestimated. Briefly put, the Test Act required an explicit denial of the Roman Catholic doctrine of transubstantiation (the belief that the bread and wine of the communion service truly and miraculously become the body and blood of Christ), the obligation to recognise the monarch as the head of the church in England, and to take Anglican communion at least once a year. By this Act Parliament sought to create a nation united by its loyalty to one creed and one king, an England in which a Roman Catholic or a Presbyterian was disqualified from holding any office under the crown.

Despite this, the continuing Catholic bias of the king's court appalled many and, after the so-called Popish Plot of 1678, anti-Catholic feeling seized the nation with a neurotic fury. Pepys caught the general mood when he noted in his Diary 'how people do cry out in the streets . . . that we are bought and sold and governed by papists and that we are betrayed by people about the king and shall be delivered up to the French'.

Opposition to the perceived threat from Catholics at home, and across the Channel in France, centred round the charismatic figure of the Earl of Shaftesbury and his protégé, Charles' illegitimate son, the Duke of Monmouth. Many hoped Monmouth would succeed to the throne if the Duke of York were prevented by an Exclusion Bill barring Catholics from succession. Shaftesbury had a genius for practical organisation while many of his followers had a flare for propaganda; together their activities took on the characteristics of a political party. The Whigs, as Shaftesbury and his followers came to be called, stood for a protestant monarchy and the liberties of the people as guaranteed by Magna Carta and maintained by a Parliament responsible to the electorate. Although the Whigs were not republican, supporters of the court responded by forming a group under the popular name of the Tories. So the seeds of modern party politics were sown.

Much of this clamorous political debate took place in the streets and inns of London. Inns were natural meeting-places (like the newly established coffee houses) where men habitually discussed both business and politics. The King's Head in Chancery Lane, for example, was the headquarters of the important Whig Green Ribbon Club, and it was from here that writers distributed propaganda tracts while others organised the enormous public processions, culminating in great bonfires and the burning of the Pope in effigy. Shaftesbury himself ran political clubs at the Swan in Fish Street, the Angel near to the Old Exchange, the Queen's Arms and the Nag's Head. This was a great age of mass petitioning and it was from the Swan, also, that a group of Whig magnates sent out a brewer called Manly to solicit signatures. To facilitate the process, a number of London inns were provided with tables, printed petition forms, pens and ink.

The Tory party, favourable to the Duke of York and greater freedom for Catholics, would meet at the Salutation in Lombard Street. Tempers on both sides ran so high that political meetings were often far from peaceable. On the Monday after Bonfire Night, in 1682, a group of some forty young Whigs arranged to dine at the White Hart before going to watch their bonfires burn. Matters turned unpleasant when rival Tory youths appeared on the scene and proceeded to extinguish several of the fires. There was a fight, and the triumphant Whigs processed through the City chanting political slogans. Inflamed by wine, victory and excitement, they attacked anything that smacked of either Toryism or Catholicism. Provocative inn signs became favourite targets. One group in Cheapside attacked the boards of the Cardinal's Head and the Duke of York's Head; another burned the sign of the Mitre, much to the delight of an onlooker who called out excitedly: 'the Mitre burns bravely'.

Nor was this an isolated incident. When Tory youths were found toasting the health of members of the royal family, including the Duke of York, at the Queen's Head near Temple Bar a fight broke out. The Whig apprentices threw stones at the inn windows and the Tories hurled back chairs and stools. The angry Whigs promptly made these into a fire before going off to pick a fight with a large gang of Tories in Covent Garden. A similar incident took place at the King's Head, the home of the Green Ribbon Club, when riotous young Tories from the Inner Temple broke the windows and pulled down the sign. The watch was summoned to disperse the crowd, but some armed watermen came to the assistance of the young lawyers and, in the ensuing brawl, serious injuries were suffered.

The great issues of the authority of the Crown, the place of Parliament and the succession of the Duke of York were temporarily settled not by street violence but by the guile of the king, who negotiated a large pension from France on terms which he kept secret but which freed him from dependence on the House of Commons. He then called the last parliament of his reign at Oxford, where the Whigs' powerbase did not extend. After little more than a week, when the members again attempted to introduce an Exclusion Bill to debar the Duke of York from the throne, Charles dissolved them. He was confident that he could both rule without them and successfully prosecute his vengeance on the Whig opposition, especially on Shaftesbury whom he was determined to have tried for treason.

A trial in London, however, meant facing the deeply entrenched Whig opposition in the City. For all that the Court of Aldermen was firmly Tory in its sympathies, the increasingly influential Court of Common Council had a strong Whig element in it which could, by winning the support of neutral members on particular issues, sometimes achieve a majority. Whigs could thus not only influence the Courts of the livery companies, but also the liverymen gathered together in Common Hall who elected the City's four Members of Parliament – a practice which ceased only in 1918. More than this, it was the right of Common Hall to nominate the two candidates for the mayoralty from which the Court of Aldermen then chose one. Finally, it fell to the liverymen in Common Hall to choose the sheriffs, and it was the sheriffs who empanelled juries. In such ways as these the Whigs exercised a very real influence within the City and were quick to demonstrate it now. The grand jury, with their Whiggish sympathies, summoned for the trial of Shaftesbury refused to be browbeaten by the prosecuting counsel and returned an *Ignoramus* verdict. The case against the great Whig leader had not been proven.

Charles in his fury responded with a decisive logic. Just as it was the chartered boroughs throughout the country (including the City of London) who returned the majority of members to the House of Commons, so it was the senior Whig members of the chartered livery companies who had ensured Charles' humiliating rebuff in the courts. What the royal hand had once bestowed the royal hand could now seize back, and in October 1683 Charles issued a writ of *quo warranto* by which all the borough and company charters were called in and examined for anomalies and abuses. If the rights the charters conveyed could be legally challenged – indeed even if they could not – then the corporations could be compulsorily remodelled to give the Crown control over the appointment of their officers and elected representatives.

For all that the City of London defended its case with courage and expertise, judgement finally went against it. From now on the capital was to be governed by a Royal Commission, and its officers were to be appointed by the king and to act only during his pleasure. Eight Whig aldermen were dismissed, the Court of Common Council was dissolved, the Mayor, the Sheriffs and the Recorder became royal appointees and, for five years from October 1683 the once proud and independent City of London was reduced to the status of a royal demesne.

*

The loss of liberty inflicted on the City at large was visited on each of the livery companies in turn. This was a particularly painful experience for the Innholders. The recall of their charter would have been distressing at any time, but it was doubly so at this moment since a few months earlier they had been pursuing plans to obtain a revised charter which would extend their authority over all innkeepers within *twelve* miles of the City and thus over the ever-expanding suburbs of London. However, during April and May, in common with most other corporations, they discussed, in the light of legal advice, the voluntary surrender of their charter, while simultaneously pleading for the withdrawal of the writ of *quo warranto.*

That the senior members of the Company were bitterly at odds on the underlying disputes which then divided London and the nation is revealed by a stark fact. The records of the meetings held between 31 August, 1682, and 18 July, 1683 have been physically torn from the Company minute book, probably because these pages dealt with debates and motions to expel members of the Company deemed unacceptable to the king. Any record of such acrimonious proceedings, smacking of opposition to the Crown, would be better suppressed in these dangerous times.

When the entries resume, the minute for 25 March, 1684 reads: 'this day Thomas Allen was sworn Clerk of the said Company, being recommended by the King'. There was clearly ill-feeling about this since only the Master and three members of the Court were present. The removal of subsequent pages, silencing forever whatever angry and seditious words might have been spoken, imply that dissension in the Company continued. Nonetheless, it is clear that Tories loyal to the king took control of the Company and, three months later, on 17 June, 'it was ordered by the Court' that the charter should indeed be surrendered to him.

If the minute book is evidence that leading members of the Company had been obliged to bow to Charles, in common with Parliament and the rest of London, the account books suggest that they had lost neither their pride nor their initiative. Plans to petition for a new charter went ahead, and more than £200 was paid out in legal fees for its preparation. The draft charter that was eventually granted extended their authority to supervise and search inns anywhere within twelve miles of the City boundaries.

On the other hand many of the other clauses diminished their powers, and the degree of supervision exercised by the City over the livery was considerably enhanced. Not only did the charter require that the entire Company be subject to the Lord Mayor and the predominantly Tory Court of Aldermen in all matters concerning the government of the City, but these dignitaries also had the duty of approving any person the Innholders wished to elect to the livery. It was also made explicit that the king could, by an order in Privy Council, remove any Master, Warden, Assistant or Clerk of the Company at his pleasure and that a place thus left void could be filled only by a candidate acceptable to the Crown.

Then, just as the new charter was about to be ratified, the king died in February 1685.

*

Despite all the earlier opposition, the Duke of York, a Catholic, was crowned James II. His brief reign was a catalogue of startling ineptitude. By 1686 he was pursuing a number of tactics to ease the lot of his Catholic subjects. Already disliked by the Whigs because his methods were of dubious constitutional legality, James alienated his natural supporters among the Tories too. Furthermore, by refusing to call Parliament, he increasingly antagonised the country at large.

Nonetheless, by 1687 he had convinced himself that, if he could pack the House of Commons with Nonconformist members, then these people who had suffered for their beliefs like the Catholics, would willingly vote for the repeal of the laws passed against them all. A propaganda campaign swung into action, while James himself set about purging his opponents from the chartered boroughs and liveries which had the right to vote against his supporters. Gerrymandering, fraud and intimidation became commonplace.

The Innholders were not immune to these manoeuvres. In September, 1687, a writ issued from Windsor declared that William Petty, one of the Company Wardens, and no fewer than fifteen of the Assistants 'are hereby removed and displaced'. Since these men were almost certainly the sort of solid, Tory Anglicans that Charles' policies had required, it is likely that James was now seeking to pack the Company with Nonconformists and others sympathetic to his cause in order to secure their vote in forthcoming elections. The restoration by royal command of five more men to the Court of Assistants (presumably those removed earlier for the bias of their beliefs) reinforces this notion. It was, however, a gross misjudgement to assume that the Nonconformists would so easily swallow their innate hatred for Catholicism.

Eventually the political nation, fearing for its faith and privileges, would stand no more, and James' daughter Mary, married to his Dutch nephew William of Orange, – both of them Protestant – were provisionally invited to sit together on the English throne.

James panicked and his last actions were those of a desperate man. He knew he had lost London to his enemies, and to lose London was to lose the mainspring of his authority. He therefore tried to buy the City back, restoring its charters and its ancient privileges. As a result, the livery companies were no longer subject to royal surveillance. But far from showing gratitude, they set about reasserting their dignity and ancient traditions. On 10 October, 1688, four days after the restoration of their rights, the Innholders' minute book records the resolution 'that this court should cause to be restored to their respective places all such liverymen of the said Company at the time of the late judgement given against the City upon the *quo warranto*'. They, like the nation at large were opposed to its king.

In November James fled to France and in February, 1689 William and Mary were proclaimed the joint sovereigns of England.

*

Despite the national euphoria the Innholders faced one final setback. In 1689, William III, seeking to assuage the damage done by the high-handed actions of his predecessors, agreed to an Act of Parliament which not only declared Charles II's writ of *quo warranto* itself 'illegal and arbitrary' but rendered any charters drawn up subsequent to it null and void. Naturally this included the Innholders' charter granted by James II and with its demise went the Company's hope of extending its authority twelve miles beyond the City boundaries. It was felt unwise to complain and better gratefully to accept with the rest of London the new status quo. Nothing bears more eloquent testimony to this than the loyal address sent by the Company to the king after a failed attempt against his life made in 1695:

> Whereas there has been a horrid and detestable conspiracy, formed and carried on by papists and other wicked and traitorous persons, for assassinating his Majesty's royal person in order to encourage an invasion from France, to subvert our religion, laws and liberty; we the Master, Wardens, and Livery Men, and other members of the Company of Innholders London ... do heartily, sincerely and solemnly profess, testify and declare, that his present Majesty King William, is rightful and lawful King of these realms. And we do mutually promise and engage to stand by and assist each other, to the utmost of our power in the support and defence of his Majesty's most sacred person and government, against the late King James and all his adherents. And in case his Majesty come to any violent or untimely death (which God forbid) we do here by further freely and unanimously oblige ourselves to unite, associate, and stand by each other in revenging the same upon his enemies and their adherents; and in supporting and defending the succession of the Crown or according to an Act made in the first year of the reign of King William and Queen Mary entitled an Act Declaring the Rights and Liberties of the Subject, and settling the succession of the Crown.

This is English, Protestant loyalty at its most heartfelt and suggests how, after all the turmoil of the recent years, the Worshipful Company of

Innholders willingly embraced the prospect of a stable and prosperous new world to be introduced by the Glorious Revolution. The Company had survived the Great Fire of London and rebuilt its Hall. It had survived the arbitrary actions of two kings. It had survived, all the same, into a world where its very existence was becoming increasingly anachronistic and its useful role ever more uncertain.

The loyal address to William was signed by 189 of the Innholders, thirty-five of them with just their mark. The City in which most of these men lived and worked was a London risen from the ashes. The ancient, dangerous maze of timber-framed buildings, each storey of which overhung that below until daylight was all but excluded from the jostling streets, had been replaced by a City of fireproof brick and stone houses, built in a modest, vernacular style along improved and often paved thoroughfares. Dotted between them were Wren's exquisite City churches while, after 1710, the skyline was dominated by the sublime dome of the new St Paul's.

To help realise this extraordinary expression of civic confidence, laws against employing stonemasons and bricklayers from outside the City were relaxed, a first indication that the long-treasured monopolies of the guilds would lose their hold on this new London.

These powers were further diluted as the capital continued to spread voraciously beyond its old boundaries. The elegant West End attracted those who could afford to live in its gracious squares; the poor continued to congregate to the east; while religious dissenters tended to move to such areas as rustic Hackney, where their worship was largely free from legal impediments. As a consequence, many of the new houses in the City stood empty and its slowly returning population rose only very gradually. In 1695 it stood at about 80,000 and had grown merely to some 87,000 half a century later.

The slow but inexorable process by which the City became a centre of business by day and an all but deserted, spectral maze by night had begun. The magnetic pull of London as a whole however – its fashionable and bustling season, its huge importance as an administrative centre, the fact that it was the hub of the nation's communications and, above all, its rapid and vigorous flowering as the greatest concentration of commercial activity in Western Europe – all ensured that the innkeepers' business flourished. The 'monster' capital city, feared by many, was a source of great prosperity to those who ran its ever more necessary hostelries and stables.

With the coronation of William and Mary, a new era opened. The vagaries of personal monarchy (all too familiar to the Innholders) would henceforth be held in check by a Protestant and sovereign Parliament which took over from the king the handling of war, religious governance, finance, and constitutional change. Its initiatives were profound and moved towards recognisably modern forms of administration, including the institution of the national debt and the creation of the Bank of England, both essential to funding William III's campaigns against the Catholic Louis XIV of France, who was protecting the now exiled James.

By the time first Mary and then William died, England and London especially, were richer and stronger than they had ever been. From 1702 Queen Anne, the last of the Stuarts, reigned over a nation governed by a professional bureaucracy of specialised civil servants, serving an autonomous Parliament in which, before long, a new figure would sit – the 'premier' or Prime Minister. It was also a nation whose deployment of capital and enterprise was expanding towards the far horizons of a great trading empire.

* * *

Chapter 7

DECLINE OF THE LIVERIES

1702 - 1776

The Innholders' festivities – Company difficulties – London and country Inns – Some awkward consequences of London's new prosperity.

In the new political world of the 18th century, religion and the Crown ceased to determine Livery life. Instead, the economics of enterprise increasingly challenged the guilds' aspirations to control their trades, and aroused growing opposition. Nevertheless the social life of the Innholders Company remained as vigorous as ever.

Festivities chiefly focused on the annual round of seasonal dinners and nothing suggests the ceremonial of these so clearly as the Company's silver headed mace. This imposing piece bears the London Britannia standard mark for 1707 and carries the inscription 'Thomas Hill, Master'. It is surmounted by a vigorously modelled horse 'regardant', one of the supporters of the Company's arms; the arms themselves appear on a large escutcheon below the horse's fore hoofs. Bearing the mace aloft the Beadle led the Master into the Hall at the start of every feast, many of which, in the 18th century, were of gargantuan proportions.

Audit, Election and Lord Mayor's Days were particularly important occasions, the last being the high point of the year. For a long time the Company had retained its own barge in the traditional mayoral procession on the Thames but this seems to have lapsed soon after the Great Fire, perhaps to curtail expenses. The Innholders nonetheless continued to play their part in the City pageantry, either in person or paying fifteen shillings to have some half a dozen standard-bearers join the procession in their place.

Fortified by a heroic breakfast consisting of three ribs of beef, four legs of mutton and a 'barrel of strong beer', many of the more senior members of the Company then watched the spectacle from their private stand erected in Cheapside. This appears to have been a considerable structure.

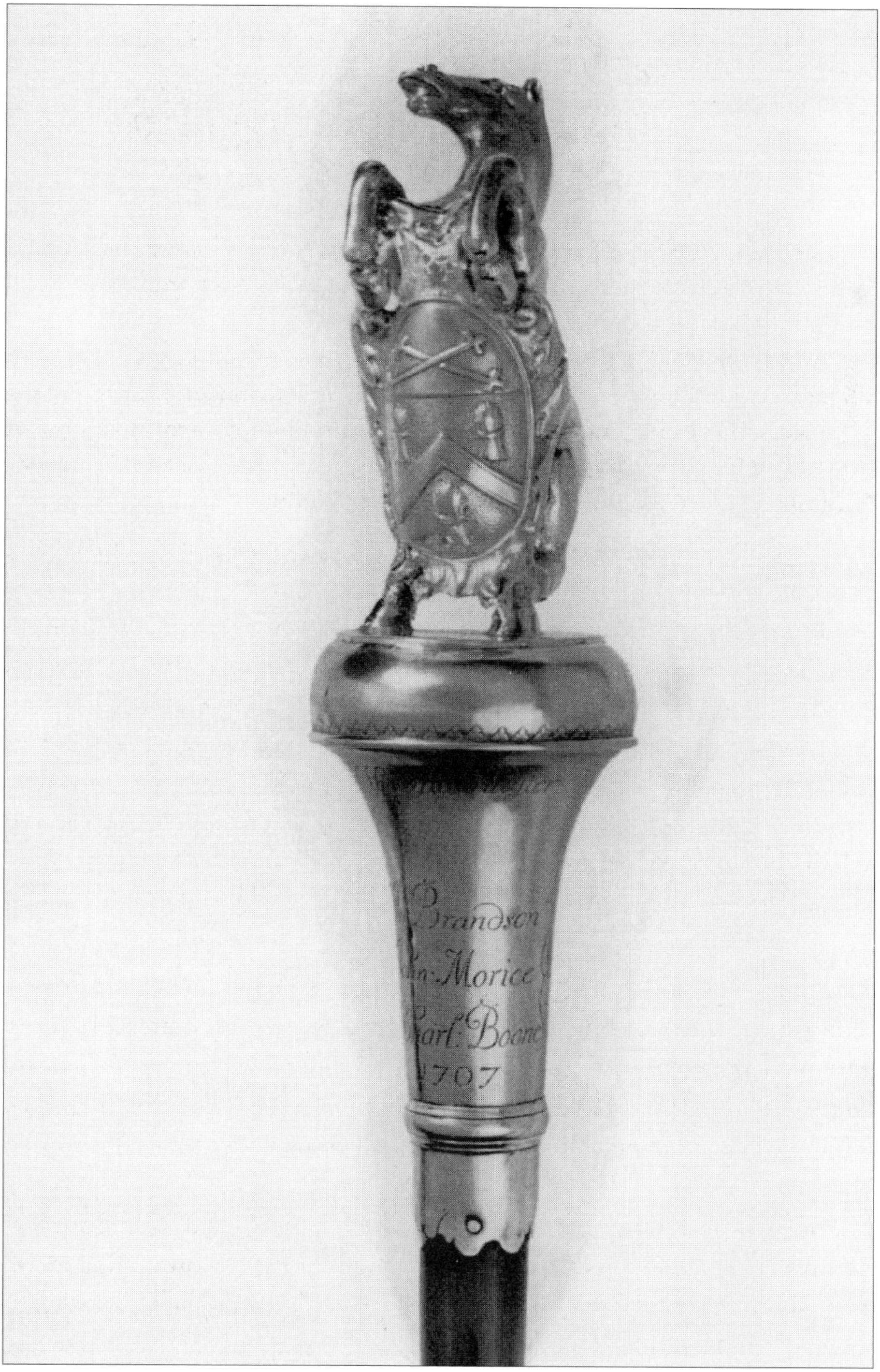

The Beadle's Mace, 1707

Raised on eleven trestles, it was surrounded by twenty-two turned wooden columns supporting a canopy gaily decorated with a valance worked in the Company colours of blue and white (based on the blue and silver of its arms). There were hand rails for those who needed them and the front of the stand was decorated with 'a blue cloth laced with white and blue lace'; the royal coat of arms was embroidered on the back. One area of the stand housed the musicians hired for the day.

To keep the stand in good repair Mr Beard, a carpenter, was hired to maintain it at an annual cost of £6, and when it became too dilapidated the Company bought the Turners' one for £33. A second carpenter was hired to put it up and to take it down, but eventually this stand, too, was discarded.

The dinner which followed the Lord Mayor's procession was lavish in the extreme. One surviving bill for a dinner, held some time around 1700, lists six dishes of 'pullets oysters', five chines of pork and turkey, five huge pigeon pies created at the vast cost of eight shillings each, five dishes of geese, each containing two birds, five dishes of mince pies and five tarts. Various other delights crowded the table, with ample quantities of wine and beer. There were twenty-four gallons of red wine, eight gallons of white, two gallons of canary, three nine-gallon barrels of ale and an eighteen-gallon 'kilderkin' of small beer'. For some sixty persons such provision was generous.

To preserve decorum and keep an eye on costs no person might bring a stranger without leave of the Master, Wardens, or Steward, to any feast 'except upon the forfeiture of four shillings to the use of the Company'. Women were apparently admitted as spectators and were provided with altogether lighter refreshment. Then – as now – for the Lord Mayor's Feast, it was 'ordered that the Master, Wardens and Assistants take their wives according as they are called on, and that no person presume to sit at table before the Company be set'. An orchestra hired at the considerable fee of £6 provided music during dinner.

Slightly less lavish feasts were held to celebrate the admission of new members to the livery, although the newly promoted sometimes complained to the Court about the costs involved. One 18th century commentator wrote: 'now a youth having taken up his freedom, if he is a popular man, he may in two or three years have the honour to be appointed Renter Warden, or Steward, which entitles him to the privilege of treating the fraternity unto an elegant and expensive entertainment'. Up to 1740 the Renter Warden of the Innholders was indeed expected to cover the entire cost of his election day expenses from his own pocket but, after 1740, this charge was limited to £18. The change coincided with a growing feeling among many liveries that the costs of accepting one of the higher offices were not altogether matched by the professional advantages which accrued from them.

*

The Innholders were not immune to these difficulties. As early as September 1690 the Court had passed a resolution ordering 'that no person shall be elected or chosen Master except he be first translated from the company he is originally free of'. Matters came to a head in August 1707 when it was proposed to elect Mr John Branstone to the Mastership. The retiring Master, Thomas Hill, refused to nominate him since he believed him not to be suitably qualified. It might be inferred from this that, in addition to the fees to be derived from the candidate's elevation to the Mastership, the further fees that Mr Branstone would be obliged to pay on being translated from the Vintner's Company would be welcome. Mr Branstone was unwilling to agree to this however and, although it was hoped to settle things amicably, John Morris was elected in his place. An aggrieved Branstone, finding himself struck off the Court, took the Company to law, arguing that he had served and been fined in all the chargeable offices of the Innholders' livery except that of Master and, as a consequence, should be restored to his place or have some of the £58 he had already spent on the Company returned. The case went against him, the judge considering the plea 'not just or proper', but it was also ruled that he might be translated from the Vintners Company if he so wished. In the event Morris remained Master.

For some considerable time there had been a large measure of uncertainty in the City about the companies' rights to enforce membership on unFreemen practising their craft or trade, to seize goods during searches and to prohibit the sale of goods made by those who had not served an approved apprenticeship with the correct company. As a result, by the early 18th century, the Companies' willingness to regulate their trades largely depended on individuals within them deciding to act either from indignation, malice or the prospect of reward. This was a highly unsatisfactory situation.

In July 1712 the City Corporation therefore resolved, in response to a number of petitions asking for a clarification of the law, to issue 1,000 copies of a new and strongly worded act. This made it clear that the corporation was determined to punish in its own courts those men not free of the City who attempted 'to use any manual occupation or handicraft or to sell or put to sale any wares or merchandises by retail in any shop inward or outward'. In other words the guilds' old monopoly powers were restored to them. Thus it was that, on 19th May, 1727, the Innholders, who badly needed to boost their numbers in order to augment their incomes, received the following order from the Common Council of the City of London:

> No person or persons whatever, using or exercising the art, mystery or occupation of an innholder or keeping any inn, hostelry or livery-stable, within this City or the liberties thereof, shall from henceforth be admitted into the freedom of this City by redemption, unless such person shall be first admitted into the freedom of the said Company of Innholders: and this to be observed as a standing order of the Court.

Such a ruling suggests that the Company had problems of both recruitment and finance, for the Court was guilty of extreme dilatoriness in handing over the accumulated sums of 2s.6d. which it was due to pay on all apprentices bound to the Company, for the use of the City fund for orphans. A list of these apprentice payments was started in 1724 but the first tranche of money, a sum of £24.2.6, for the binding of 193 apprentices, was not paid until 1748. The following year the fine for obtaining the freedom was raised by 60% to £2.14.4. It is clear from such statistics that the financial health of the Company was far from good.

In 1757 the Company's right to exercise its powers in an area three miles outside the City boundaries was challenged in the courts. In June the Clerk was required to make a copy of such papers 'as relate to the Company's prescriptive rights and bye laws' so that a committee of the livery could consult their legal advisor, a Mr Field, who was paid three guineas for his services. However the courts decided that the powers exercised by the Company outside the City boundaries were not founded on custom and were, besides, an interference with the rights of the subject under common law. In such a way was the Company's monopoly shown to be in conflict with the new world of enterprise.

For all that, a Livery List of 1756, preserved in the Guildhall Library, shows that 93 out of the 118 Innholders counted were practising innkeepers – a very high proportion.

*

If the authority of the Company, like that of other liveries, was declining, for the majority of its members the 18th century was a golden era. Many had rebuilt their establishments after the Great Fire or erected new inns in the new style, which required relatively plain brick with stone fronts and trim sash windows. An archway still led into the courtyard where the increasing number of visitors arriving by coach were deposited. London, ever expanding and ever more sophisticated and diverse, was a magnet of immense power drawing tourists not only from across the country but from the mainland of Europe as well. In the words of a contemporary, the capital was 'the centre to which almost all the individuals who fill the upper and middle ranks of society are successively attracted'.

London provided for all of their needs. 'Business, interest, curiosity, the love of pleasure, the desire of knowledge, the thirst for change, ambition to be deemed polite, occasion a continual influx into the metropolis from every corner of the kingdom'. The Thames and the Port of London were log-jammed with ships that had sailed from every part of the globe. Tea, china, cotton, spices and sugar were brought from the East Indies. Rum, coffee and cocoa were imported from the West Indies; while from Africa came fruit, oils and 'elephants' teeth'. A thriving Navy kept the seas safe for British trade, while the ever more sophisticated financial institutions of the City raised capital for entrepreneurs and guaranteed credit on an unprecedented scale. From such energies as these the City's innkeepers could greatly profit.

They did not hesitate to advertise their presence and many famous London inn signs were, or claimed to be, the work of some of the most conspicuous artists of the day. These included a sign allegedly painted by Hogarth for the Man Loaded With Mischief in Oxford Street. Like many of Hogarth's more certainly attributed works, this sign was richly loaded with moral and allegorical detail. It showed a sad-faced man bearing a large and drunken woman on his shoulders who blithely waved a glass of gin in the air as a monkey and a jackdaw set about attacking the man's head. In the background could be seen two quarrelling cats, a sleeping sow, a pawn shop, and a public house crowned by a pair of horns and clearly labelled the Cuckold's Fortune. The artist who created Gin Lane had clear and strong ideas about the dangers of drink.

Many inn signs were designed to be hung on elaborate iron brackets across the pavement in front of the house which they advertised. The middle years of the 18th century however saw this ancient practice made illegal in London. There was a good reason for this. In 1718 a particularly heavy sign in Bride Lane, just off Fleet Street, had fallen down taking with it a large part of the front of the house and killing four people. Something had to be done and, in obedience to the Acts of Parliament of

BEER STREET.
Beer, happy Produce of our Isle
Can sinewy Strength impart,
And wearied with Fatigue and Toil
Can chear each manly Heart.
Labour and Art upheld by Thee
Successfully advance,
We quaff Thy balmy Juice with Glee
And Water leave to France.
Genius of Health, thy grateful Taste
Rivals the Cup of Jove,
And warms each English generous Breast
With Liberty and Love.
PAWN BROKER

Beer Street by William Hogarth (1697-1764)

1762-70, the huge number of often expensive and elaborately designed hanging signs were taken down. Safety was purchased at the loss of one of the capital's most distinctive features, and from henceforth the proprietors of inns were obliged to signify their presence by boards fixed flat to the fronts of their buildings.

Both the famous and the forgotten left accounts of their visits to London, and some provide a delightful picture of the sort of hospitality expected. John Kersley Fowler, for example, recalled his boyhood when his father occasionally took him to the Old Bell at Holborn, which exuded a quiet air of masculine comfort. The inn boasted a mahogany lined coffee room divided into 'boxes' that could accommodate anywhere between two and eight people and in which they could dine. Guests would sit on stuffed horsehair seats and there was a fixed dining table in the centre of each box. The waiter was obliged to hand the excellent food and drink over the diners' shoulders, while the proprietor himself, Mr Bunyet, brought in the post-prandial bottle of port and very often joined his guests in a glass.

Visits to London frequently combined business with pleasure. Fowler's father would make up a small group of friends, scrupulously booking places on the early morning four-horse coach so as to arrive in town in time for a lunch of mutton chops.Business was then conducted, and the party would return to the Old Bell at around five o'clock for a dinner ordered for six o'clock sharp. These meals were extremely agreeable, consisting of mock turtle, cod and oysters, or salmon and lobster sauce, followed by a rump steak and pancakes, with Cheshire or Stilton cheese to finish. Thus replete, the company went on to the theatre, preferring above all to watch whatever was being performed at Drury Lane. When the show was over it was time to go home in a cumbrous old coach whose driver was magnificently provided with a coat of four or six capes to protect him from the weather.

The roads remained, for the most part, in a deplorable condition during the 18th century. Attempts to improve them were made after 1750 when a series of Turnpike Trusts were set up, each by a separate Act of Parliament, whereby groups of local people undertook to keep their stretch of road in good order from dues collected by a keeper at the toll gate.

Simultaneously the design of coaches developed, as more and more people found it necessary to travel. Passengers now sat on the top of the vehicle, three side by side at the front of the roof, while a further three perched precariously on the back, with nothing to support them but their own iron nerve. A luckier seventh passenger often sat beside the coachman. The perils of all this were recounted by Mr Jingle in *Pickwick Papers:* 'Dangerous work – other day – five children – mother – tall lady, eating sandwiches – forgot the arch – crash – knock – children look round – mother's head off – sandwich in her hand – no mouth to put it in – head of a family off – shocking, shocking!'.

Foreign visitors, in particular, were appalled by the condition of English travel. Carl Phillipp Moritz, a young German pastor, described a nightmare journey from Leicester to Northampton. Immediately the party set off, he fancied he saw certain death before him and as the vehicle bowled along he crept down from the roof to secrete himself in the basket behind. For a little while he was more comfortable but, as the coach began to run downhill, so the iron-nailed and copper-fastened boxes around him began to dance about, bruising him terribly. 'At last we came to another hill, when, quite shaken to pieces, bleeding and sore, I ruefully crept back to the top of the coach to my former seat'. Then it began to rain and the poor young man ended his journey soaking wet, frightened and depressed.

Moritz's experiences in Eton, Slough and Windsor were particularly unfortunate. At Windsor he was charged 6s for a wretched supper and a further 3s for a bedroom that he was obliged to share with a fellow guest who returned very late and very drunk, and who staggered into bed without taking off his clothes or boots. The following morning Moritz was sworn at by the waiter to whom he had offered a paltry tip, something he did not extend to the surly chambermaid who, when she asked that he would remember her, was told he would never forget her ill-mannered behaviour and shameful incivility.

It was only when Moritz reached Oxford that matters improved. Signing the visitor's book at the Mitre (still an attractive eating house on the High) Moritz found the place to be 'full of clergymen, all with their gowns and bands on, sitting round a large table, each with a pot of beer before him'. The following morning with a sound hangover, Moritz declared that his treatment had been 'prince-like' compared to what he had earlier experienced, the management even washing his linen for him.

Today, as then, the Mitre announces its presence with an elaborately carved wooden mitre suspended over the pavement on a wrought iron bracket. Other inn signs of the period were even more conspicuous, including the one put up by the White Hart on the main road into Norwich. Constructed at a cost of £1,057, this was reckoned to be the noblest signpost in all of England. In form it was what was known as a 'gallows sign' because it arched across the road like a double gibbet. This simple shape was then elaborated with a plethora of some twenty-five carved figures of classical deities who, in turn, supported the armorial bearings of a dozen prominent East Anglian families.

The proprietors of many successful coaching inns were people of substance able to invest in local enterprise. Their work brought them into contact with the nobility, the clergy, the magistracy, and the local gentry, whom they would welcome with the offer of a glass of wine over which they would then exchange news and opinions.

Coaching inns were complex businesses to run and their proprietors had to be expert judges of horses, wine and food, to have a sound knowledge of character, and to be able to maintain discipline over their employees. The more enterprising therefore possessed considerable commercial vision.

Thomas Fletcher, for example, the proprietor of the George in Walsall, procured an Act of Parliament whereby the road from Walsall to Stafford was constructed, thereby ensuring that the George itself stood on one of the main traffic routes in the area. Inspired by this success, Fletcher also had the Birmingham road widened and straightened to encourage passing trade. Similarly, Robert Lawrence of the Lion in Shrewsbury succeeded after great efforts in having the main route between London and Dublin run through his town greatly to his profit. His feat was recorded for posterity on his tombstone which praises his 'public spirit and unremitting exertions for upwards of thirty years, in opening the great road through Wales between the United Kingdoms'.

Some odd sidelights on the quirks and curiosities of life in 18th century inns have come down to us. No visitor to the Unicorn in Ripon forgot Tom Crudd, the 'boots' of the establishment, whose excessively long nose all but touched his extremely protuberant chin. Turning this misfortune to his advantage, he would appear before newly arrived guests with a pair of slippers in one hand and a boot-jack in the other offering, in return for a coin, to amuse them by balancing it between the tips of his deformities.

In 1744 the second Duke of Chandos witnessed a far more profound drama on his way back from Bath to London, when he stopped overnight at the Pelican in Speenhamland. Then a widower, he and a friend had just sat down at the dinner table when they were interrupted by sounds of excitement rising up from the innyard. Deciding to investigate, they found to their amazement that a man was auctioning off his wife. Intrigued by so bizarre a circumstance, Chandos and his friend looked on as a 'brutal ostler' led out a handsome and modest-looking woman with a halter round her neck. The duke fell instantly and violently in love with her. Setting all thoughts of social position aside, Chandos promptly bought her for an undisclosed sum and made her his duchess on Christmas Day. The marriage was apparently a happy one, the couple producing a daughter.

Visits to inns by members of the aristocracy could have unexpected and disconcerting consequences for proprietors and their regular guests. When the elder Pitt, dignified as the Earl of Chatham, was returning from Bath after an unsuccessful attempt to cure his gout, he decided to break his journey by staying at the Marlborough Castle. Finding that the place suited him, he resolved to remain there for several weeks on the condition that the entire staff of the inn be clothed in his livery, and that the whole place should be put at his disposal. The proprietor felt unable to resist such a profitable if outrageous demand from one of Britain's finest war ministers, its leader in the Seven Years War with France and a great defender of civil liberties against the new King George III.

After a break in the fighting the French ambassador travelled from Dover to London in order to negotiate a peace treaty, and stopped for the night at the Red Lion in Canterbury. He ordered for himself and the dozen members of his entourage a supper of oysters, fowls, boiled mutton, poached eggs and fried whiting. The following morning he was presented with a bill for over £44. Disdaining to squabble over such a matter, the ambassador paid the bill.News of how the Frenchman had been fleeced rapidly spread across the country and the culprit found himself notorious. His fellow innkeepers in Canterbury disowned him and all the local gentry, who had once been the mainstay of his clientele, boycotted his establishment. In vain he protested and wrote to the newspapers; he was condemned as a pariah and, within six months, he and his business were ruined.

The meals for all these distinguished visitors had, no doubt, been cooked in a kitchen of a type familiar across the entire country at this time. Meat still had to be roasted on a spit before an open fire and clockwork jacks were becoming popular. But many cooks still resorted to the old and cruel expedient of having their spits powered by a terrier in a wheel. The dog was first placed inside the wheel along with a live coal which burnt his legs if he stood still, while if he ran too fast it would spin over and fall on his paws. Eventually, by dint of much painful experience, he discovered a happy medium. A spell on the treadmill was a savage sentence, for a sizeable piece of beef takes at least three hours to roast.

The 18th century inn could be a civilising place all the same. During the spring of 1776, Dr Johnson and the ever-faithful Boswell were making their way from Oxford on the road to Worcester and Lichfield. The weather had been particularly unpleasant, their journey was a long and tiring one, and it was while sitting before a blazing fire at the 'excellent inn at Chapel House' – called, appropriately enough, the Shakespeare's Head – that Johnson began to hold forth on 'the felicity of England in its taverns and inns'. He was at his most relaxed and magniloquent:

> 'There is no private house', said he, 'in which people can enjoy themselves so well as in a capital tavern . . . No man but a very impudent dog indeed can as freely command what is in another man's house as if it were his own, whereas, at a tavern, there is a general freedom from anxiety. You are sure of a welcome; and the more noise you make, the more trouble you give, the more good things you call for, the welcomer you are. No servants will attend you with the alacrity which waiters do, who are incited by the prospect of an immediate reward in proportion as they please. No, sir, there is nothing which has yet been contrived by man, by which so much happiness is provided as by a good tavern or inn'.

*

The proprietors of London's inns were inevitably caught up in the political, social and economic currents of their times. The capital continued to expand inexorably; in the century from 1700 its population rose from 575,000 to 960,000. Four times as many of these people lived in Westminster or the suburbs as in the City itself, a process greatly helped by the building of two bridges (Westminster in 1750 and Blackfriars in 1769) which opened up areas south of the river that had previously been all but inaccessible.

The rise in population provided the manpower for the continuing expansion of London's economy. At the beginning of the 18th century the capital was the largest manufacturing centre in Europe, a myriad of crafts and trades being practised there, involving some 40% of London's labour force. The import and export business, centred around the Pool of London, was another important employer. In addition to these, the capital's financial services continued to mushroom; specialised contractors raised vast and ever-increasing amounts of money to fund government loans.

Jonathan's coffee house in Change Alley became a highly sophisticated money market which grew to such an extent that, in 1773, the brokers acquired their own premises known as the Stock Exchange. Meanwhile private bankers in the West End – Hoare's, Coutts' and Drummonds' – lent money to the aristocracy and gentry, while other firms in the City financed trade and acted as clearing houses for the growing number of provincial banks. By 1775 their business was so extensive that they were obliged to set up a central clearing house in Lombard Street. Marine, fire and life insurance also flourished. The result of so much expansion was that wage-earners in London had higher living standards and more purchasing power than those anywhere else in the country and this, coupled with the fact that London continued to be a centre of fashion and conspicuous consumption, meant that the capital thrived.

This was nowhere more evident than in the West End. Here luxurious shops displayed the newest and most sophisticated wares. Many establishments still famous today had their origins in the 18th century: Aspreys, Christies, Hamleys and Hatchards all date from this period, while a host of other traders provided exquisite furniture fashioned from rare hardwoods, beautiful china, elaborate clocks, elegant clothes, stout boots and the latest masterpieces of English literature bound in finely-tooled leather. When shopping palled there were a host of other activities to beguile the time. Men could go to their clubs: Brooks's, Boodles or Whites. The city's many parks were the resort of fashion, while its pleasure gardens at Ranelagh and Vauxhall provided fireworks and music as well as the opportunity for less reputable diversions. There was sport in plenty too: bull and bear-baiting, cockfighting, boxing (including the novelty of female boxers) and, inevitably, cricket.

In such a climate as this innkeepers could flourish and early 18th century London was reckoned to have 207 inns, 447 taverns, 5,875 beer houses and 8,659 brandy shops. While such figures suggest that individual innholders might well be prosperous, the very proliferation of London meant that their Company found it increasingly difficult to regulate the trade and the problems that arose from it, not least the terrible epidemic of alcoholism which began to grip the capital.

Thousands of desperate people sought oblivion in the cheap gin sold in shops that proclaimed the promise of 'Drunk for a penny, dead drunk for twopence, straw free'. Prodigious quantities were consumed. By the 1740s the total was said to average two pints a week for every man, woman and child in the capital. Hogarth's *Gin Lane* shows a helplessly inebriated mother allowing her baby to fall out of her arms and into the gutter below. The novelist Henry Fielding observed that gin was 'the principle substance' of more than 100,000 Londoners, adding that 'the intoxicating draught itself disqualifies them from any honest means to acquire it at the same time and that it removes sense of fear and shame and emboldens them to commit every wicked and desperate enterprise'.

In an attempt to confront the crisis the Excise authorities resolved to introduce licences and duties on spirits and it was debated whether it was necessary for members of the Innholders Company to obtain them; the court of Aldermen ruled that they should – adding that only those who were actually members of the Company could be granted them. It was gratifying support for the Innholders' belief in their social utility as an association which could help ensure law and order through their powers of search and punishment. But the major problem of 18th century London was on too great a scale for such medieval measures to be effective. The Innholders alone could not stem the tide and control eventually had to be exercised not by the City of London but through central government. The episode was a synecdoche of the plight of the livery companies in general and of the Innholders in particular.

If the epidemic of gin drinking was eventually brought under some

The statuette of St. Julian, mounted above a leaden cistern embossed with the Company's arms and the date, 1685

degree of control, there was much continuing discontent in the capital, not only among the poor but among the ranks of the 'middling sort' too. Many of them (including some Innholders) felt aggrieved at their lack of adequate political representation. Angered by the placemen who swelled the ranks of government, they chafed in particular at the grossly unfair way in which a number of small constituencies returned a disproportionately large number of members while the vast population of London was badly underrepresented.

Perhaps the most vociferous of these critics was a figure famous in the annals of London radicalism: John Wilkes. For all that he was an unscrupulous demagogue, constantly in debt, in prison or in exile, Wilkes is a figure of exceptional importance for it was on him that demands for parliamentary reform focussed. He was elected Lord Mayor in 1774 and the cry 'Wilkes and Liberty' which echoed round London was not unknown at the Innholders' Hall. By 1776 Wilkes was MP for Middlesex and proposing elections by adult male suffrage, a hugely important step in the history of democracy. The Innholders of the day, like many liverymen of the lesser companies, were enthusiastic in his support and were determined to help further his career.

The minute book for 1776 records that on 23 February a motion was made by Mr Waddington and seconded by Mr Parke that the Company's Hall (its external facade and other features newly remodelled two years before in a contemporary Georgian style and at a cost of £100) 'be opened at the expense of the Company on Friday and Saturday mornings next in order to support the election of John Wilkes, Esq., our late worthy Chief Magistrate, to be Chamberlain of this City'. They further requested 'that the Clerk do sign an advertisement inviting the Livery of the Company with their friends to meet on each of these mornings and breakfast with the Master and the Wardens and to proceed from thence to the poll for the said Mr Wilkes – the same was put up and it passed in the negative'. What the Court objected to was not the Company giving their open support to so radical a figure as Wilkes but the expense involved. When the motion was put a second time and other arrangements were proposed for the cost of such canvassing the motion was agreed. Such conspicuous efforts were in vain, for Wilkes was defeated by 400 votes. Nevertheless the lucrative post he sought in the effort to relieve his financial embarrassments became his three years later.

The first seventy-five years of the 18th century were thus a period of mixed fortunes for the Innholders. Slowly the Company realised that if it were to survive in the new political and economic climate then it would have to admit that it could no longer claim to regulate its trade and would have to attract new blood in new ways, relying on the income it thus received in return for the prestige and the freedom of the City of London which it could still provide.

On 3 December, 1771, the Clerk was empowered 'till further order at any time to admit and swear into the Company such persons who are not innholders or stable-keepers or entitled by patrimony or servitude to their freedom as shall desire or be brought for that purpose, and that he may be empowered to reward any person who shall bring such a person with any sum not exceeding one guinea and a quarter'. Thus the Innholders accepted, like most other liveries, that its ancient *raison d'être* was no longer relevant; instead it must look for new means to survive. While it did so some of its leading members were set to flourish as the golden age of the mail coach inn began to dawn.

Chapter 8

THE MAIL COACH ERA
1776 – 1837

A glorious and turbulent age – The world of mail coaching and its inns– The first hotels – A cry for reform – The City and the Innholders examined by the Royal Commission of 1833 – The Commissioners' verdict

George III was the first of three monarchs to preside over the England of the mail coach era. His son, who assumed the regency in 1811 when his father descended into madness, became George IV in 1820. Lastly William IV, the 'Sailor King', ascended the throne in 1830. This was a glorious, turbulent, dangerous, period.

Abroad, it saw the loss of America during the War of Independence; the establishment of India as the jewel in the imperial crown, following the victories of Clive and later Wellesley, the future Duke of Wellington; and, above all, the long-drawn-out campaigns by sea and land of the Napoleonic Wars, which eventually culminated in the Battle of Waterloo.

At home, this was a period of unprecedented expansion driven by that huge and often terrible phenomenon known as the Industrial Revolution. But they were also years of repression induced by the fear of violent revolution on the streets after London experienced the Gordon Riots in 1780. The fact that our traditional Catholic enemies, France and Spain, had joined with the Americans and appeared to be threatening Britain itself, ensured that the restriction of dissent remained the government's dominant policy. The authorities methodically suppressed the activities of leading radicals, their societies and the vast public meetings they were occasionally able to organise. 'One insurrection and all is lost' muttered Prime Minister Lord Liverpool as he stared down at the angry metropolis from a window in his townhouse.

Victory at Waterloo did not at first ease the worries of the great or the resentment of the poor, for in places there was widespread unemployment. It was a time for the Innholders and other liveries to sit quiet.

*

Nevertheless, the businesses of many individual innkeepers thrived. With the end of the Napoleonic wars the country was once again open to a wide range of visitors and a Dutchman, newly arrived at Harwich in 1815, provided a vivid picture of a Regency inn.

> 'I have just landed and have been shown into the White Hart Inn. . . . I ring the bell and a person dressed like a gentleman comes in. He served up a most elegant breakfast. There was a teapot of a kind of black earthenware, which I have since learnt to be of Wedgwood make, with a low relief of classic figures; the cream pot was of silver, the cup and saucer of Staffordshire ware. The tea-caddy was of neat lacquer work, and, in the divisions, I found excellent green and black tea with a scalloped silver spoon for ladling out the exact measure. There was a china plate with toast, top and bottom, upon a china basin, and another with slices of thin bread and butter, also a basin of a very fine loaf sugar. All this was brought to me on the neatest tray.'

The rooms at the White Hart were carpeted, and the Dutchman found that he was to sleep on a magnificent mahogany bed ornamented with pretty curtains and covered with a counterpane that was as white as snow. The remaining furniture in his room consisted of a bow-fronted mahogany chest of drawers on which stood a finely wrought mirror. There was also a washstand with a blue Staffordshire jug and basin, and two neatly folded towels draped over a convenient towel-horse.

The food at the White Hart was abundant. The table was set for ten persons. At its head stood an enormous and rather daunting joint of roast beef with its attendant pickled onions and walnuts while, at the other end, there was an imposing leg of mutton. There were two large dishes of potatoes served with a butter sauce, french beans, various fruit pies and, among all of these, a mahogany wagon in which rode an enormous Cheshire cheese. The drink consisted of London porter and port mixed with brandy. When the first course was over a dessert of grapes, walnuts and apples was produced on highly decorative plates. Replete and satisfied, the Dutchman made his way to bed.

The following morning he found the bill to be 'most reasonable' at twenty six shillings a day, but he was slightly put out by the number of servants who accompanied him to the door as he was leaving. The cook, the chambermaid, the under-waiter, the headwaiter and the boots all pressed for their tip, a claim which the Dutchman was able to satisfy by distributing ten shillings among them.

Another foreign visitor to England, the delightful Sophie V. La Roche, also landed at Harwich and was equally impressed. 'The transport arrangements for London are excellent' she wrote, describing how the distance of some seventy four miles was divided into five stages. She describes how the host of an inn kept horses, grooms and coaches who would work as fast as lightning to see that each newly arrived coach was prepared for the next stage of its journey, and how it was both well-built and handsomely lacquered. Four horses and two postillions carried her 'along the best roads and through the finest of landscapes'. At one point she watched the Colchester mail-coach arrive. 'Its name', she wrote, 'is quite rightly the Colchester Machine – seating six people inside, in front, outside behind the coachman, four more, and at the back, where trunks usually go, as many again within a neat enclosure with benches, while eight people were sitting above on deck, their feet dangling overboard, holding fast with their hands to screwed-in brass rings'.

The mail-coaches were the glory of the Regency roads which had been hugely improved by the spread of Turnpike Trusts all over the country. Developing these, the engineering skills of Telford and McAdam ensured that the country was criss-crossed by fast, metalled roads, necessary for the rapid expansion of travel, carrying traffic from London to the ports, to the great industrial centres, and to fashionable spas and sea resorts, like

Bath and Brighton. These good new roads were also essential to the fast conveyance of mail.

Earlier, the carriage of mail had been a royal monopoly, entrusted only to postmasters who supplied horses for post-boys riding at about six miles an hour at a cost of about 3d a mile. This monopoly had been ended in 1780 and an entrepreneur, John Palmer, planned a series of mail-coaches which would not only travel at nearly twice the speed of the post-boys but which, by taking paying passengers, would greatly reduce the costs. By 1784 a coach service from Bristol to London, by way of Bath, concluded its journey to the capital at the famous Swan with Two Necks in Lad Lane. Competition swiftly followed and, by the following year, services in and out of London were running to Norwich, Leeds, Manchester, and Birmingham, Wales and the West Country. By the autumn of 1786, a service to Edinburgh had been established which ran along the Great North Road, via York.

These coaches were extremely smart and the presence of an armed guard appeared to reduce the dangers posed by highwaymen. The coaches were, nonetheless, uncomfortable but kept amazingly good time due to the overwhelming emphasis on speed. An irritable German professor wrote:

> Picture to yourself that we were obliged to cover 124 English miles from Yarmouth to London in fifteen hours without a single stop, except about halfway, at Ipswich, where we were suffered to refresh ourselves for half an hour. Even the most urgent demands of nature had to be suppressed or postponed in order that there might not be a minute's delay in changing horses, which happened about every ten miles. If a traveller wished to get down and disappear for a moment, he was faced with the danger that his luggage might be carried on to London without him. The postillion seemed to recognise no other duty than to arrive punctually. Whether

> his travellers, whose money had very wisely been collected beforehand, arrived with him was their concern, not his. The fresh horses were harnessed in a flash, and away we dashed without any inquiry as to who was on board.

It is hardly surprising under such circumstances that accidents were frequent. No fewer than nine coaches were overturned during the February of 1835 alone.

Nonetheless, the London coaching inns thrived on the new trade and the roll-call of the most famous is a list of some of the finest establishments in the capital. They included the Bull and Mouth in St. Martin's-le-Grand, the famous Bell Savage on Ludgate Hill (now known as the Belle Sauvage), the equally famous Swan with Two Necks (more properly the Swan with Two Nicks, so called from the two nicks that were the mark used for identifying birds belonging to the Dyers Company), the Spread Eagle in Gracechurch Street, the White Horse in Fetter Lane, the Blossom Inn in Lawrence Lane, the Bolt-in-Tun in Fleet Street, the Golden Cross in Charing Cross, the George and the Blue Boar in Holborn, the Bull and the Three Nuns in Aldgate, and the Saracen's Head and the King's Arms on Snow Hill. The most luxurious of all these was reckoned to be the White Horse Cellar on the corner of Arlington Street, close to the present day site of the Ritz, from where wealthier passengers departed for the West Country.

The Belle Sauvage, run in the early 19th century by Robert Nelson, continued its long tradition of innovation and entrepreneurship. The immense stables now accommodated four hundred horses which drew coaches to Bath, Cheltenham, Brighton, Cambridge and Manchester. The competition was fierce, and Nelson decided that his best suit was to promote the highest standards of modern luxury and convenience. To this end the 'Beehive', the coach he ran to Manchester, was 'fitted with spring cushions and a reading lamp, lighted with wax, for the accommodation of those who wished to amuse themselves on the road'. The seats them-

The Royal Mails preparing to start from the Swan With Two Necks, 1831, by James Pollard (above) and *The Brighton Coach leaving the Belle Sauvage* (below)

selves were padded with hair cushions and, to avoid the old problem of passengers squabbling with each other over the seats, Nelson introduced a system of numbered cards so that no one should be in doubt as to where they should sit.

Two great figures of the coaching trade, William Chaplin and Benjamin Worthy Horne, also made their fortunes in this period and became eminent members of the Innholders Company.

Taking over the Swan with Two Necks sometime around 1825, Chaplin went on to acquire the White Horse in Fetter Lane along with the Spread Eagle and the Cross Keys in Gracechurch Street. Although the inn yard of his first establishment was extremely difficult to approach, being situated at the end of a narrow lane and hidden behind a low arch, his business flourished and Chaplin was extremely ingenious at finding methods to ensure its continuing expansion. In particular, he built underground stables for two hundred horses, and such was his relentless energy that, by dint of working night and day, he became a major London employer and an extremely prosperous man.

By 1830 Chaplin had some two thousand people working for him and owned in whole or part upwards of sixty eight coaches and 1800 horses. Nearly half of the twenty seven mail coaches which left London every night were drawn by beasts from his stables and there were those who reckoned that his annual turnover was something in a region of half a million pounds. As time went by his dramatic and successful attempts to ensure he kept his concerns abreast of new developments led to his fame, and he became Master of the Innholders Company in 1854.

One of Chaplin's principal rivals was Benjamin Worthy Horne. In 1828 Horne inherited a substantial coaching business from his father consisting of the Cross Keys in Wood Street, the George and Blue Boar in Holborn and, the pride of the family, the Golden Cross on what is now Trafalgar Square. As the owner of a coaching concern working over 700 horses he constantly looked out for opportunities to expand.

His most prized inn, the Golden Cross, has a place in literary history for it was from here that Mr Pickwick and his companions set out on their adventures. The actual establishment had a chequered history and a chequered reputation. There had been an inn on the site since at least 1643, when zealous puritans demanded the removal of what they considered to be the offensive sign of the golden cross. The inn itself stood in what was then the little village of Charing, midway between the separate and distinct cities of London and Westminster. A painting of the area by Canaletto executed in 1753 shows the Golden Cross as a large but hospitable looking building with a handsome range of coffee-room windows looking out over the street.

Mr Pickwick and his companions were not its only Dickensian patrons. David Copperfield, travelling up to London from Canterbury by coach, also stayed here, somewhat to his discomfort, for the inn is described in the novel as 'a mouldy sort of establishment', while his bedroom 'smelt like a hackney-coach, and was shut up like a family vault'. Such criticisms of the Golden Cross were not infrequently made. Although it was extremely well known, and *The Epicure's Almanac* for 1815 claimed its fame had spread 'from the Pillars of Hercules to the Ganges; from Nova Scotia to California', others maintained it was 'a nasty inn, remarkable for filth and apparent misery'.

Perhaps it was this reputation which prompted Horne to rebuild the Golden Cross when it became his in 1828, replacing its Queen Anne style with a stuccoed box ornamented with gothic details. Unfortunately, his new building almost immediately fell victim to the remorseless pressure to improve London and make it a capital worthy of the empire it ruled. Under the terms of the Charing Cross Improvement Act, by which the tumbledown buildings in the area were cleared and the magisterial development of Trafalgar Square begun, the Golden Cross and some associated buildings were purchased for £30,000 and demolished. Yet another inn of the name was immediately erected a little to the east – a smart building of five stories in the approved Georgian style, later demolished to make way for South Africa House. Benjamin Worthy Horne continued his ambitious career, joined the Court of the Innholders in 1840 and was elected Master, shortly after William Chaplin, in 1858.

Two formidable women were also major figures in the world of Regency London's coaching inns. Both owned inns mentioned by Dickens. Mrs Ann Mountain, widowed in 1818, was proprietor of the Saracen's Head on Snow Hill. Here Nicholas Nickleby found the school-master Mr Squeers, principal of Dotheboys Hall, breakfasting luxuriously on toast and beef, while his diminutive and wretched charges were expected to make do with milk, water and slices of bread and butter.

Mrs Mountain ran her business assisted by her son Peter and was clearly the dominant force behind its success. It was she who, in 1823, put the Tally-Ho coach on the London to Birmingham run, making sure that it made the journey of 109 miles in eleven hours. This feat so roused the competitive fury of Benjamin Horne that he set up his own Independent Tally-Ho on the same road, requiring it to set out a full hour and a quarter earlier than Mrs Mountain's vehicle in order to snatch her customers from under her nose. She was not, however, a woman easily daunted and continued to operate with great success – thirty coaches a day leaving the Saracen's Head. Many of these vehicles were built in her own factory while others were leased out to partners at the rate of threepence half-penny a mile.

Mrs Ann Nelson, who ran the Bull in Aldgate, was almost as formidable. Her splendid establishment maintained the highest traditional standards. Charles Harper, the devoted historian of English inn life, praised it in the warmest terms. The Bull, he declared: 'presented the picture of a typical old English hostelry, and its coffee-room, resplendent with old polished mahogany fittings, its tables laid with silver, and its walls adorned with numerous specimens of those old coaching prints that are now so rare and prized so greatly by collectors, it wore no uncertain air of that solid and restful comfort the new and bustling hotels of today . . . are incapable of giving.' Harper's was indeed a panegyric for a lost world and he went on to declare how 'everything at the Bull was solid and substantial, from the great heavy mahogany chairs that required the strength of a strong man to move, to the rich old English fare, and the full-bodied port its guests were sure of obtaining'.

It was from the Bull that Dickens' Tony Weller, father of the more illustrious Sam, drove a coach down to Ipswich. As so often, Dickens rooted his fictional events in historical fact, for Mrs Nelson ran the greater number of the coaches leaving London for the eastern parts of the country, while her son George drove the 'Defiance' down to Exeter. Her coachmen, along with their attendant guards, had a room specially set aside for them in the Bull, where they lived in a lordly manner, dining in as much style as the regular guests and observing strict rules of etiquette and hierarchy. It was always the oldest coachman who proposed the loyal toast, while all of those under him were never referred to by their names but by the destinations to which they drove. Thus there might be gathered in the room figures variously known as 'Oxford', 'Ipswich', 'Manchester' and 'Devonport'. Another curious custom of the Bull is worth noting. Under no circumstances whatsoever would Mrs Nelson ever allow her establishment to be referred to as an 'hotel'. In this she was distinctly behind the times.

*

Early in the 19th century two important developments occurred simultaneously in the world of innkeeping. The first was the rise of the commercial inn or hotel, designed to cater for the needs of a growing phenomenon – commercial travellers who usually drove about the country in their own vehicles. They came to expect preferential terms in the establishments which they regularly used and, in time, it also became the habit of these hotels to set aside a special room for them.

The second innovation was the emergence of altogether more comfortable, stylish and exclusive inns which were also referred to as hotels. These often catered for officers home from the Napoleonic Wars. Only private travellers, with their own vehicles, would actually stay the night in them, but others could use them briefly as staging posts, while the horses of the public coaches in which they were passengers were being changed. Many hotels had continental connections. For instance, by the opening years of the 19th century there was The German Hotel in Suffolk Street just off Pall Mall and a French establishment in Leicester Square called La Sablonnière. Regency London was not well provided with hotels, most people preferring to stay in cheaper rented accommodation, and for the time being the best hotels were found in such spa towns as Tunbridge Wells, Epsom and Bath.

As London slowly came to be better provided with hotels so they developed their own distinctive style. They were easily distinguished from the old coaching inns as they had no common dining room, thereby allowing greater privacy. One of the most notorious affairs of the early 19th century also attempted to shroud itself in the privacy of a London hotel, for while Sir William and Emma Hamilton lived together in Piccadilly, her lover, Lord Nelson, stayed at Lothian's Hotel close by. A little later, before he set sail for Trafalgar, the admiral moved to Gordon's Hotel.

One of the most pleasing of these early hotels still preserves much of its discreet atmosphere. Brown's Hotel in Dover Street was founded in 1837 by James Brown and his enterprising wife, whose early experience had been shaped by being a maid to Lady Byron, sometime wife of the notorious poet. Mrs Brown made sure the hotel was a conspicuous success from the start. There were sixteen suites, each characterised by a quiet sense of luxury and convenience; accommodation was provided for every visitor's personal servant, and also for the entourages of visiting diplomats.

*

By the 1830s the hotels and inns of London, as in the rest of the country, were catering for a new world. Sections of the British population had grown rapidly and acquired access to enormous material assets and power, especially in the North which had spearheaded the revolution in manufacture and business enterprise. This meant that the antiquated electoral system, represented ever more inadequately those large and newly influential sections of society which produced so much of its wealth. The cry for reform grew louder, and increasingly pressing: the reform of Parliament and the reform of local government, especially.

The Reform Bill of 1832 – supported by William IV and improbably by the Duke of Wellington – significantly remodelled parliamentary representation. Fifty six of the old 'rotten boroughs', those underpopulated constituencies that Wilkes had complained about, were abolished, and thirty others lost one of their two members in the Commons. Forty three further boroughs which had previously been without representation now achieved it, including Manchester, Birmingham, Sheffield and Leeds. The industrial middle classes – those whose money lay in manufacture rather than land – were thus given a more adequate voice in the running of the country, while the cities in which they lived were given modern systems of administration.

The 1835 Municipal Reform Act required borough councils to be elected by ratepayers and staffed by professional officials. In the same year the City of London reduced the fee for its freedom to £5, and its grant was made independent of the membership of a Livery Company. But in many ways, as so often, London remained an exception to the general rule.

'The present condition of this huge metropolis exhibits the most extraordinary anomaly in England', declared one contemporary. 'Abounding in wealth and intelligence, by far the greater part of it is as yet absolutely without any municipal government whatever.' A plethora of small local councils or 'vestries' dealt with a wide range of parochial concerns, while individual entrepreneurs provided ramshackle sanitation, lighting, and transport. There were many who believed that this combination of free enterprise with small, decentralised, elected bodies cut costs. Nevertheless widespread complaints of inefficiency were directed against the Corporation which continued to function in a manner very little changed from the Middle Ages.

There was criticism too of the City hierarchy. There was still a Court of twenty six Aldermen, elected for life, who retained considerable authority, although the majority of decisions were taken by the Court of Common Council, made up of 234 Freemen elected annually from the wards. Having chosen to reject the expanding suburbs and to concentrate only on the square mile, the Corporation continued jealously to guard its traditional powers and to resist all encroachments from national government. Change was unwelcome.

Just as the City fought to defend its ancient rights, so did the Innholders, as a petition of 1819 from the Company to the Court of Common Council illustrates. Some three dozen proprietors of central London inns were greatly concerned that the capital's so-called Ticket Porters (an ancient and robust fraternity) were spoiling business by claiming 'on the pretence of privileges granted to them by your honourable Court' that they had the right to deliver across the capital goods transported to London in the innkeepers' coaches. As a result, the innkeepers' work had been 'vexatiously obstructed and interrupted'.

The petition gives an insight into one often neglected aspect of the innkeeper's business: the carriage of goods. 'The trade of your petitioners', it declares, 'consists principally in the accommodation of public carriages, and in the receipt, custody and delivery of goods conveyed to and from the City and to and from the various parts of the kingdom'. It goes on to state that for the purposes of the trade, the proprietors 'are under the necessity of maintaining numerous establishments of servants, and of occupying premises of the most extensive description, and as the convenience of the public requires that these should be situated in the most central parts of the City, the rent, rates, taxes, and other expenses are particularly heavy'. The Innholders then allege that profit from 'the receipt and delivery of goods' is their chief source of income.

They were determined to bolster their case by presenting themselves as men of substance, not only the proprietors of the vehicles involved but, unlike the Porters, figures of professional calibre. In the effort to downgrade the Porters, the Innholders' concluded by stating that the Porters 'contribute neither to the capital nor the expense with which your petitioners' trade is conducted. The Innholders finally asserted that the Porters' claims 'are repugnant to the plainest principles of equity'.

The matter was very fully investigated and the final ruling was balanced in the extreme: 'No case has been made out so as at present to induce this Select Committee to recommend any alteration to be made in the existing laws for the regulation and government of the Ticket Porters, as the governor and rulers [of the Porters] have the power to punish all vexatious obstructions or interpositions of any individuals of the fellowship of the Ticket Porters, and no applications having been made to the said governor and rulers upon any occasion of complaint'.

It is clear that the Committee believed the Innholders had been somewhat peremptory, but they nonetheless upheld the common sense view that 'the Innholders should be permitted by themselves and their servants, or otherwise to deliver all goods consigned to their care for that purpose.' Fair Trading was to be encouraged and the law was not to be used as a blunt instrument in a highly competitive world.

*

Mounting public pressure for the preservation of competition and the suppression of privilege and restrictive practices, led to the establishment in 1833 of a Royal Commission to 'inquire into the existing state of the Municipal Corporations in England and Wales'. In particular, the apparently anachronistic nature of the City of London Corporation became the object of zealously critical eyes; and, because of the central role they played in its functioning, Livery Companies such as the Innholders were a special object of the Commissioners' concern. Their scrutiny allows us to look at the operation of the Company in some detail.

During the first decades of the 19th century the annual intake of

Freemen fluctuated widely. From about 40 per year in the first years admissions rose to over a hundred between 1825 and 1830. However in 1831 it suddenly dropped to 61 and then averaged about fifty a year until the number dwindled further in the next half century.

By far the majority of these entrants obtained their Freedom by Redemption (Purchase) – 97 doing so in 1825. Admissions by patrimony – the right of an Innholder's son – were very few, varying from none to seven in the years 1801 to 1830. The figures of entry by Apprenticeship tell the same story; although eleven Apprentices were admitted in both 1828 and the following year, the annual average for 1801 to 1830 was about five.

New members were needed since healthy admission figures were important to the financial well-being of the Company since fines were payable on entry to the Freedom. These were fixed in 1808 at £3.4.0 for entry by Patrimony or Servitude, and at £5.6.0 for entry by Redemption. Fines were also set for taking office. In 1823 those elected Assistant (of whom there were twenty excluding the Master and Wardens) were fined at £31.10.0, but acceptance of the office was now voluntary. The Renter Warden was not liable to any fine on taking office because he had to pay £24 towards the cost of his dinner, but he was liable to a fine of £20 if he refused the office. The Middle Warden paid £5 on being sworn in and £2 on going out of office, but candidates were also liable to a fine of £10 for refusing the post. Finally, the Upper Warden and Master paid £2 each on being sworn in and £2 each on quitting the post, they too were liable to a fine of £10 each if they refused to take up office. In addition to these fines all members of the Company paid 'quarterage' fees of 6d a quarter, this money being collected by the Beadle.

Such fines and fees were a vital source of income. In 1834, for example, fees from Apprentice bindings amounted to £15, those from the admission of Freemen to £124.4.0, fines on the senior members of the Livery totalled £105, and quarterage collections brought in a further £50.4. 0. This total £420.8. 0 was only very slightly less than the £423. 17. 0 derived from the

Company's rental income, the two figures combining to provide the Innholders with an annual receipt of £944.5 0.

How was this money spent? The single most expensive item in 1834 was the £232 paid out to the Master, Wardens and Assistants for attendance on Court days. The next rather loosely accounted item was the £161. 18. 2 for 'expenses at the meetings of the Court, repairs, tradesmen's bills, and general and casual expenses'. Immediately below this came the Clerk's remuneration of £100; while that other important official, the Beadle, received £28. Entertainment was a further sizeable item, a dinner for 153 Freemen, exclusive of wine, costing £85, while the replenishing of the Company's cellars in 1834 cost £92. 'Gifts to poor members in addition to £86.15. 0 charity money and poor's box' amounted to £28.3.0, while printing and insurance were costed at £18.13. 0 and £4. 10.0 respectively. Out of their surplus income the Company bought £100 in stocks, leaving it for that year with a cash balance of £50.2. 3.

Who were the people gathered together in this clubbable if not conspicuously charitable body? The Innholders themselves were at pains to point out that 'in the government of the Company they have always been actuated by a desire to uphold the character and respectability of the Company', adding that they were constantly 'ready to give admission to every person of proper character requiring the freedom'. Nonetheless, as the Commissioners somewhat acerbically pointed out, 'no opposition has ever been made, and no refusal is recollected; yet, in theory, the admission is still a matter of discretion, except where the applicant is a keeper of an inn, hostelry, or livery-stable, in which cases the admission is matter of right'.

This reference to the trade was important, and careful distinctions were still drawn. 'Under the act of Common Council persons keeping eating houses or beer-shops' were not considered as being entitled to automatic membership of the Company, 'the test of being entitled to admission as an Innholder being the 'receipt and entertainment of travellers'.

The Company still had the right to compel innkeepers within the City to join their body and 'the process of compelling a party . . . to enter the

Company', is by summons requiring him to attend a Court of Assistants, and take up his freedom, and such person is liable to a fine for refusal, which is recoverable by action; but it has not recently been necessary to resort to legal proceedings' – indeed, many innkeepers, even if they lived outside the area covered by the charter, joined the Company readily and out of a natural interest, preferring 'this Company on account of its bringing them into connection with others of the trade'. As a result, 'seven out of the present twenty four members of the Court are, or have been, of the trades . . . specified, and the proportion of all the members of the Company belonging to these trades is greater than those not belonging to the same'.

So much was sensible and agreeable, and the Innholders were wisely determined to maintain their present status and reputation and not push their rights and obligations in a way that might disturb them. For example, although the Company had very extensive rights to examine the business of any innkeeper whom they thought was dealing in unlawful measures, or otherwise operating illegally, 'no search has been made within 20 years'.

Very wisely too, in view of the developments to come, the Innholders continued their charitable work, distributing the interest on monies left to them for this purpose. Thomas Lewis, Master in 1806-7 left £500 to be distributed among the poor. John Jones, his successor, left £200 for the relief of poor widows of the Company. £500 was left by James Newton in 1827 for the relief of poor Freemen and their families; Richard Flour Bayley left £100 for a similar purpose; and Thomas Hinde of the Spur in Southwark left a yearly rent charge of £5 from his business to help the poor and decayed. This was continuing an ancient tradition and an honourable one. It was a quiet expression of the genuine social concern that went hand in hand with the Innholders' conviviality and fraternal bonds.

It must have seemed to the Innholders – as to the other Livery Companies – that the arguments they had put to the Commissioners to justify their existence and privileges were persuasive.

*

The Commissioners delivered their main report on the Municipal Corporations in 1835 but delayed their report on the City of London until 1837, no doubt on account of its complexity and scrupulous thoroughness. They were impressed by the functioning of the City Corporation as a whole, but their view of the institution of the Livery Companies was quietly damning and written very much in the contemporary spirit of reform.

They were particularly galled by the fact that, for all the Freemen of London were 'very numerous', they were 'but a part of the householders of London'. It seemed inequitable that such a random selection of people should enjoy the 'right to take part as electors in the concerns of the Corporation, in . . . exemption from certain tolls in the City and elsewhere, in. . . exemption from impressment, and in their exclusive right to exercise retail trades, or act as Brokers, within the City'. The fact that the Freemen could elect members of the Corporation while that body itself had little if any control over them was equally objectionable and smacked, besides, of self-interest, the fees payable on entry to the freedom being, in the Commissioners' words, 'no more than a troublesome and capricious method of taxing the inhabitants of London for the emolument of the Companies'.

All three methods of obtaining the freedom – Patrimony, Redemption and Apprenticeship – came under attack. 'Birth and apprenticeship have been supposed to raise the presumption of a permanent interest in the City; but inhabitancy for a definite period furnishes evidence much more simple and direct, and much less liable to fallacy' As for obtaining the freedom by purchase, 'it is practically a tax upon the retail traders of the City, who are compelled to take up the freedom; and whatever advantages may be attributed to such a tax, as a test of the competence of the party contributing, or a compensation for the convenience of a residence within the City, these, admitting them to be advantages, might surely be obtained by a much less circuitous and more equitable process'.

The real point at issue here was the Commissioners' strong distaste for the fact that the right to vote in the City's elections was something that could be bought by joining a livery company. It seemed like a question of votes for sale. The Commissioners were prepared to countenance the idea that some form of property or wealth qualification for electors might be desirable, but they believed that this 'could be better obtained by a more direct means; and we can therefore see no disadvantage in severing the guild franchise and the municipal franchise, and in permitting all the privileges of the City to be obtained independently of the Companies'.

They had other objections too. For all that the companies had once been intimately connected with the trades they represented, nowadays 'very few comparatively exercise any substantial control over their proper art or mystery, or retain more than a nominal connection with it.' Worse still, the companies' regulations implied a limit on free trade while the suggestion that they also tried to run something like a 'closed shop' were equally unattractive to them:

> It may not be irrelevant to remark that several of the rules in the bye-laws of the Companies as, for instance, the limitation of the number of apprentices, are entirely analogous to those which workmen often attempt to force upon their employers by means of their Trade Unions. Whether these practices are more or less mischievous when sanctioned by charters conferring legal incorporation, or when insisted on by unauthorised associations, is a question not unworthy of the attention of the Legislature; but it is evident that, in the present enlarged state of the Metropolis, any powers which are confined to the City and Liberties, must, from that circumstance alone, be inefficacious, and that no exertions on the part of the Companies, under the imperfect powers granted by their Charters, could have enabled them to retain whatever utility they may be supposed to have formerly possessed.

Basically the Commissioners saw in the Liveries only anachronism, irrelevance and privilege. What had served the Plantagenet capital well could not (or perhaps should not) survive into Hanoverian London. It was their view that 'the only useful functions which remain to the Companies, and more particularly to the larger and more opulent of these bodies, are the management of the charities which are vested in them as specific trusts, and the dispensation of the 'voluntary benevolences which issue from their own funds'.

At the end of their four years' hard work the Commissioners' views were ignored and their report was greeted with a resounding silence. To be sure, it had laid bare faults in plenty: but before long, the moment for decisive action passed. The Whig Prime Minister, Lord Melbourne, was satisfied that he could safely do nothing, certain in his belief that 'whenever you meddle with . . . ancient rights it appears . . . that for the sake of remedying comparatively insignificant abuses you create new ones and always produce a considerable discontent'. Besides, it seemed to him as to many others that a solution to the City of London's administrative problems was intractable, and Melbourne feared the idea of replacing an old if rickety system with a new and monolithic authority. It seemed best to let sleeping dogs lie and to rely, if on anything, on a process of piecemeal reform.

In 1837 the report was shelved and William IV died. Melbourne, altogether more interested in the future, turned his attention to initiating the newly crowned, eighteen-year-old Queen Victoria into the ways of the great new age which, in time, would bear her name.

Charles Druce
Liveryman 1784, Clerk, 1785-1835, Master 1840
portrait by H.P. Briggs, RA, (1791-1844)

Chapter 9

VICTORIAN LONDON

1837 – 1901

The Liveries languish as the country flourishes – The railways and London's grand new hotels – A second Royal Commission on the Liveries, 1880 – The Innholders' response to the Commissioners – The Commission's verdict, 1884 – The restoration of Innholders Hall – Three Lord Mayors – The end of an age.

When Queen Victoria ascended the throne, the leading livery companies remained exceptionally rich and influential, but others were in steep if not terminal decline. In 1837 the Commissioners had listed a total of eighty-nine liveried bodies but, fifty years later, thirteen of these were extinct and the overall livery list had virtually halved to barely 5,500.

This process can be illustrated by figures from the Innholders' records. A report on the Company issued by the Inspector of Charities in 1865 declared that 'the Freemen are diminishing, the new admissions not exceeding three or four a year', and a table was produced to illustrate this trend. From a high point in 1832, when there were 466 liverymen in the Company, membership had fallen decade by decade, and by 1862 there were merely 184. This decline continued until, by the close of 1880, there only remained 134 in the Livery, admissions during the previous decade amounting to a meagre 23. In the same period, only 20 men had been granted the Freedom, eleven by Redemption and nine by Patrimony or Apprenticeship.

This was a sad story but it was far from untypical. A number of companies even less fortunate were obliged to reduce the size of the quorum required at their Court meetings; at the Tinplateworkers sometimes only the Master and the Clerk were present. There were several reasons for such a decline: the alteration of the Freedom regulations had taken away from the companies the sole power to grant that privilege; the constant threat to withdraw a Liveryman's right to vote in local and parliamentary elections made membership decreasingly attractive; and finally, as the gulf between the companies and their trades widened, so it seemed to many that there was little commercial reason for joining them.

Yet it was not a story of unmitigated decline. Some once flagging companies showed signs of revival and expansion. This was true of the Basketmakers, the Makers of Playing Cards, the Shipwrights, and soon the Innholders, for the more vibrant companies could still offer opportunities to the thrusting and thriving businessmen who brought so much energy and enterprise to Victorian London.

In the middle years of the 19th century London became the most important and influential city in the world, its population eventually rising to close on four and a half million. 'This vast bricken mass of churches, and hospitals, banks and prisons, palaces and workhouses, docks and refuges for the destitute, parks and squares, and courts and alleys, which make up London' left the reforming journalist Henry Mayhew awe-struck as he surveyed it from a balloon. He declared that he could not 'tell where the monster city began or ended, for the buildings stretched not only to the horizon on either side, but far away into the distance... where the town seemed to blend into the sky'.

To the men of Mayhew's generation, London was above all an imperial city, the capital of a vast manufacturing and trading empire. The Great Exhibition, housed in the glass and iron wonder that was the Crystal Palace, proclaimed that Britain was the workshop of the world and the centre of innovation. That its capital was the hub of the planet was given symbolic expression three decades later when an international conference agreed that the meridian line, passing through the observatory at Greenwich, should be the point from which Longitude would be measured and Standard Time across the world determined.

Manufacturing and trade aside, the future of London's wealth and importance lay in its hugely proliferating financial sector. Commercial services thrived. National banking groups administered the flow of short term funds across the country, the empire and beyond. Growing numbers of jobbers and brokers in the Stock Market helped finance loans to foreign governments and lend unprecedented sums to companies managing gold mines, tea plantations, railways, telegraphs, telephones and, as we shall see, the vast and luxurious hotels that were soon to become a hallmark of the age. The time was rapidly approaching when a bill on London was deemed to be a better currency than gold itself, more economical, more readily transmissible, more efficient.

Much of the commercial activity funded by the City depended on ships, and the time was approaching when nearly half of the world's merchant fleets were owned and controlled from London. As a direct result, marine insurance flourished, some two thirds of this business passing through Lloyd's. Fire and life insurance boomed equally and, with them, the careers of a host of associated professionals: accountants, liquidators, company lawyers and their vast army of clerks. It was no exaggeration to describe Lombard Street as 'by far the greatest combination of economical power and economical delicacy the world has ever seen'. Deposits in London banks were ten times those in Paris and, for the time being, three times those in New York. The pound sterling was the world's currency.

If there was one single innovation which made this expansion possible, it was harnessing the power of steam: steam drove the mills, the looms and, above all, the railways. The first steam powered passenger railway in London ran from the capital to Greenwich and was opened in 1836. The Midlands had seen its first tracks laid a decade earlier, but it took men of foresight to realise the enormous significance that the railways would have for London. One such man was William Chaplin, the Innholder, and now the hugely successful proprietor of one of London's greatest coaching concerns.

Chaplin realised that opposition to the railways would be fatal to his business and, in the year after the Greenwich line opened, he approached his great rival, Benjamin Worthy Horne, with the daring proposal that they pool their resources and throw in their lot with the railways. With a

THE DRIVER OF 1832

Two Victorian aquatints by Henry Alken (1852) comparing the Mail Coach Era with the new Age of the Railways

THE DRIVER OF 1852

bluntness born of real acumen Chaplin argued that they would lose £10,000 apiece if they resisted the forces of change.

Horne was eventually won over and the firm of Chaplin and Horne won the contract for the parcel agency on the London and Birmingham Railway, which grew and prospered. Together they demonstrated that the 19th century livery companies could indeed attract men of the highest calibre, willing to embrace a new industry that was to alter profoundly the nature of the innkeeping and hotel business in this country.

*

There were three reasons why the Victorian railway companies encouraged the building of hotels. Long distance travellers by train were eager to stay and rest in station hotels before the next stage of their journey. Furthermore, trains were not yet famous for their punctuality and it was necessary to offer somewhere to sleep to passengers arriving late, along with those who were to leave early in the morning. Finally, and perhaps most importantly, the stiff competition that soon sprang up between the various railway companies prompted their owners to attract customers to their lines by siting hotels at their stations. As a result railway hotels, particularly in London and the major cities, soon vied with each other in size, ostentation and modernity.

There was, however, one sad victim of this new expansion: the coaching inn. As the railways snaked their way through the country, drawing travellers off the roads and transporting them at ever faster speeds across land where no vehicle other than a farm cart had ever been before, so the yards of the old coaching inns ceased to echo to the sounds of ostlers and stableboys. Grass grew among the cobblestones; increasingly desperate landlords turned to making a meagre living in some other way; premises once proud and prosperous became synonymous with decay and despondency.

Otherwise the surge in hotel building was a welcome innovation since, in the words of Dickens 'in proportion to its size, London is still worse provided in this respect than most of the great Continental or American towns. Almost every great railway however, with the exception of the South Western, has now a handsome hotel in connection with its terminus'.

The first of the capital's railway hotels was that erected for the London and Birmingham Railway, at Euston, in 1839. It consisted of two separate buildings, one of which was for dining and passing time in (there was, for example, a splendid coffee room) while the other comprised quarters described as 'dormitories', many of which had a sitting or dressing room attached. This early Euston hotel, grand though it may have been for its time, was a modest affair in comparison with those that were to follow it.

Three great London railway hotels of the Victorian period call for particular mention. The first is the Great Eastern Hotel in Liverpool Street, now (at the time of writing) the only hotel in the City of London. Designed by Charles Barry in 1884, it was built to serve Liverpool Street Station. An extension by Colonel Robert Edis was added in 1901, and the complete Victorian ensemble gives an excellent notion of the luxury combined with modern efficiency at which the proprietors of the railways aimed. Guests dining in the Great Eastern were much impressed by the elaborate glass-domed restaurant complete with dancing sylphs and two Masonic temples, but would have been barely aware of the service areas. During the night the hotel's own railway system, situated in an area called 'the backs', deposited the large amount of coal the hotel consumed and took away the quantities of clinkers and rubbish it produced. The night train also brought in the supply of sea water needed for its much vaunted salt water baths.

The second of these railway hotels, the Grosvenor on Victoria Station, is impressive even today when its external glories have become blackened with grime. The building is a masterpiece of imitation French High Renaissance architecture – all pavilion roofs, statues and writhing stone chiselled with fruit and flowers. But the Grosvenor had – and still has – a rival altogether more fabulous, a building so quintessentially Victorian that its sheer magnificence and nerve cause the passer-by to stare in wonder and the guest to know that he has done more than dream, if only briefly, that he dwelt in marble halls.

The Midland Grand Hotel, at St Pancras, was designed by Sir George Gilbert Scott. His Gothic masterpiece is one of the wonders of London, as the *Quarterly Review* recognised when it wrote that 'the building inside and out is covered with ornament, and there is polished marble enough to furnish a cathedral'. Visitors alighting on the specially soundproofed road outside entered a world imperious in its expensive modernity, which offered walnut pianos in all the best sitting rooms, expensive clocks ticking on the mantelpieces, and a bank of passenger lifts installed at £710 each. The total of costs amounted to a massive £450,000. With investment made easier by the passing of the Companies Act the age of the Grand Hotel had arrived.

One of the grandest was the Langham at the top of Portland Place. Accommodating 500 guests, it was half as big again as the Grosvenor and occupied ten floors. When it was opened on 10th June, 1865, the Prince of Wales came to inspect it along with some 2,000 other visitors, including a correspondent of *The Times* who was loud in praise of its exquisite hydraulic lift; its great saloons for balls, wedding breakfasts and receptions; its three main dining rooms and its 300 water closets.

In the vast basement there were the bake houses, the laundry and packing offices, the servants' hall which could seat 260, and the enormous kitchens in which fifty joints could be roasted at a time before being carved and served on the 2,000 plates warming in the ovens. A 'quaint little tramway' speeded up the transport of goods through this labyrinth.

The life led by the staff of these hotels, especially the more lowly of them, was gruelling in the extreme. The Shop Act ensured that young people under eighteen could only be worked for a maximum of twelve hours a day for five days of the week and fourteen on the sixth. A total of seventy hours was nevertheless regarded by many managers as too few compared to the one hundred hours that had previously been expected.

Wages were pitifully small. A cook might expect £5 a month, a head waiter £4, while a maid would receive perhaps £1.10.0. Tips (an acronym for the phrase *To Insure Promptitude)* helped to increase these paltry sums. The management was perfectly well aware of this, with the result that many of the staff – waiters, for example – were not paid a wage at all but had to rely entirely on the generosity of the guests and were even, in some cases, obliged to pay the hotel a commission in order to retain their posts.

If hoteliers and innkeepers had few obligations towards their employees, it was different when it came to their guests. In the words of a contemporary writing for the Incorporated Association of Hotels and Restaurants, 'the legal position of an innkeeper today is complicated and uncertain'. For instance, it had been the custom from the earliest Middle Ages for an innkeeper to assume responsibility for all his guests' goods. These did not have to be put in the hotel safe, while the fact that keys to the rooms were left hanging in unguarded places made theft all too easy.

Happily, in 1863 the law was changed. Hoteliers were now deemed to be responsible only for the first £30 of a guest's losses, provided that a sign explaining the law was clearly displayed. In addition, they were no longer considered responsible for their guests' animals and carriages.

Another important change was made in 1878 when the Inn Keepers Act laid down that a hotelier seizing the property of a guest who had failed to pay his bill might sell it after six weeks and the placing of a notice in the newspapers to advertise his intention. For a long time it was not difficult to run up a large bill without being wholly aware of it. Finally a list of hotel tariffs had to be printed and displayed – and many objected that these newly enormous hotels were run, as they had to be, with the efficiency of a factory. As a result the personal touch was often felt to be missing.

The very best hotels sought to avoid this, supreme among them the one opened by D'Oyly Carte in 1889: the Savoy. He was determined that it should be the last word in modern luxury. There were six hydraulic lifts running 'at all hours of the day and night, perfectly safe, their movement smooth, rapid and pleasant'. The perfection of these lifts enabled rooms on all floors to be chargeable at a uniform rate. The luxurious rooms were lit with electricity powered by the hotel's own generator: 'the supply will be continuous during all hours of the day and night not only in sitting rooms but in bedrooms, the button or switch being so placed that the light can be turned on or off without getting out of bed'.

The Savoy was exceptional in another way, too. After considerable effort D'Oyly Carte managed to persuade César Ritz to come to London as his director. Ritz brought with him not only Echenard, the best maître d'hôtel of his day, but Auguste Escoffier, perhaps the greatest chef de cuisine of all time.

*

There were many reasons why the livery companies continued to exert their deep and subtle appeal to the entrepreneurs of Victorian London and a society which had a taste for such large and luxurious hotels.

In an era when the Houses of Parliament were rebuilt in Gothic style, the romanticised allure of the guilds, rooted in the Middle Ages, exercised a strong fascination. Here were tradition and continuity, the comforting notion that the mighty 19th century metropolis had its origins in small groups of honest tradesmen pursuing their business in a simpler age. For many the social side of company life offered a decent and desirable sense of fraternity and trust. Livery dinners and public occasions were, besides, excellent opportunities to entertain and perhaps impress business colleagues and clients, and so help advance a career. For others, in an age deeply concerned with public welfare but lacking a system of social security, the charitable activities of the liveries were distinctly appealing. Finally, the Companies could still confer the Freedom of the City, with its right to vote in parliamentary and civic elections.

In this lay a great and familiar cause of contention, exacerbated by the lesser charge that the livery companies were guilty of gourmandising and gross self-indulgence. Curiously, one of the most strident voices of criticism rose from among the ranks of the Innholders. In 1872, J. R. Taylor, a radical member of the Company, peevish and embittered because he believed he had been denied his rightful place on the Court on account of his views, vented his dissatisfaction in a publication called *Reform Your City Guilds.* Perhaps disingenuously, he stressed the innocence of his intentions, but his line of thought was clear. The City companies – including the Innholders – would have to find ways to be 'useful' if they were to survive; they must reform themselves if the government were not to do it for them.

Others saw the companies in an altogether more hostile light – as a dead weight on the inevitable march of progress – and campaigned vigorously for their abolition. Determined on the thorough reform and modernisation of London, such people only had to glance across at continental Europe to find a multitude of precedents for the suppression of the guilds. The National Assembly had destroyed the guild structure in France in 1791, and those of Belgium and Holland followed soon after. The guilds of Spain and Portugal were abolished between 1830 and 1840. Germany and Austria followed in 1859-60, and Italy succumbed to their example in 1864.

Those in England who thought in a similar way, Liberals by nature, looked at the results of the recent City elections and saw London becoming a Tory stronghold firmly opposed to change. In 1874 only one Liberal was elected, six years later none at all. The cry of 'faggot votes' echoed round the streets as the Aldermen permitted the companies to expand membership of their liveries beyond their original limits. It was feared their newly swollen ranks would march out to vote for what many in the Liberal camp saw as the reactionary forces of the *ancien regime.*

By 1876 the formidable J. F. B. Firth had taken up the issue in his swingeing book *Municipal London.* There, in the third chapter especially, he launched his attack on the City guilds. Firth was a firm advocate of the notion that London should have a centralised metropolitan authority. He found it preposterous that the mighty Victorian capital should be governed (or, in his view, misgoverned) by a jumble of authorities dating from the Middle Ages. As a result, he dedicated his energies to the removal of what he considered to be the moribund City Corporation. It was self-evident to him that the Livery vote in Common Hall was a cornerstone of this hated body and so he argued that the guilds would have to be abolished too. This last was particularly attractive to him since it was known that some of the companies were very rich; once destroyed, their confiscated wealth could subsidise his projected new municipal council. A necessary innovation could thus be achieved without cost to the ratepayer.

Fired by such ideas, the City Guilds Reform Association was set up and campaigned vigorously against the companies, luridly describing them as dens of gluttony and fraud. Pages from Firth's book were reprinted and distributed as flyers and pamphlets at meetings of such institutions as the St Pancras Workingmen's Club. Tradesmen were urged to turn against the guilds that had for so long neglected their real interests. Letters in the radical press (almost invariably written over a pseudonym) repeated the cry, and figures were adduced to prove that the companies evicted the poor from their homes in the City, forcing them to live in squalor so that their tenements could be converted into prestigious offices. All of these reformers urged that there was only one way of dealing with the matter: a Royal Commission of Enquiry, regardless of the fact that the previous commissioners had already examined the issues only forty years earlier.

A commission required parliamentary action, and agitation for guild reform now grew louder in the corridors of Westminster. Eventually, in 1876, the radicals found a spokesman in W. H. James, the Member for Gateshead. In May of that year he rose in the chamber to demand details of the companies' income and property, averring as he did so that he did not wish to see them 'obliterated and swept away', but hinting darkly that 'they should be more fully alive to the altered circumstances and necessities of the present day'. James was addressing a Conservative majority and he was obliged to withdraw his motion.

However, he had interested a number of leading Liberal grandees, including the towering figure of Gladstone. Although he realised this was dangerous ground, Gladstone was convinced that much of the revenue of the livery companies was 'positively and utterly wasted, and very imperfectly and doubtfully bestowed'. Like James, he too believed that the companies should not be utterly abolished, but speculated on their likely fate if they continued in their absolute resistance to change. The following year James mounted a second attack, but a request for a 'full investigation' into the affairs of the guilds was heavily defeated, the Solicitor General declaring that such a 'general communistic enquiry' was a threat to private property. Nevertheless James raised the issue a third time early in 1879. He argued that to give men the vote as a consequence of their buying their membership of a Livery Company was disgracefully to sell the City franchise and was a clear abuse. He was again defeated.

In 1880, with the return of a Liberal government, it seemed that his time might have come. Gladstone, the Prime Minister, remained interested in the issue and the still angry Firth had his ear; in May the government resolved on setting up a Royal Commission to investigate the Livery Companies.

The commission was made up from a highly distinguished collection of leading aristocrats, judges, bankers and politicians including James and Firth. They proceeded with that remarkable thoroughness so characteristic of Victorian commissions. Lengthy questionnaires were sent out to the Liveries who, despite protesting on legal advice that they had no duty to make public their title to their private wealth, returned sufficient information to fill four stout volumes.

Then the board began to hear the oral evidence. The all-important Charity Commissioners declared themselves by and large satisfied with the way in which the companies discharged their formal commitments, but suggested that there was slackness in the way in which corporate income was invested. Critics of the companies were then summoned to present their case for abolition of the Liveries and for the distribution of the resulting assets to what they considered worthy causes.

Representatives of these hopeful causes themselves were then summoned. They included a number of educational bodies eager to share the good fortune of the City and Guilds Institute which had been set up by the Corporation and sixteen of the leading companies in 1877-78. The Lord Chancellor, the Institute's chairman, and three company Clerks (all of them closely associated with the Institute) then put the case for the defence and, finally, the guilds themselves were allowed to present their own memorials, letters and deputations.

*

The Innholders Company responded fully to the Commissioners' numerous and often probing questions but, like several other liveries, attached 'a protest against the legality of the inquiry' to their reply. Their private concerns were about to be made a matter of public record, an intrusion which they found uncomfortable and even threatening. In fact the Innholders had always conducted their affairs honourably and decently, as the Commissioners' comprehensive picture of the Company makes clear.

It shows the Master and the three Wardens, annually elected on the first Tuesday in every August, heading a Court of twenty Assistants appointed for life, men who had risen through the ranks of the Company by chronological seniority. Such means achieved continuity and security which the Commission apparently disliked, since they did not allow new and less experienced voices to be heard. The Commissioners further declared that 'no attempts have been made to throw open the Court, or to alter the present right of suffrage'. A hint of the complacent, even moribund, is palpable. But there is no suggestion of corruption.

The Innholders' Court met monthly, discharged its necessary duties, paid its members a comparatively modest fee of £1 for their attendance, and then threw a luncheon or a dinner to which these men could invite a friend. The Commissioners listed the Court's business as including 'the admission of persons to the freedom', which now cost £6.16.6 if it were obtained through purchase and £7.7.0 if it were sought through patrimony or servitude. Admitting Freemen to the livery, with a view to their eventual eligibility for the Court, was another regular item of business, although the six most recent Assistants had waited for periods of between eleven and twenty-seven years before reaching it. Assistants often had little if any connection with innkeeping, the Commissioners commenting that 'no particular trade is now represented by persons becoming members' – an observation reinforced by the fact that although the Court still had the authority to bind apprentices, none was bound between 1871 and 1880.

The Commission listed the other functions of the Court as being 'the general management of the Company and its property and revenues and charities'.

The most valuable of its holdings were its properties numbers 72 and 73 Coleman Street, which had recently been cleared for the erection of 'a new building intended for warehouses, and offices, built by Messrs Colls the builders, under agreement for a lease'. The Company had owned this site since the reign of Henry VIII when it had been willed to them by Thomas Baylie, and the rent of the new buildings was expected to be worth £350 a year. Out of this an annual payment of £2.8.0 was made to the vicar and churchwardens of St Lawrence Jewry. The Company also owned ten properties in Moorgate Street, each comprising a house and a shop, which brought in rents varying from £33 to £120. Finally, there were two properties in College Street, numbers 29 and 30, which were let out at 'rack rent' (ie a rent annually equalling the full value of the property) along with their separate cellars, and those under the Company's Hall which were leased by a basket maker.

In addition to these rents the Innholders derived net annual receipts of £13.3.9 from stocks and shares which were 'the absolute property of the Company', and a further £111.8.7 from various 'bequests and donations and accumulations' which were, in turn, set aside as a 'fund for rebuilding the Company's Hall etc'.

Next there was the revenue which the Company derived from internal sources: from admissions to the Freedom, the Livery and the Court, on promotion to office, and from fines on those who refused office. A table of the annual revenue is shown on the following page. Omitting both charity and trust income, and any balance brought forward, it amounted to about £1,000 per year. Below the income table is an account of the Company's income and expenditure for 1880.

Compared with the Great Companies, this income was paltry. In the same year the Drapers' corporate income was £50,141 and the Fishmongers' £46,913. Among the lesser Companies the Leathersellers received £16,393 and the Saddlers £10,245. It was not, however, insignificant that of the ten companies worth over £1,000 a year, only three were more prosperous than the Innholders; twenty-four companies had incomes of less than £1,000 a year; while the Makers of Playing Cards had barely £50 a year, the Blacksmiths £61 and the Gold and Silver Wyre Drawers £62. In terms of overall income the Innholders' revenue roughly measured up to its ranking as number 32 in the order of precedence among the Liveries.

The Innholders also had some £220 of trust income which was dedicated to charitable causes. In comparison to the charity incomes of the other minor liveries (nineteen of which had none at all) this was an appreciable sum which had been substantially increased in 1846 by a gift from Henry Scambler, who had been elected Master in 1833. Its nature was excellently described by the Charity Commissioners nineteen years later. The passage in their report on this particular trust is a fascinating insight into the workings of Victorian charity: a combination of generosity, shrewd investment, and an insistence on respectability as a condition for the relief of poverty.

INNHOLDERS' ACCOUNTS
ANNUAL INCOME 1871 – 1880

	£	s	d
1871	837	16	2
1872	858	14	2
1873	957	4	2
1874	980	13	11
1875	1,024	7	5
1876	1,017	3	9
1877	905	4	3
1878	928	14	9
1879	937	14	10
1880	1,326	13	7

BALANCE OF INCOME AND EXPENDITURE 1880

INCOME	£	s	d	EXPENDITURE	£	s	d
Admissions	12	10	0	Taxes	106	5	9
Quarterage	-	-	-	Court money	184	0	0
Rents	566	16	1	Provisions	222	8	5
Building fund balance	10	10	0	Investments	-	-	-
Interest and dividends	132	7	6	Casual expenses	253	15	3
Fines	183	10	0	Salaries	150	0	0
Casual receipts	421	0	0				
TOTAL	1,326	13	7	TOTAL	916	9	5
Last year's balance	84	14	7	Unspent	494	18	9
	£1,411	8	2		£1,411	8	2

Here is the wording of Henry Scambler's legacy:

> Henry Scambler, by his will of the 9th April 1845, bequeathed to the Company £6,000, upon a trust to lay out same in the Government funds; and he directed them to divide the dividends to arise from time to time between as many of the most respectable poor members of the Company, or their widows, who should have paid the livery fines; that is to say, eight of the most respectable to have £25 a year, and the four next respectable to have £10 a year, and so in a proportion until the dividends were exhausted; such payments are to be made in equal moieties twice every year, for the respective lives of the said annuitants.
>
> The legacy duty was deducted, and the residue of £5,648.0.11 invested on the 26th April, 1846, in 3 per cent consols. The dividends amount to £169.8.8. The supplies beyond the £160 directed to be divided have been annually added to the capital, which now amounts to £5,696.3.7 in 3 per cent consols, which stands to a separate account in the corporate income of the Company.
>
> The fund is divided between 12 liverymen, or widows of liverymen, of whom eight have £15, and four £10 a year each, in half-yearly payments. The pensioners are chosen by the Court, and remain on the list for their lives.
>
> A payment of £1.1.0 per annum is made to the Clerk as an indemnity for the petty expenses and charges, and the rest is invested as above stated. There are always far more applicants than can be satisfied by the gift. There is at the present time one vacancy among the £15 annuitants, which will be filled up in January next.

Apart from this gift Henry Scambler also presented his company with a fine silver punch bowl and ladles for their feasts.

From a myriad of details such as these the Commission built up its overall picture of the livery companies. The single most important fact to emerge was that the companies, as a body, were spectacularly wealthy, their total annual income of £750,000 – £800,000 being greater than that of the universities of Oxford and Cambridge and their various colleges combined. The estimated capital value of the companies' property, from which much of this income derived, was reckoned to be £15 million, a figure which the Commissioners believed would rise steeply over the next twenty-five years.

The most tendentious matter was, naturally enough, how these resources were used and controlled. The Commissioners came up with the following figures. £200,000 (27%) of the liveries' income was held in trusts explicitly committed to charitable causes, and of the freely disposable income a further £150,000 (20%) was spent on good works. In other words nearly 50% of their income was devoted to philanthropy. The remaining income was spent on 'maintenance', a category which included not only repair to the fabric of their properties but fees for attendance at Court, and the salaries of the companies' various officers. A sizeable £100,000 was spent on entertaining.

To men of a modernising, centralising and interventionist turn of mind the thought of such riches being at the disposal of private and often ageing conservative hands was distinctly uncomfortable. The Commissioners were quick to point out that a mere 1,500 of the current 7,500 liverymen sat on the Courts which controlled these resources. As they wrote in an ominous paragraph: 'considering the amount of their patronage, the importance of the trusts which they administer, and the large funds which they have in some cases under their absolute control, the constitution of the Courts of the companies is an important matter'. However, the evident desire of many of the Commissioners to take over the running of the Courts and to grasp their funds (or at least distribute them in ways which seemed to them more equitable and efficient) faced legal objections from the most impressive quarter.

Lord Chancellor Selborne, who was himself a Mercer, told the Commissioners it was his belief that the City companies were the 'absolute and perfect masters of their own property'. Under the law they could use any of their funds that were not held in trust as they pleased. His firm reasoning nonetheless contained an important rider. While legally the companies' incomes were theirs to do with as they chose, Lord Selborne believed that they were under a moral obligation to 'promote objects which were for the public interest'. The Commissioners leaned forward with newly concentrated interest.

'You acknowledge a great moral responsibility to the public in the case of private property, but not any greater legal right?', they enquired.

'That is my impression', the Lord Chancellor replied. 'I do not know that I can express it much better'.

To the assembled liverymen this was a relief. The highest legal authority in the land had given it as his opinion that their wealth was their own responsibility, as was the realisation of the obligations that went with it. On this basis they elaborated an argument by which they presented themselves as private philanthropists rather than public charities, friendly societies set up for the protection of their membership, companies that were in truth independent of the City Corporation rather than a constituent part of it. They were, besides, bodies who had discharged their charitable duties with scrupulous care and often with generosity. A number of the Commissioners were minded to agree with them and presented a conclusion which supported the companies' case. The rights of private property, they averred, should be protected at all times, nowhere more so than in the case of the livery companies which were, they made clear, honourable and public-spirited institutions.

Reasonable as this proposition may have seemed, the majority of the Commissioners disagreed with it. J. R. Firth, of course, was the most outspoken of them. He failed to see 'what useful purpose can be served by the continued preservation of such companies as are disassociated from trade'. They were an anachronism, an abomination (or, at least, a stumbling block in his pursuit of centralised government) and he considered that 'the best course to pursue will be to dissolve them and vest their property in an Official Trustee unless or until a Representative Municipal Authority be established in London'.

The majority of the hostile Commissioners were not prepared to go quite so far. Although they were ready to declare their belief, based on a number of distinctly tendentious arguments, 'that the State has a right at any time to disestablish and disendow the companies of London, provided that the just claims of existing members to compensation be allowed', they considered it undesirable to pursue policies so nakedly draconian. They were resolved, instead, to be more circumspect.

To secure the control they desired over the companies, they prepared a four-pronged attack. First they would take steps to prevent the companies from alienating their property. Secondly they would set up mechanisms to secure 'the permanent application of a considerable portion of the corporate income thence arising to useful purposes'. Thirdly they would go about 'declaring new trusts in cases in which a better application of the trust income of the companies has become desirable'. Finally they declared that: 'we think that no future admission to the livery of a company should confer the parliamentary franchise'. In other words, the livery companies were to lose their autonomy, and hence their prestige and their pride. Ancient traditions were to be surrendered to modern bureaucracy, individual enterprise would be sunk in corporate decision making.

To implement their financial plans the Commissioners proposed, first, that the companies should be prevented by an Act of Parliament from alienating their more ancient property. Next, a second Act of Parliament should set up a commission to control the companies' affairs, and compel them to divert their income 'to the support of objects of acknowledged public utility'. Because of the companies' close association with London and the City, these objects should be largely metropolitan, focussing especially on education and scientific research, amenities such as museums, libraries and parks, the improvement of working-class housing, and making contributions to working people's benefit societies. In order to maximise the income for these purposes, the new commission should have the power to reallocate and reinvest ancient charitable funds. Finally, the Commissioners declared that all of the companies' accounts should be made available for public inspection and that the Courts which supervised them should be 'rendered as efficient as possible'.

The debate had been opened and the interested public looked on eagerly after the Commission's report was published in 1884. When the Conservatives took office in the following year, the Home Secretary, faced with questions from all sides, observed that the ministry was 'not only willing, but anxious to deal with the subject'; the government would turn to the matter 'at an early date'. But the government had other and more pressing concerns: further reforms to the franchise at home and urgent issues abroad – in Ireland, Egypt and Afghanistan. Besides, the matter of the Liveries was complicated, delicate. Attempts by radical members of the opposition to introduce legislation failed and then, with agitation for Irish Home Rule becoming ever more vehement, the government fell.

During a brief year in office Gladstone had no time to attend to the Livery Companies before the Conservative and Unionist parties were returned in his place. The new Prime Minister, Salisbury, was both too busy and too shrewd to risk annoying the City by grasping so dangerous a nettle as the reform of the Liveries. He left the last word on the subject to the Chancellor of the Exchequer, Lord Randolph Churchill, who declared superciliously that he would not 'feel justified in saying that the attention of the government has hitherto been very closely given to the Report of the Commission'. The report was shelved. The Livery Companies survived – by the skin of their teeth.

*

Throughout this period (and for many years afterwards) the Innholders' beautiful Hall was repeatedly in jeopardy. In 1839 a sum of £50 had been left for necessary maintenance on the building, and, three years later, work commenced under the supervision of William Tite, costing a total sum of £700. The thorough restoration was almost immediately threatened by an outbreak of fire in the cellar occupied, as we have seen, by a basket maker. Unfortunately, the Court had not informed their insurers about the nature of this tenancy and they immediately disputed the claim on the grounds that they were unaware of the highly flammable materials of the basket maker's trade stored there. Eventually a compromise was reached and the Company accepted that they would have to make good the damage partly from their own resources.

Altogether more serious was the discovery, in 1882, that the Hall needed fundamental repair. The Company was fortunate in having, in J. Douglass Mathews, an architect of skill, taste and ingenuity who loved the building through long association. He reported that the Court faced two options. They could demolish the whole structure and reuse the site for a smaller Hall, to be built and serviced from the rents of premises erected on the remainder of the site. Alternatively they could carry out a judicious piecemeal rebuilding of the existing property. The Court took their time before making their decision and fortunately they chose the latter course. The work, which cost £5,000, was completed in 1886.

Much of the exterior was rebuilt in a typically Victorian interpretation of the Georgian style, a solution that allowed for the retention of the large, light and handsome windows with their double-hung sashes. Although it was necessary to demolish and reproduce the brick door-case, the original arms and canopy above it were taken down and refixed. The old door, frame, and its carving, were also taken down, stripped of encrusted paint and re-used.

Fortunately the dining hall could be largely preserved with most of its original oak panelling; however a new roof, ceiling and windows in the west wall were needed. Below the windows stood a "buffet", a piece of furniture used in the Middle Ages – and adopted again in the 18th century – for the display of the Company's plate. Above it, on a pinnacle, stood the 17th century wooden statue of St Julian, now in the entrance hall. Beside it was placed the substantial iron chest, an elaborate locking mechanism set into its lid, which the Court probably acquired in 1667 for the safekeeping of its charters after the Great Fire. An 1888 watercolour of the hall interior shows the triple west windows glazed with the coats of arms of Henry VIII, Charles II and Queen Victoria in stained glass.

To cater adequately for the banquets held in the hall, the basement below was refitted appropriately with kitchens, a wine cellar and serving areas. The new ovens – despite the introduction of modern electric ones in 1997 – are still in occasional use and were marvels of contemporary engineering, being fed by a two inch gas main and an enormous plug valve; they made wonderful soufflés for eighty or more people. While the restoration was in progress the Company met in nearby Dyers' Hall, a return of favours, for the Dyers had used the Innholders' Hall while their own was being reconstructed in the 18th century.

The beautiful old Court Room, opening off the hall, presented the architect with his most difficult problems, for he had not only to remove the original oak panelling in order to rebuild three of the walls, but also replace the timbers from which the superb plaster ceiling – one of the finest examples of its kind in London – was suspended. In the end he achieved this, preserving the authenticity of both the mellow woodwork and the glorious, gilded plasterwork ceiling. It remains a place of quiet dignity amid the bustle of the City. From now on courts were held in the room above, enlarged for the purpose during the work of rebuilding.

The old Court Room was furnished with some of the Company's heirlooms, including two 17th century armed chairs, with leather upholstery and barley sugar woodwork. Standing in a corner was a double domed grandfather clock with an arched dial, dating from about 1679 and bearing the signature Josephus Franklin.

A number of pictures hung in the room. Of these the most important

The Hall restored in 1886 looking West (above) and East (below),
(John Crowther, 1887)

(and in many respects the most attractive) is Francis Sartorius' racing scene which, according to the inscription painted across the foot of the canvas, represents: 'Totteridge (the property of Mr Bott, was got by Dungannon out of Marcella) winning the King's Plate of 100 guineas for horses, etc., not more than 6 years old, carrying 12 stone, Newmarket, May 4, 1791, 11 to 8 on Totteridge, who won easy'. The picture was completed the following year. Of more general interest is a painting by George Jones of William IV and Queen Adelaide opening the new London Bridge in 1831. It is probably an oil sketch for the larger picture commissioned by Sir John Soane and now in his museum. A third oil (now on the stairs) depicts an early 19th century Lord Mayor embarking for a river pageant. The Sartorius and Jones now hang in the Reception Room next to the original Court Room.

The picture which will probably be most familiar to members of the Company, however, is that of the Charles Druce whose impressive portrait by H. P. Briggs, RA, still hangs over the fireplace in the Hall, its shrewd and kindly face having stared down at generations of diners. Charles Druce served as Clerk to the Company between 1785 and 1835 – a grand total of fifty years. Like his father before him, he also became Master, holding the position during 1840-41. Indeed, the Druce family association with the Company is both exceptionally long and extremely distinguished. Alexander Druce, the first of the line, was apprenticed to the Company in 1712, and his descendants have provided no fewer than six Clerks and six Masters over nearly 300 years. The association continues to this day.

*

In all, five Innholders during this century and the next, rose to become Lord Mayor, a considerable achievement for a company of only a hundred or so liverymen, and this may be a convenient place to discuss this distinguished office within the governance of the City.

(above) Racing Scene by Francis Sartorius, 1792
(below) William IV opening London Bridge, by George Jones

The Lord Mayor of London is the head of the oldest municipal corporation in the world. He is the City's chief magistrate and, within the City itself, takes precedence over everyone except the sovereign with whom he has the constitutional right to seek an audience through the Lord Chamberlain. He is, in addition, Head of the Lieutenancy, Admiral of the Port of London, Chancellor of the City University, and one of those to whom the password of the Tower of London is confided. The Lord Mayor is also and principally chairman of the City's two governing bodies: the Court of Aldermen and the Court of Common Council. The position is held on the basis of an annual election called for Michaelmas Day, 29th September, when the liverymen of the City companies meet in Common Hall in the Guildhall to nominate for the post two Aldermen who have previously served as Sheriffs.

The first Innholder to become Lord Mayor was Sir Chapman Marshall, a wholesale grocer with premises in Upper Thames Street. Chapman Marshall was knighted in 1831, was Master of the Company in 1835, and became Lord Mayor in 1839. The second Innholder to rise to this eminence was Alderman David Williams Wire, Lord Mayor in 1858.

The third, Sir Thomas Scambler Owden, had a strong family connection with the Company. Born at Cuckfield in Sussex in 1808, his father died when he was a child and he was brought up by his uncle, Henry Scambler, whose generosity to the Company we have already noted. Scambler himself was a highly successful livery stable owner operating from 62 Bishopsgate Street Without. He left his business to his nephew (who also ran the Thames Freight and Navigation Company) and Sir Thomas, finding himself to be a wealthy man, devoted the greater part of his time and talents to the City and the Company. He was Master in 1853-54 and Lord Mayor in 1877. He was a twinkling, heavily bearded, diminutive figure possessed of great natural authority, a vigorous admiration for Disraeli and the Tory party, and a nature which modestly delighted in doing good deeds by stealth.

Sir Polydore de Keyser was an altogether more flamboyant character and a figure of the greatest interest. He was born in Belgium and, for all that he was educated in Fulham, he never lost his native accent. His father ran the Royal Hotel at Blackfriars which was a sufficiently profitable exercise for him to go on to build the magnificent de Keyser Royal Hotel, which stood on the Blackfriars Embankment, a site now occupied by the Unilever building. The new hotel was opened by the King of the Belgians in 1874. Sir Polydore himself seemed at first to move effortlessly through the upper echelons of City life. He was naturalised in 1862, was elected to the Court of Common Council ten years later, and in 1882 was elected both an Innholder and Alderman for the ward of Farringdon Without, defeating an ex-Sheriff named Sir Sidney Waterlow in the process. It was at this point that his problems began.

So incensed was Waterlow at losing to a foreigner and a Roman Catholic that he dug up an ancient regulation from the time of Richard II to the effect that tavern licence holders could never become Aldermen. To call the de Keyser Hotel a tavern was an arrant insult but presented the City Fathers with a problem they solved with deft wisdom. They admitted the validity of the regulation but then declared that Sir Polydore's case should be an exception to it. His path to Lord Mayor was thus cleared and in 1887 he became the first Catholic holder of the office since the Reformation. He had shown himself throughout to be a man of great energy and distinction, being a member of no fewer than six livery companies, and campaigning tirelessly for a great many City institutions such as the Guildhall School of Music. He regularly made gifts of clothing to the poor children in his ward and was a governor of a number of hospitals. In recognition of his many services and interests he was given, in addition to his knighthood, fellowships of the Society of Arts and the Royal Geographical and Statistical Societies.

*

De Keyser received his academic honours at a time when the country – wealthy, strong and governing a vast empire – was able to undertake the greater part of the world's research. The nation's prestige was at its height and the romantic pageants that celebrated Queen Victoria's Golden Jubilee in 1887 and her Diamond Jubilee in 1897 were expressions of what had been achieved through two generations of unprecedented development. Materially, the industrialisation of Britain had enriched its people and extended its influence across the globe.

When the old Queen died in 1901, there was an inevitable sense that an era was coming slowly to a close. The country's industrial and commercial supremacy were being challenged; new territories could only be added to the empire at considerable financial cost; and the early humiliations of the Boer War showed the world that Britain might not be invincible, while the size and might of its imperial power (especially its navy) provoked the increasing enmity of Germany.

The shadow that hung over Queen Victoria's deathbed was therefore not simply one of grief at losing the woman who for so long and for so many had symbolised the nation's greatness, it was also the ominous shadow – perceived by too few – of an impending and terrible war.

* * *

Sir Polydore de Keyser, Innholder
Lord Mayor 1887

and the de Keyser Hotel (below)

Chapter 10

WARS AND PEACE

1901 – 1950

The First World War – peace and recovery – the new popular hotels
the Second World War: bombs fall on the Hall
a Prime Minister joins the Livery – the Company's recovery.

Few images better capture the sense of self-confidence, power and wealth which pervaded London at the beginning of the 20th century than *The Heart of Empire*, painted by the artist Niels Lund in 1904. It shows the densely packed and prosperous City going about its orderly business in the Square Mile, symbolically crowned by the magnificent dome of St Paul's Cathedral.

By now membership of the Innholders bore almost no resemblance to its original composition. The association with innkeeping, and later the hotel business, had survived for more than three centuries. As late as the 1830s there were still seven members of the Court and more than 50% of the Livery so qualified, but by 1900 this distinction seems to have become almost, or entirely, obsolete.

The Company's previous histories are silent about the criteria by which men were chosen for the Freedom and Livery. It is, however, apparent that the most powerful element which drew and held them together was family connection. As in other companies which had virtually lost touch with their original trades or crafts, probably 70% of the membership were linked by blood or marriage.

Most of them were drawn from the ranks of Middle England, or rather Middle London – able men of the middle classes, rising to share the status and security, rewards and setbacks, of the characters John Galsworthy brought vividly to life in his *Forsyte Saga.* Instead of innkeepers they were accountants, stockbrokers, bankers, insurance brokers, property developers and shipping agents; lawyers, doctors, engineers, architects,

The Heart of the Empire, 1904

by Niels Moeller Lund

View of London looking west from the Royal Exchange, with the Mansion House in the foreground, to the left and St. Paul's Cathedral in the middle distance

wine merchants and men of business. If a large majority of them worked in the City, – with 400,000 others –almost none lived there, but many came in from Harrow, Hampstead, Ilford, Bexley, Chislehurst, or Croydon. The rest commuted daily from Buckinghamshire, Hertfordshire, Essex, Kent, Sussex and Surrey. Nevertheless they were as loyally and meticulously bound to the company, and conducted its business as scrupulously, as any generation in the past.

Every autumn the Master retired from his office, his three Wardens each rose up a place in the hierarchy, and a new Renter was elected – usually the senior Assistant. In October 1908, after a lapse of many years, the Court, Clerk and Beadle, together with some of the Livery and their ladies, processed along College Street to the church of St Michael's Paternoster Royal, to solemnise the new Master's installation.

Founded in 1209, rebuilt by Richard Whittington in 1409, and rebuilt again by Wren in 1689-94 after the Great Fire, St Michael's has been the setting of most installations since. Only for a brief period was this annual ceremony necessarily transferred to St Mary Aldermary, Queen Victoria Street, where a stained glass window now incorporates the Company Arms.

The opening of the First World War in August 1914 coincided with the election of Sir Charles Johnston – the fifth Innholder – as Lord Mayor. His family ran a packing and export business in London and Liverpool, and he immediately concentrated the authority he now commanded on galvanising the City's war effort; this included its support of the Red Cross and the establishment of a National – or Home – Guard in the capital. At the end of his year of office Sir Charles was elected Master of the Innholders.

By the middle of 1915 the German army had overrun Belgium, nearly driven a wedge between the French and British armies in northern France, and were close to Paris; casualties began to mount alarmingly. And then something quite new in the history of war occurred. The Germans sent over zeppelins, great gas-filled airships, cruising at over 10,000 feet and at about 50 m.p.h., to drop bombs on London. During the course of the next three years 600-800 people were killed in the capital, over 1,000 were badly injured, and 174 buildings were severely damaged. The Innholders' Hall escaped a direct hit but its brickwork was scarred by the fragments of a bomb.

The deaths and destruction inflicted by the zeppelin raids were, of course, merely a hint of the massacre and devastation which were to follow less than thirty years later – just as the casualties on the Western Front up to 1915 were only a fraction of those killed and wounded by November 1918, the British alone losing 500,000 men. Another 1,500,000 were seriously wounded, maimed, gassed or shell-shocked. It is surprising that a horror of this magnitude, which virtually left no community or family in the country unscathed, seems not to have claimed a single life among the Innholders.

*

In the two decades which followed the First World War, the Company, like London and the rest of England, had first to recover itself and then combat the great economic slump or depression of the early 1930s. Livery numbers were under 100; on average only two new members were elected each year; the Company's investments – in government securities – stood at about £20,000, with a further £10,000 held in the name of its charities. Rents brought in no more than £450 a year.

Nevertheless, by very careful management the Company could still maintain its modest Court fees, its traditions of hospitality, and a yearly covenant of about £400 to its charities. For a time Richard Harding, previously a chef at the busy Great Eastern Hotel on Liverpool Street station, was employed as Beadle, Hall Keeper and caterer, in charge of the kitchen, service and wines. When he retired, his son briefly succeeded him, but his health soon failed and in 1934 Gordon Marsh – with his wife Hilda and young son Paul – took over. They had no idea of the adventure which lay ahead of them.

If the Company no longer practised its Mistery of Herberging or Innkeeping, it still preserved its time honoured mystique of close-knit fellowship, generosity and good will. There were several tangible expressions of this in the years between the two World Wars. First, in 1921, W. D. Cronin, then Master, and John Wylde, whose family had a long association with the Company, presented to it the adjoining freeholds of 29 and 30 College Street, which they acquired from the Merchant Taylors. They were then occupied by the City Dispensary, chemists funded by the Corporation and a church charity, to supply the poorest residents of the City with prescriptions and other medical supplies at prices which they could afford, or sometimes free.

As a further gift, in 1931, A. S. Ruston, who had been Master several years earlier, paid for the new Court Room upstairs to be handsomely panelled. Next, in 1937, Austin Balls presented four silver wine cups, specially designed at the College of Arms, to be used by the Master and Wardens. The cups were to commemorate the election of his daughter as a Freeman of the Company. This gift was later to be followed by far greater benefactions from both him and his daughter.

The original charter, granted to the Innholders by Henry VIII, is explicit that both women and men may join the Livery. However up to the time of writing there is no record of women being invited to do so, although well over twenty Livery Companies now regularly elect them. On the other hand, during the 20th century daughters frequently received the freedom of the Innholders, and currently nearly thirty women enjoy it.

In 1937 the Company discovered that once again the beautiful plaster ceiling of the Old Court Room was in a parlous state. The necessary process of restoration was best described by the architect responsible, Jefferiss Mathews (son of H. E. and grandson of Douglass Mathews), in an interview he gave to the *Evening Standard.* 'We took up the floor of the room above', he said, 'and found that the laths had been ruined by furniture beetle, and that the key of the plaster was also rotten. It was confirmed that the ceiling had been for years unsupported.' Remedial action was urgently needed and Mathews went on to describe how 'we first shored up the ceiling from underneath with a number of timbers, and between the timbers and the ceiling we inserted felt pads'.

What then followed was ingenious in the extreme. To safeguard the suspension of the ceiling Mathews constructed a lattice of laths to the same dimensions as the floor above. He used copper wires to suspend it from the beams, securing it beneath with pennies in which he had drilled holes for the purpose. The lattice and upper side of the ceiling plaster were then bonded with a mixture of adhesive and newspaper. As Mathews himself commented: 'the task took a long time because we had to work slowly enough to avoid any strain on the painted surface of the original ceiling. We have been successful, for there is not a crack on it'.

*

The Company did retain one tenuous link with inns and hotels during the years between the wars. In 1921 the celebrated author Hilaire Belloc joined the Livery. Novelist, travel writer and essayist, he is probably best known for his verses *A Bad Child's Book of Beasts* and *Cautionary Tales.* But he also wrote appreciatively of food and drink and poignantly (in his essays *This and That*) on inns.

> From the towns all Inns have been driven: from the villages most... change your hearts or you will lose your Inns and you will deserve to have lost them. But when you have lost your Inns drown your empty selves, for you will have lost the last of England.

Soon England did lose many of its inns, but one of their usurpers or successors, a hotel, was the centrepiece of *Imperial Palace,* a novel by Belloc's contemporary and friend Arnold Bennett. In it Bennett explored the complex management of a large and luxurious hotel together with the fortunes of its guests.

For a time Sir Polydore de Keyser had insisted on personal introductions before he accepted bookings in his hotel. The owners and managers of some of the exclusive and imposing London hotels which opened in the 1920s and early 1930s were less demanding. Among these, after the London home of the Dukes of Westminster was sold and demolished in 1927, the Grosvenor House Hotel was built on its site. It was a fine two-wing building with a colonnaded west facade designed by the eminent architect Sir Edwin Lutyens. For a few years it boasted a skating rink, and it was the first hotel in London to have a swimming pool. The Great Room of the Grosvenor House Hotel remains a splendid venue for grand occasions both public and private.

The Park Lane Hotel was opened in the same 1927 season, guests staying in the rooms immediately behind the large pillared portico enjoying a splendid view over Green Park. A few years after this, on 18th April, 1931, the Dorchester Hotel was built and opened on the site of the erstwhile Dorchester House, on the edge of Mayfair and overlooking Hyde Park.

But high quality hotels were not confined to the capital. One of the most influential ventures in the hotel trade was started in 1922 when the remarkable John Fothergill took over the Spread Eagle Hotel at Thame in Oxfordshire. Fothergill aimed at the very highest levels of furnishings, service, food and wine. He was in many ways a difficult man – a dreamer and a snob – but his vision of what an English country hotel might be like was and remains extraordinarily influential, and his memoirs, *An Innkeeper's Diary*, is essential reading for anyone seriously interested in the subject. Above all it shows the exceptional dedication and hard work which are required to run such enterprises. Fothergill took it as axiomatic that the good innkeeper should be willing to work fourteen or even sixteen hours a day to ensure scrupulous attention to detail. He believed a willingness to take risks and shrug off failure were also essential.

The popularity of country hotels was stimulated by the introduction of a phenomenon which rapidly became fundamental to the industrial, commercial and social life of the 20th century: the motor car. By 1925 William Morris was selling upwards of 50,000 cars a year from his Oxford factory. Touring the countryside in private cars and charabancs was adopted with such enthusiasm that small individual hotels opened everywhere to accommodate the swelling numbers of motorists and holiday makers. Hotel chains also began to cater for the market. In 1924, for example, the Trust Houses started to hang their familiar sign of a stag rampant against a sun and star (an emblem evoking St Julian) outside their numerous properties. A modern hotel industry was rising from the roots of the nation's historic business of innkeeping.

If the birth of the car spelt the doom or decline of the railways, the birth of the aeroplane had sounded a knell for the majestic steamships which still carried their passengers from continent to continent. But before the airliner could usher in the age of mass tourism, war broke out in 1939 and aeroplanes became its tools of destruction.

*

Unlike the outbreak of the previous World War, the early months of the second were deceptively quiet. It was not until May 1940 that the Germans launched their lightning attacks across Belgium and Northern France, to take the channel ports. By the end of June the entire British Expeditionary Force had been evacuated through Dunkirk.

Immediately the Germans let loose their bombers, escorted by squadrons of fighters, on raids over Southern England. The Battle of Britain had begun, and raged for three months. On Saturday 7th September a raid on London began in the afternoon sunshine and only ended when the last wave of bombers turned home on Sunday morning. By then they had killed more Londoners than the zeppelins had in four years. It was a taste of things to come.

The raids continued virtually without intermission for the following seventy-six nights. The East End was at first the principal target but, by late December, 1940, the City was being regularly 'fired'. The Guildhall and eight Wren churches were destroyed during one raid. Five months later, on Saturday and Sunday 10–11 May, 1941, 550 German bombers maintained a merciless onslaught for five hours, killing over 1,400 people, destroying the Chamber of the House of Commons, and causing very considerable damage to the Innholders' Hall.

Before he had joined his regiment, Jefferiss Mathews had been asked to protect the building and its treasures against such a disaster. He did so with typical family ingenuity. Externally he covered each of the windows and doors with vertical wooden slats, so that the force of a bomb's blast would pass through the crevices, leaving the wooden boards to resist any debris, or fragments from the bombs themselves. At the same time the building would remain safe from pillage. To safeguard the delicate plaster moulding of the Old Court Room ceiling, he had prepared an army sand table whose contours exactly complemented those of the moulding; this was gently jacked up and held in place by supports.

Although Gordon Marsh, the Beadle, was well aware of the dangers once the Blitz got under way, he insisted on living in the Hall, sleeping upstairs with his wife while his ten-year old son Paul (who succeeded him as Beadle thirty years later) spent his nights in the huge safe down in the basement. Marsh gave a graphic account of the night on which the Hall was hit; the Germans seemed to be concentrating on the area between Cannon Street and Southwark Bridge.

> Our first narrow escape was when an oil bomb fell on the premises of Messrs George Berridge, Printers, our neighbours in Little College Street. This quickly flared up, and served as a target for the following machine, which sent down two high explosive bombs, one of which again struck Berridge's and scattered the flaming oil bomb to surrounding premises. The other bomb struck the building opposite the Hall, in Little College Street, and as this building collapsed, burning parts of it 'leaned' against the wooden protection of the Hall's stained glass windows, at the west end of the Hall, setting fire to the wooden protection, and to the Hall ceiling inside.

Because he was already on the premises Marsh was able to summon what he called the Mutual Fire Party of locals; they quickly put out the flames at the west end of the dining hall, and assessed the damage. Almost everywhere the doors, windows and their frames had been blown in behind their slatted protection, while the boards remained in place. When the All Clear went on Sunday morning Marsh found that round the corner on Dowgate Hill the Tallow Chandlers had been hit by one bomb, and the Skinners by another, which killed a fire watcher there. At the opposite end of College Street St Michael's Paternoster Royal had been wrecked by incendiary bombs. Fires raged in all the surrounding streets throughout Sunday and, with too little water to fight them, they blazed almost unchecked.

Marsh went on:

> At about 6pm the Nelson Financial Trust Building, at the corner of College Street and Dowgate Hill - which had been burning all day - became completely enveloped in flames. This set the City Dispensary alight, and for the second time brought the fire next door to this Hall. The mass of flame completely shut the eastern end of College Street, and the Dyers' Hall was evacuated, also the Warden's Post.

Nothing, it seemed, could halt the encroaching inferno and soon the Innholders' pantry, on the south east corner of the Hall, was ablaze. The gallant fire fighters fought desperately to contain the damage.

> After all the extinguishers had been used, the fire caught the stained glass windows at the eastern end of the Hall. The flames, after destroying the windows, began to come into the Hall. Buckets of water were handed from the ancient tank in the front lavatory, but this proved useless. Most determined efforts were made by all to save the Hall, even one or two of the old waiters appeared from somewhere and gave willing hands to save the place where they had worked for so many years.

It was at this point that Marsh took the decisive action which has secured his fame for ever in the Company's annals. As Beadle and Hall Keeper he had full responsibility for the property, its furnishings and treasures, and now he appealed to an officer of the Enfield Fire Brigade to help save this historic building, shrewdly suggesting that samples of the Company's wine stock might assist the men's efforts. 'Help us to put this fire out, and we'll help you to something which will put you out!' he declared. The promise of this 'liberal entertainment', as he called it, did the trick.

> . . . some water was found, and pumped from a good distance away, and after some two hours' work, during which the water failed again we had the pleasure of seeing the last of the fire put out and knowing that, as there was nothing left around us that could burn, the Hall was safe.

When the dust had settled, the Renter Warden, C. R. Wylde, tactfully agreed that a quantity of the Company's wine stock had been 'blitzed'.

A full survey of the building revealed that the dining hall ceiling was wrecked, its chandeliers destroyed and its west wall shattered. The pantry at the back was burnt out, its domed glass roof lying in huge globules on the floor. After the mess was cleared up, bare brick walls remained open to the sky. A local builder came with tarpaulins to cover over the fallen areas of the main roof, draping them down the sides of the building. A wooden beam was brought in to shore up the remaining rafters, and a giant wooden prop to support the west end of the hall.

About one third of the City's offices were destroyed in the Blitz. But however melancholy a sight, rising from the greater wreckage all round it – not unlike the aftermath of the Great Fire – the Hall remained the centre of the Company's life without a day's interruption. Somehow Marsh and his staff saw that there was always a meeting room and a meal ready for the Court, the Livery, and any other City company in need of a hall and its amenities.

The only Innholder to die from enemy action during the Blitz was

Two pictures of the damage caused by the Blitz to St. Paul's Cathedral (above) and the Innholders' Hall (below), having lost its roof, with Cannon Street Station behind

Francis Druce. He had been Clerk from 1910-1926 and was actually Master of the Company when he was killed at home in Chelsea by a bomb in 1941. He was the fifth member of his family to hold each of those two offices. Although Liverymen were serving in the navy, the army and the air force all over the world, and several were badly wounded, none was killed in the fighting.

Four years after the Blitz reached its climax, Winston Churchill, the Prime Minister, was able to preside over the allied victory in Europe. Later that year, defeated in a general election, he was succeeded by his deputy war leader, Clement Attlee. He, in August 1945, pronounced the final victory over Japan.

*

Soon after he became Prime Minister, Attlee was elected to the Livery. Arriving to visit the Hall, he looked up for a moment at the portrait of Charles Druce, staring imperturbably out over the charred dining hall, and said in his softly spoken voice that he had refreshed his mind about the history of the Innholders. His father and his brother had been partners in the solicitors' firm of Druces and Attlee, and his association with the Company was therefore close. It continued to be so. Following these words the Master presented the Prime Minister with a casket made from timber used in the rebuilding after the Great Fire.

A tea party had been arranged to honour the new Liveryman and in line with the policy of his government he requested that it be a modest one. There were fish paste sandwiches and cups of tea. Attlee could not stay long and the moment he left, Gordon Marsh went downstairs and up came a choice of crab or cucumber sandwiches, with cream cakes to follow, so that the afternoon became, as Marsh put it, 'a proper Innholders' occasion'.

In a sense Clement Attlee came from typical Innholder stock of the period, serving as a major in the first war and later becoming Mayor of

The Rt. Hon. Earl Attlee,, KG, PC, OM, CH
Liveryman, Prime Minister

Stepney. Rising to the highest office in the country, he never lost his innate modesty which later prompted him to scribble this short verse for his son.

> Few thought he was even a starter,
> There were many who thought themselves smarter,
> But he ended PM,
> CH and OM,
> An Earl and a Knight of the Garter.

Thoughtful, conscientious and decisive, he gave India its freedom, nationalised the country's major industries and utilities, and introduced the welfare state. If his economic policies have not stood the test of time, his sense of social justice and compassion survive, and his values are discernible in some of the Innholders' activities today.

Just as the whole fabric of national life required reconstruction between 1945-1950, so did the Innholders. The devastation around College Street had been appalling, and dangerous structure notices were served on the Hall and the miraculously preserved ceiling of the Old Court Room. Then the town planners got going. Large sections of the City, including the area round Innholders' Hall, were potentially subject to compulsory purchase and redevelopment. College Street was made a 'declaratory area' and it looked as if Innholders' Hall and the little flattened building of the City Dispensary next to it would be removed from the Company's control.

Fortunately however, an authority decided to list the building as an 'Ancient Monument' and Jefferiss Mathews, who had done so much to protect the Hall was now commissioned to effect the extremely delicate and demanding task of restoring it. The west wall of the banqueting hall had almost been demolished, the ceiling had fallen, and most of the panelling on the south wall was down and broken. The wreckage was such a shambles that it would not have been worth cleaning and re-using the old bricks; Mathews therefore used modern high quality ones. He restored the ceiling and the panelling as closely as possible to their state after the 18th century repairs.

To remain healthy, traditions must sometimes revitalise themselves

GOLDEN CROSS
THIS HALL WAS REBUILT 1668 – 1674 AFTER THE GREAT FIRE
DAMAGED IN WORLD WAR 1914 – 1919
SEVERELY DAMAGED IN WORLD WAR 1939 – 1945
IT WAS FULLY RESTORED IN 1950
C.W. HALL M.C. MASTER

The new west window of the Hall
erected as a memorial to John Wylde and Cecil Wylde (Master 1943)

with innovations of their time – a solution applied to the triple west windows of the dining hall, which were themselves a Victorian gloss on the original 17th century building. Their replacement was commissioned as a single chequerboard of plain and engraved glass. The largest, centre, panel was to be engraved with the Company's arms; spaced round it were engravings of some of the signs sported by early Innholders – among them William Chaplin's Cross Keys, Benjamin Worthy Horne's Golden Cross, and Robert Briscoe's Ram, in which the Company's plate had been kept safe during the Great Fire.

The engraved window, not completed and installed until 1961, was endowed in memory of John Wylde and C. R. Wylde. Its design allows a fine light to enter the hall on spring and summer evenings and affords a pleasant view, across the little green outside, to the tower and pinnacle of St Michael's Paternoster Royal. Such a vista only became possible when the planners decided not to rebuild the houses destroyed by the bombs which fell on the opposite side of Little College Street, leaving open the area of what was once a little harbour where the Walbrook flowed into the Thames.

By the time the principal restoration of the Hall was completed in 1950, John Bentley, an energetic new part-time Clerk from Druces and Attlee, had succeeded Jack Druce in the office. He encouraged a new generation, not just in age but in experience and outlook, to apply for the Freedom of the Company. The intake each year was nearly double the pre-war average. Nevertheless, finances were still tight and the ruins of 29 and 30 College Street, the site of the City Dispensary and adjoining the Hall, could not be rebuilt, and let out as offices, until 1958.This accomplished, the Court and the Clerk turned their eyes to the future.

Chapter 11

THE COMPANY RENEWED

1950 - 2000

The Company's inheritance – The Master Innholders' Association, 1978
A windfall – The Hall redeveloped, 1990 – Company patronage
A new millennium.

As the City of London approached the two thousandth anniversary of its foundation by the Romans, the Innholders were within sight of celebrating five hundred years since the grant of their charter by Henry VIII.

Like other Liveries of ancient plumage, the Company's wings had been steadily clipped through the centuries and it had twice seen its Hall go up in flames. But as Archbishop Cranmer says of the phoenix in Shakespeare's *Henry VIII,* "when the bird of wonder dies. . . her ashes new-create another heir". The Innholders' postwar restoration ensured that the next generation would be able to draw fresh strength and inspiration from their history.

The original charter entitled them to have "custody of lands, tenements and rents". Through wisdom and good management they still possessed valuable freeholds, pre-eminently their Hall, with 29 and 30 College Street next to it. In addition the Company owned a small property in Birchin Lane, and buildings between Coleman Street and Moorgate, rented out since the 16th century. The charter had also incorporated it as a "fraternity or guild" practising "the art or mistery of St Julian the Herberger" but, by the 20th century, it had virtually forfeited its status as a trade guild. Only two members could claim to be innkeepers, though together they represented the twin branches of their profession - one at The Coach and Horses inn, Trumpington, just outside Cambridge, and the other at the Grand Hotel, Leigh-on-Sea.

On the other hand, as members of a charitable guild, the Liverymen still honoured their patron saint. In 1952 Austin Balls had left the residue of his considerable estate to the Innholders after the death of his daughter; in 1958 Lieutenant-Colonel James Rydon willed his estate to the Company; and in 1965 the Court continued to distribute the proceeds of various charitable endowments and set up a General Charity Fund to which the Company covenanted to pay "a substantial part" of its income.

A Livery is, in essence, a curious entity, being neither a business nor a charity; but its Court is under an intrinsic obligation to be as businesslike as a commercial enterprise and as conscientious as a trust. Furthermore, John Bentley warned the Court not to invite from the current Labour government the kind of political strictures twice levelled against the Innholders by the Whig and Liberal commissioners in the previous century.

The composition and procedures of the Court had remained unchanged since they were laid down by Charles II's charter in 1663. Each year, in the first ten days of August, the new officers were elected - the Master, Upper, and Middle Warden each moving on a place, and the senior Assistant becoming Renter. On the rare occasions when the Upper Warden was unable to serve as Master his predecessor was elected to a second term rather than that anyone should pass an office as Warden. The Renter retained his traditional role of arranging the Company's hospitality. Formal installation of the officers took place in the first week of October.

The full complement of Assistants remained at twenty. As stipulated in the original charter a replacement was to be elected if a member of the Court died or was discharged, should this be "necessary or expedient". A minimum quorum of thirteen was required, with the Master casting two votes in the event of an impasse.

No Livery can function without a Clerk, who attends its Court meetings, records the decisions, and oversees their execution. The management of the Company's property, finance, charities, staff, Hall and social activities, all fall on his shoulders. In 1980 John Bentley died suddenly, but was immediately succeeded as Clerk by his assistant, John Edwardes Jones, a partner in his firm, Druces & Attlee, who had provided the

Company with Clerks for two hundred years. For the next twenty years, until 2000 when he was elected to the Court directly as Renter Warden (a rare departure from precedent), Edwardes Jones helped the Court plot the Company's course. At first reefs of insolvency sometimes threatened, but when the tide turned he advised and encouraged successive Masters and Wardens through two of the most eventful and successful decades in the Livery's history.

The Beadle, like the Clerk, has always been at the centre of a Livery's life, especially its ceremonial. In 1979 Paul Marsh, with his wife June, succeeded his father as Beadle, Hall-Keeper, and caterer. In addition, like his grandfather and great-grandfather, he was a Ward Beadle. He would clothe the Ward Alderman in his robes for the Lord Mayor's procession and other City ceremonies, and then attend him with his mace, clad in his own resplendent robes, bonnet and cape. When the Marshes finally gave up the catering and moved out of the Hall in 1989 both were awarded the Freedom of the Company. Robert Fox, a warrant officer from the Rifle Brigade, took over as Hall-Keeper, with his wife Julie.

During these years the number of Liverymen rose to 140. Their horizons were wider than those of the pre-war generation. Some had fought in Europe, Africa or Burma, others had served on the seven seas, and one of the airmen had survived a collision with a second plane over the Atlantic. Many more than in the past held university degrees; they regularly travelled the world on business or pleasure; and they began to cultivate a keen personal interest in hotels, a taste for more sophisticated food, and an interest in the relative merits of the wines they drank in the Hall, from Alsace, the Loire, Bordeaux, Burgundy and the Rhone.

In short, the Company could now draw on a lively reservoir of varied talents, expertise and ambitions, to make the most of its assets in the light of economic opportunities which dawned towards the end of the 1970s. It was then that the country emerged from the gloom of an oil crisis, industrial unrest, recession and alarming inflation, and then too that Margaret Thatcher began to undo forty years of nationalisation, regula-

Paul and Gordon Marsh in their uniform and bearing the maces of Ward Beadles

tion, high taxation and exchange controls. Optimism surged, and the Innholders seized the moment.

*

In 1977 Derek Balls was elected Master and quickly persuaded the Company to take one of its most significant decisions since the 17th century. As the great-nephew of Austin Balls, the son of another Master, Burgess Balls, and a Member of the Court of Common Council himself, he was well placed to do so.

In recent years he had observed at close quarters how several Lord Mayors and their Aldermen had actively encouraged a flow of fresh enterprise into the Liveries. Only one new company had been chartered in the 17th century and none in the 19th. However, between 1900-1970 eight new Liveries had been created, all of them comprising practising professionals, including the Airline Pilots and Navigators (1929), the Solicitors (1944) and the Farmers (1952). Then, between 1972-1979, there was a remarkable run when another eight applicants were successful, all of them associated with the economic confidence then flooding Britain. Among these were the Environmental Cleaners, the Constructors, the Actuaries and the Insurers.

At the same time the Mansion House urged the older Companies to revive their concern for their original crafts or trades, with which most had lost touch. Balls was determined to respond to the challenge. He had seen his family wine business develop from the import of port and sherry, first into the retail and then into the wholesaling of wine, while he and his brother (also an Innholder) had opened four successful wine bars in the City. Not a hotelier, he initiated a plan with a recent young Liveryman, David Locket, who was one. Together they discussed a variety of ideas with the country's most influential trade body in the field, the Hotel, Catering and Institutional Managers' Association (HCIMA). As a result, the concept of an organisation parallel to the élite Masters of Wine, affiliated to the Vintners Company, began to take shape, and was approved by the Court in 1977.

The formation of a Master Innholders Association finally crystallised after months of research and debate, and was announced at a lunch for the great and the good of the hotel industry in 1978. In deciding to help, encourage, and promote excellence in hotels the Company felt it should concentrate on individual owners or General Managers. The Court committee overseeing the scheme therefore invited a selection of notable hoteliers to apply for membership. The candidates were to submit a paper on a basic element of the profession, and attend an interview about their approach to hotel management. Great attention was focussed on their personal engagement in recruiting, training, the promotion of business and public relations, through working closely with local schools, technical colleges and tourist boards.

To establish the committee's qualifications as selectors they co-opted the hotelier Douglas Barrington, who had established a reputation since the war for the outstanding style, standards and success of his hotel The Lygon Arms, at Broadway in the Cotswolds. He was also invited in March to be the first Master Innholder. Shortly afterwards David Locket became the Association's Secretary (later Clerk or Chief Executive).

The foundation of the Master Innholders has brought wide and lasting benefits to its members, the hotel industry, and also to the Company. The Association has grown steadily and membership is eagerly sought after. It now numbers over seventy on its past, present and overseas lists, representing virtually all the most famous or distinguished London, city and country hotels. Gradually they have become one of the most effective voices in the hotel industry. At their request, in 1993, the Innholders contributed financially (as they have since done regularly) to the first conference for hotel General Managers ever held in the United Kingdom. Now an annual event held in one of the great London hotels - for instance the Dorchester or the Savoy – it draws more than two hundred hoteliers and attracts expert speakers from all the relevant disciplines: investment, accountancy, insurance, employment, management, training, communications, marketing and travel. From time to time a Secretary of State, too, addresses the conference, recognising that in this age of mass tourism the leisure industry, of which hotels are a vital element, rank third or fourth as net earners in Britain's business league table, and employ some ten per cent of the country's work force.

The immediate and continuing success of the Master Innholders restored to the Company its original raison d'être. This new connection with its founding trade is genuine, not cosmetic, and in the 1990s half a dozen members joined the Livery or Freedom and the Court plans steadily to strengthen these links in the years ahead. Further financial aid was also on the way, but that had to wait until a fresh source of funds could be found.

*

The economic turbulence which came to a head in the late 1970s tested the business abilities of the Innholders to their limit, although by then their modest property and investment portfolios, both corporate and charitable, had grown more substantial and elaborate. In the same way their limited income from stocks, rents, Livery fees, and letting the Hall to other companies, had improved – but not sufficiently to cope with inflation, which was then averaging 16% each year, (see Inflation Table, page xxx).

In fact the charities were now better off than the Innholders themselves. There were two reasons. First, the trusts had no heavy, regular commitments to meet from their income, and the Company charged them no administration costs. Secondly, the Court had used bequests from Liverymen to buy two properties, both of great potential value, as homes for the elderly.

The first of these, in Wimbledon, was acquired in 1958 and named after its benefactor, Lieutenant-Colonel James Rydon. When adapted and enlarged it housed some twenty men and women, who were looked after by The Friends of the Elderly, a charity which already managed a similar house adjoining it.

The Innholders' second acquisition, a house in Tunbridge Wells, stood on twenty-four acres of garden, woodland and fields; next to it was a nursing home, Laverstock House, owned and run by the Distressed Gentlefolks Aid Association. The property was bought in 1971 with a legacy of a past Master, F. W. Porritt, and the house was named after his wife. It was divided by the Company into seventeen small self-contained flats for elderly residents, who managed for themselves but could rely, in need, on the reassuring presence of a resident warden.

In 1972 Austin Balls' daughter, Violet Halliwell, endowed a purpose-built residential home for the elderly in the gardens of the Tunbridge Wells property, which gave about twenty residents their own bed-sitting rooms and basic facilities, but with a communal lounge and eating arrangements. Named Florence Balls House after her mother, it was staffed and managed, at the Company's request, by the Distressed Gentlefolks Aid Association. Six years later, when Violet Halliwell died, the final tranche of her father's bequest enabled the Company to add to Laverstock a wing containing thirty-two beds, two sitting rooms, a dining room, a physiotherapy unit, and a chapel.

The three Tunbridge Wells homes owed much to John Bentley, who continuously urged individual Innholders and the Company to endow charitable enterprises of this kind, and then helped to plan and manage them. After his death the entire estate was therefore called John Bentley Park.

The running expenses of both Rydons and John Bentley Park were met by the residents and the charities managing them, nevertheless any annual deficits and the maintenance of the buildings and grounds, fell to the Innholders. Such charitable liabilities were unpredictable and therefore potentially hazardous; furthermore,by 1980, the Company had its own internal and immediate problems to deal with, for its running costs were rising steeply. They included Hall maintenance; the payment of staff, fuel, rates and tax; and, not least, funding the Company's hospitality. Unlike many Liveries, individual Innholders have never been expected to pay for their food and wine. The task of reconciling these costs with the Company's income was especially challenging, since the system of financial forecasts was still rudimentary.

The Livery's income consisted of dividends, fees, and rent from three properties, in Moorgate (owned since the 16th century), in Birchin Lane, and next to the Hall in College Street. Together they brought in £37,000 a year, the annual rent from Moorgate being £10,500. Like the Birchin Lane building, its 99-year lease still had many years to run; as a consequence the prospect of raising the rents or turning the leases into cash seemed extremely remote.

However, the Innholders were lucky to have on the Court an enterprising property expert, Horace Mellery-Pratt. It was providential, too, that the economic tide was now flowing in their favour. The streets of the West End were lined with "For Sale" boards, while the City had become a nightmare of scaffolding, cranes, pounding pile-drivers, chutes of thundering rubble and asphyxiating dust as old buildings came down and new ones went up.

Early in 1983, supported by a small Court committee, Mellery-Pratt approached the tenants of the Moorgate property, in an attempt to buy back the end of their lease and develop the site. To his delight he discovered that they were already planning to move into Mayfair, and so began intense and complex negotiations which were steered to a triumphant conclusion in October 1984.

Put simply, the Innholders bought out their tenants for eight million pounds (which the Company did not have). Wates City of London Properties put down the eight million for the right to raise a major new building on the site, with a series of intricate leases attached to it. By way of these, the Innholders recovered the entire costs of the exercise and, when the new building was soon let to a bank, received an annual income of about half a million pounds.

For the first time in its history the Livery was able to meet all its current obligations, lay the foundations for a secure economic future and make a substantial contribution to the well-being of the industry to which it owed its existence.

*

This sudden flush of new wealth, after its recent financial anxieties, brought home to the Court how urgent it was to overhaul, and then review regularly, its financial policies and management.

Its obligation towards its charitable trusts was palpable, but its duty towards the Livery was both arcane and more worrying for, due to the Company's legal status, the Court enjoys absolute authority to bind the Company to whatever commitment it chooses, but allows ordinary Liverymen no right to question or overturn by a vote any action to which they object. Furthermore, in the event of bankruptcy the entire Livery may be held liable, without limit, for the Company's debts. It was obviously necessary to devise businesslike practices to grasp this particular nettle. It was also desirable to develop the newly forged relationship with the hotel industry and to plan the best use of the Company's financial windfall.

A committee or board of twenty-four members, such as a Court of Assistants, is too large a forum in which effectively to analyse and debate solutions to such fundamental issues. However able the Master as chairman of his Court, there will always be up to a dozen past Masters who will see themselves as honorary managing directors. At the same time the small Master and Wardens Committee, influential at the summit of Company affairs, cannot tackle the wider ranging problems on its own. The Financial and General Purposes Committee was therefore invoked under its new chairman, Geoffrey Hughes, a professional accountant who, from now on, supervised the Company's financial procedures, and who prepared the annual accounts with the assistance of his firm.

As the first priority the committee received unanimous acceptance of their proposal to modernise the Hall. Since it had been rebuilt in 1670, the Hall had undergone major repairs every hundred years or so: in 1774, in 1886, and after the Blitz. Much more radical alterations were called for now. By modern standards of hospitality and employment the facilities were simply not good enough. Receptions before dinners obliged over eighty people to press into the Old Court Room, nose to nose and shoulder to shoulder; if it was tricky to raise a glass, it was difficult to hear a word spoken and impossible to circulate. The Clerk worked from a small desk in the windowless cellar.The catering staff were given no acceptable changing, washing or toilet arrangements. The carpets were threadbare.

Of over 100 Liveries only 39 still own halls and it has long been apparent that the possession of one, as the home and centre of a company's life, contributes significantly to its pride in its history, its spirit of brotherhood, and the confident performance of its business. The Innholders also saw theirs as an asset to be shared with Liveries who had no premises, like the Blacksmiths, and also the Cooks, who keep their Company treasures in a special safe in the Hall. When the Blacksmiths were recently obliged by their growing numbers to dine elsewhere, they presented the Company with a magnificent metal inn sign, made by a member of their court to commemorate their association with the Hall; this now hangs above the entrance in College Street. Apart from other Companies, the Lodge of St. Julian, composed almost entirely of Innholders, meets in the Hall and is only one of many Masonic groups to use it regularly.

It was obvious that to secure a regular letting income from such bodies, standards of comfort and entertainment expected in the competitive world of modern hotels and restaurants would have to be provided. The Court therefore decided to spend two million pounds on redevelopment, raising the capital by selling investments and borrowing the balance from the bank until it could be repaid from rent on the Moorgate property.

The plan was a bold one. Since the leases on the buildings next to the Hall fell in at that moment, they and the entire eastern end of the Hall would be gutted. Only the dining hall, Old Court Room, and the Court Room above would remain little altered; the original front door, door casing and canopy would be blocked but left in situ; the new entrance would be to the east of it. The project would take eighteen months to complete, during which time the Company would meet in other halls.

The architect chosen was Sam Lloyd. He specialised in the refurbishment and modernisation of historic buildings, and smooth relations with the authorities at English Heritage were essential. The Innholders asked Stephen Druce, whose family had been continuously members of the Company since 1712, to oversee the contractors.

The new building consisted of five levels: the basement comprising the kitchen and facilities; the reception rooms occupying the ground floor; the Court Room and a new flat for the Master on the first floor; the Beadle's flat and four bedrooms for the use of the Livery on the tsecond; and an entirely new set of offices for the Clerk at the top. The key structural decision was to instal a lift, which left room for only a single staircase which had to be fireproof and serve every floor.

For reasons of period and style, the refurbishment worked back from the dining hall. Its small 17th century minstrels' gallery was moved with its balusters from the north east corner to the centre of the east wall, with a larger space behind it. This entailed careful patching and matching of the oak panelling which is one of the Hall's most striking and attractive features. Originally put up in 1670, it has become something of a palimpsest – considerably restored in 1774, it had to be repaired in 1886, and again after the bomb damage in 1941. The removal from the fireplace of a heavy Victorian overmantel, and the decision to set the Druce portrait into the panelling above, improved the appearance of the south wall. Later, when air conditioning was introduced, the units were enclosed in wooden casing, skilfully moulded, stained, and polished to blend imperceptibly with the panelling.

The ceiling was much simplified, its crossing beams and coffers paint-

The Dining Hall laid for dinner

ed white to bring it closer to its original design. The three chandeliers, branched and gilded copies of 18th century originals in the Queen's Drawing Room at Kensington Palace, were left in place. However, as they now obscured the new minstrels' gallery from the Master and his guests at the high table, electric motors were installed in the loft above to raise them during a musical performance.

Blue has always been the Company's primary colour, and this was chosen for the dining hall curtains, for the background of its specially woven Elizabethan Bible pattern carpet, and for the leather of its chairs, whose woodwork was stained darker to tone with the panelling.

Little was done to the Old Court Room. However, the old entrance hall adjoining it was converted into a reception room. Its walls were moulded with 18th century-style, honey coloured, plaster panels to provide a sympathetic transition between the new white entrance hall and the dark oak panels of the 17th century apartments beyond.

The new front door, numbered as 30 College Street, opened into a lobby whose short flight of steps led up to the ground floor. At the top of these a cabinet displayed the coats of arms, in 17th century stained glass, of two Liverymen – one of them John Knott, Master in 1670, the year in which the rebuilt Hall was opened after the Great Fire.

The main entrance hall leading off this was a large new open space hung with Henry VIII's Charter and the Grant of Arms from Charles II. Between these was placed the wooden figure of St Julian, above a lead cistern dated 1685, a survivor from the rebuilding after the Fire. A bronze portrait head of Earl Attlee stands on a bracket nearby. In the staircase lobby on the far side of the entrance hall is the Charles II charter of Inspeximus, the great iron chest, and an oriel window celebrating Queen Elizabeth II's Silver Jubilee in 1977, commissioned that year from three past Masters of the Glaziers Company. The centre panel, with the Queen's head taken from the postage stamp issued for her coronation in 1953, is by Michael Farrer-Bell. The surrounding inn signs illustrate such familiar

The new Reception area(above)
and The Court Room with the new Millennium furniture (below)

names as Bag of Nails (corrupted from Bacchanalia) and Pig and Whistle (from Piege Wassail, Anglo-Saxon for Hail to the Virgin).

It was almost without precedent that an operation on this scale should be completed on schedule and within striking distance of its estimated cost, but the Hall reopened as planned in September 1990.

*

Five or six years elapsed before the costs of rebuilding the Hall were paid off and the investment portfolio consolidated as an essential precaution against all the Company's eggs being left in its property basket. During these years the Court was obliged to look very carefully at its charitable properties for two reasons. First, the needs and social behaviour of the elderly were changing. For example, the improving health and lengthening lives of the old led them to remain longer in their own homes, only moving as a last resort to a residential or nursing home. As a result, by 1994, the sheltered flats in Esther Porritt House were virtually empty. Secondly, governments constantly tightened the regulation of institutions that cared for the elderly, which entailed ever increasing and often exorbitant expense.

Since the fabric of Esther Porritt House was by now unsound the most appropriate course was to sell the building for demolition and replacement by flats. Meanwhile, the expense of running Rydons at Wimbledon rose alarmingly. In the end the cost of introducing new fire doors and escapes, wheelchair access, tighter standards of hygiene, and higher staff levels (while working hours shrank and wages increased), became prohibitive, as they did for the Friends of the Elderly in the neighbouring house. More or less simultaneously the Company and the Friends decided that the only sensible option was to close the doors of both houses. Happily the Friends of the Elderly could offer all the residents an alternative home.

This experience confirmed the growing view in Court that it was unwise to go on shouldering open-ended commitments of this kind, and shortly afterwards it closed Florence Balls House at Tunbridge Wells, after making sure that the residents could find accommodation with the Distressed Gentlefolks Aid Association (now renamed the Elizabeth Finn Trust).

One chapter in the history of the Company's charities had thus closed; but now another one opened. Rydons, bought for £6,500 in 1958, sold for £2,000,000 forty years later. The twenty-four acres of John Bentley Park had cost £24,000 in 1971; after thirty years Esther Porritt House, and an acre of garden, fetched £350,000, and Florence Balls House is expected to make several times as much. In the meantime the Company had received substantial legacies from Liverymen, including Sidney Bishop and Ronald Wates; it had also amalgamated half a dozen trusts two or three centuries old. By 2000 its charitable investment capital totalled about five million pounds.

Once the cost of rebuilding the Hall had been paid off the Company, on average, transferred £100,000 each year from its corporate to its charitable account, so that with the investment income from its charity capital it had at least £300,000 to spend annually on its adopted causes A charity committee continued to sift the plethora of appeals which came in each year, and make appropriate donations to a carefully chosen few. The Company also made an annual contribution to the funds of a Territorial Army unit, the 31st (City of London) Signal Regiment (Volunteers).

However, the greatly increased income called for an entirely new strategy and the Court asked Stephen Druce to form a Patronage Committee to research the options and recommend how the money might be spent appropriately. As a result the Company decided to direct its charity towards three broad ends: the continued care of the elderly; helping the young, in situations of special need; and to support the hotel industry's efforts to raise its standards and service.

Writing so soon after this policy was framed, it is only possible to give a brief outline of what was achieved in the first five years. Nevertheless, it reveals the Company's concern with a wide variety of the social problems facing London and the rest of the country.

In the ambit of the Company's help for the elderly, the closure of Rydons and John Bentley Park was a great wrench, for the Homes Committee chaired by Ian Haire, the Masters, the Wardens and the Clerks had always taken a warm and personal interest in the residents and staffs of both places. A donation of £100,000 was therefore made to the Friends of the Elderly for their home at Woking and a significantly larger gift granted to the Elizabeth Finn Trust. Many lesser grants were made towards apparatus to aid the old and the sick, and for training those who nurse the dying. Annual sums were also given to pensioners from the hotel industry experiencing special hardship.

Help for the young was an entirely new departure, but the Patronage Committee quickly identified four quite different initiatives to help meet specific and urgent needs among them.

One of the greatest causes of distress in society, and one of the heaviest financial burdens on the state, is the result of harm suffered by babies as a result of their mothers' exposure to under-nourishment, violence, or the abuse of alcohol, nicotine and drugs. The most efficacious treatment for a baby so damaged is often to provide it with specially formulated surrogate milk to nourish its brain. A unit at North London University, researching this treatment under Professor Michael Crawford, has been granted £35,000 a year for three years. The results will help fight this battle all over the world.

Older children, in the poorer boroughs of London, are disadvantaged more generally. Many of the local state schools there, short of funds and teachers, simply cannot offer their abler children the secondary education they deserve to fulfil their potential. This deprivation was accentuated when the government put an end to assisted places in private schools, which had previously offered a lifeline. The Innholders therefore undertook to meet the entire fees of three pupils each at the City of London School for Boys and its sister school for girls, throughout their attendance from the age of 11-18, at a total annual cost of about £45,000. It is a condition that each child should receive an unqualified recommendation from their primary school and pass an entrance exam; in addition the combined income from his or her parents must not exceed £15,000. The children chosen have so far received exceptional reports.

There is a widespread belief that nowadays a combination of cramped living conditions in cities, epidemic addiction to television, the disappearance of playing fields, and the discouragement of competition in our national school curriculum, have tended to stifle enterprise and the spirit of adventure among many of the young. The Sail Training Association has been one of the most effective organisations to challenge this trend. Their courses at sea, on their tall ships, have inspired a generation of boys and girls with a new self-reliance and confidence in embarking on their lives. Each year the Innholders send a number of young on these courses and recently contributed £50,000 for the cost of a galley in a newly launched ship.

The largest grant has been a pledge of £250,000, payable over three years, to Shaftesbury Homes and Arethusa, a charity dedicated to the reclamation of children adrift in society or on the wrong side of the law. The grant has enabled them to triple the sum with funding from other bodies, including the government and the European Union. With this endowment they have set up a unit of highly motivated and qualified staff to befriend, educate, and train for a craft or some other career, boys and girls who might otherwise never have recovered from their early setbacks or disasters. One of the first young men to emerge from this unit - known as The St Julian Educational Training Scheme – has won national recognition for his brilliant response to the opportunities he has thus received.

The final sector of the Innholders' patronage is concerned with the hotel industry's constant effort to improve its performance. The big chains have naturally evolved their own methods of training at every level but, without the same resources, the independents often cannot afford to spare their employees for advanced training. After prolonged research, the Master Innholders Association therefore advised the Court to fund a handful of carefully selected young hoteliers, well on their way up the ladder, to attend general management courses at Cranfield College in the UK, or Cornell University in the USA.

The first results proved remarkably successful and ten hoteliers each year now attend these courses, at a total annual cost of about £100,000, rather more than half borne by the Company, and the balance by the Savoy Educational Trust and the Master Innholders themselves. The first thirty recipients of the scholarships have been so enthusiastic about the experience that they have formed themselves into a group of alumni called "St Julian Scholars", who aim to promote the benefits of the scheme throughout the industry.

*

At the end of every banquet the Beadle announces a toast: "The Worshipful Company of Innholders, root and branch, may it continue and flourish for ever". If not eternal, the Livery has so far proved durable, but to remain so it must move with the times. It is only recently, for instance, that it has responded to the Victorian Commissioners' charge: "No attempt has been made to throw open the Court".

While society has placed the reins of decision and power in ever younger hands, life expectancy has ironically lengthened: meanwhile the average age of the Innholders' Court inexorably rose, and still seniority remained its only criterion for election. As a consequence the day came when seventeen past Masters sat down in Court to the right of the Master and his three Wardens, with only three Assistants to their left. In three years there would be no Assistant to assume the office of Renter. A few months later the seven senior past Masters agreed to resign at six-monthly intervals, until an appropriate balance was restored. With the balance recovered the Senior Past-Master now retires annually in the autumn, so that when the new officers are installed in October, the entire Court moves up a place, leaving a vacancy for a new Assistant.

After this the Court recognised that it had a fiduciary obligation to find new criteria for elections. Its activities were more complex and demanding than in the past. There was a clear need for a wider range of professional skills and experience to manage them. It was felt that the Company's business might be more suitably conducted by Court members closer in age to their opposite numbers, who were so often of a younger generation. In addition there was a fourth, and quite different, reason for abandoning the time-honoured precedent of seniority. Candidates were stemming from a period in which four Freemen had regularly joined the Livery each year, but logically (in fairness to those who had joined in later years) there was only room for one of them on the Court. How to choose him?

The new requirements, applied empirically at first, but later expressed as three principles, were these. To be successful a candidate must, first, command the Court's confidence that he would make an effective and suitable Master. Secondly he must reach the Mastership by the age of seventy. Thirdly he should possess the necessary qualifications to meet the current and future needs of the Company.

In such ways as these the Worshipful Company of Innholders of London entered the new millennium confident in its fundamental aims which the Court recently defined as 'the perpetuation and enhancement of the Company, its spirit, financial strength and Hall'. Strong in their traditions the Innholders could welcome the future with convictions expressed by commissioning for the New Court Room a handsome set of tables and matching chairs from one of the country's finest contemporary furniture makers, John Makepeace. Changes in personnel also ensured that traditions continued with new energy. In 2000 Dougal Bulger was appointed Clerk and, the following year, Robert Fox became Beadle. An annual newsletter enables all members of the Livery to keep abreast of such developments and reflects not only the Company's concern with its own, internal affairs but with its contacts in the City and the wider world.

With the turn of the millennia these connections were perfectly exemplified by two notable events. One was the reopening of the Great Eastern at Liverpool Street Station, to become the only substantial hotel in the Square Mile. At a cost of sixty-five million pounds Charles Barry's splendid west block, originally opened in 1884, and Colonel Edis's east block of 1901 were refurbished to offer 267 bedrooms, four restaurants, a gymnasium and twelve private suites, decorated in styles ranging from high Victorian to the understated simplicity of modern design. Furthermore its managing director was Nicholas Rettie, a Liveryman of the Company and a recent chairman of the Master Innholders Association. The hotel, like generations of inns over the past five centuries, instantly became a crowded meeting place for workers in the City, while visitors from every continent booked into its rooms.

The second event is integrated historically and administratively with the very fabric of the City Corporation but will also contribute to the projection of London's thriving image and reputation throughout the world. Every one of the City's Freemen with more than a year's standing has the right to vote for its chief magistrate, the Lord Mayor. The Company has therefore watched with pride the sixth of its own Liverymen, Robert Finch, Alderman for the Coleman Street ward since 1922, approach that great office.

A senior partner in one of London's largest international law firms, a Commissioner of the Church of England, and a Sheriff of the City of London in 2000, Robert Finch will become eligible for election as Lord Mayor in 2003. Besides being head of the Corporation of London, Chief Magistrate and Chancellor of the City University, the Lord Mayor also travels the world as ambassador for the country's financial services, which are a vital element of its Gross Domestic Product.

Nevertheless he also sits as the elected representative of every Liveryman, and is consequently the focal point of their loyalty to the City. In today's world their Companies, both ancient and modern, not only sustain their crafts, trades and professions, but through these help to strengthen the business and the quality of life of the communities surrounding, and inextricably linked with, the City.

Robert Finch has recently said of the Liveries: "By the generosity of their grants to medical research and the arts, and particularly through their charitable activities in the field of education, frequently concentrated in the most deprived areas, the Companies make an outstanding contribution to the nation's social and cultural well-being, and to the preservation of London as one of the greatest civilised capitals in the world."

These are heartening words, an expression of pride and confidence in the continuing life and relevance of ancient and essentially British institutions. They are also a fitting conclusion to a history of the Innholders themselves. They allow us to appreciate how a Company with a hall occupying a place on the quay of the original Roman capital evolved from the Saxon guilds into a medieval mistery that flourished through the sixteenth century and then survived the vicissitudes of civil war, plague, fire, political hostility and two World Wars to emerge as a valued and valuable part of the modern world – a guild dedicated to maintaining the highest standards of its original trade along with the well-being of all those whose lives it touches. This is a noble tradition and, in the words of the Company motto: *Hinc Spes Affulget* – Hope Shines Out From Here.

APPENDIX I

Badges of Office

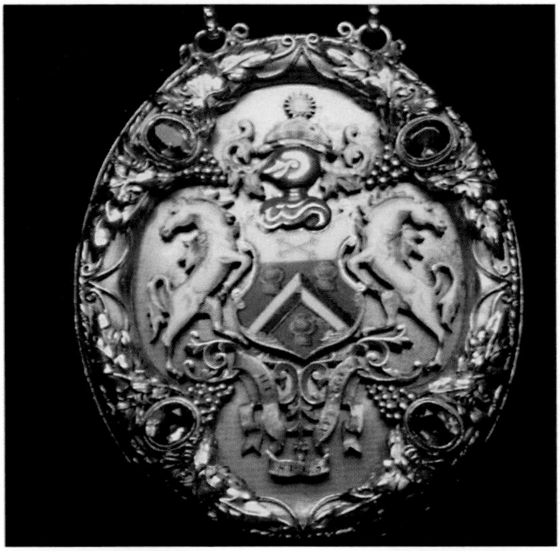

Top row:

Renter, Middle and Upper Warden

centre:

Master's Badge

Bottom row:

Clerk's and Chaplain's Badges

APPENDIX II

MASTERS OF THE INNHOLDERS' COMPANY

The record of Masters is consecutive only since 1653, at the time of the Commonwealth, owing to the loss of earlier documents in the Great Fire of London.

From other references, the following Masterships are also known: 1617 John Sweete; 1627 Edward Lycorise; 1634 Nicholas Cooke; 1641 William Lether; 1642 Henry Worthington; 1647 Richard Reeve.

Consecutive list from 1653 to 2001, with year of election

1653	THOMAS ASTILL	1687	- STEWARD
1654	AUGUSTINE BRYAN	i688	JOHN BOOTH
1655	WILLIAM PENNINGTON	1689	HUMPHREY LEA
1656	THOMAS MALCHER	1690	- BRANDON
1657	- JENKINSON	1690	RALPH COMBS
1658	THOMAS CHARLETT	1691	- CARWARDEN
1659	THOMAS HANSON	1692	JOHN CLARKE
1660	JOHN WHITTURNE	1693	WILLIAM WILKINS
1661	ISAACK BENNETT	1694	JOHN SHELLEY
1662	OLIVER MARKLAND	1695	JOHN GRAUNT
1663	ROBERT WHITBORNE	1696	SAMUEL WILLIS
1664	JOHN KNOTT	1697	CAPTAIN WARREN
1665	ROBERT BRISCOE	1698	WILLIAM LEAKE
1666	THOMAS ECCLESTON	1699	JAMES COOPER
1667	RICHARD PENNER	1700	THOMAS EADES
1668	ROBERT HUDSON	1701	THOMAS HIGGS
1669	RICHARD ELLIOTT	1702	JOHN WALKER
1670	JOHN KNOTT	1703	PETER MORRIS
1671	EDWARD SHALLER	1704	JAMES CARPENTER
1672	WILLIAM DUNSTON	1705	URIAH ANDREWS
1673	THOMAS HALL	I 706	THOMAS HILL
1674	WALTER COLEIR	1707	JOHN MORRIS
1675	WALTER COLEIR	1708	JOHN ROBERTS
1676	PHILLIP STOWER	1709	MARTIN BARNES
1677	JOHN CHOLMLY	1710	HUMFREY BELL
1678	WILLIAM GARFIELD	1711	WILLIAM WEBB
1679	EDWARD FAWCETT	1712	JOHN BLINCKHORNE
I 680	WILLIAM WEEKES	1713	THOMAS TRAUNTER
1681	HUMPHRY LEA	1714	JOHN DRURY
1682	SAMUEL NEWTON	1715	JONAS WHITLEY
1683	CHRISTOPHER JOHNSON	1716	SIDNEY POTTS
1684	ROBERT APPLEGARTH	I717	WILLIAM AMES
1685	EDWARD NORMAN	1718	WILLIAM BOULTON
1686	ROBERT BUCKLAND	1719	JOHN HOLMES

1720	JOHN ABORMAN
1721	SIDNEY CHARLES
1722	WILLIAM THOMPSON
1723	WILLIAM BIGSLY
1724	HUGH HUNTER
1725	ARTHUR JOYCE
1726	EDMUND PEPPERCORNE
1727	HENRY HEARDSLEY
1728	JOHN CHAPMAN
1729	ROGER PRESCOTT
1730	THOMAS NIXON
1731	JOHN COOBAN
1732	ROBERT TAYLOR
1733	WILLIAM PEMBERTON
1734	JOSEPH HARRISON
1735	WILLIAM NEVILLE
1736	ROBERT JOHNSON
1737	CHRISTOPHER WOODROFFE
1738	THOMAS ANDERSON
1739	RICHARD ALLEN
1740	JAMES MILLER
1741	JOHN NOVIL
1742	JOHN BARKER
1743	RALPH CHAMBERLAIN
1744	THOMAS MINET
1745	GEORGE DYSON
1746	RICHARD FENTON
1747	JOHN PARS
1748	HENRY COTHERY, SNR
1749	THOMAS WISKER
1750	JOHN ARMISTED
1751	THOMAS ROBERTS
1752	HENRY TAME
1753	RICHARD ROYBOLD
1754	WILLIAM ILIFFE
1755	THOMAS LEWIS
1756	CHARLES CREMER
1757	RICHARD MORRELL
1758	DANIEL SMITH
1759	MOSES NETHERWOOD
1760	ALEXANDER SMITH
1761	JOHN PISTON
1762	JOHN GREENHOW
1763	DAVID DE CAUX
1764	ABRAHAM DAKING
1765	JAMES BISPHAM
1766	JOHN POULTNEY
1767	THOMAS DALE
1768	ABRAHAM BRECKNOCK
1769	JOSEPII PLAISTS
1770	HOLLOWAY BRECKNOCK
1771	ALEXANDER BELL
1772	GEORGE WADDINCTON
1773	GEORGE RHODES
1774	JOHN MILLER
1775	WILLIAM NORTHROPE
1776	JOHN STOCKALL
1777	BRYAN GREEN
1778	THOMAS MAUDLEY
1779	JOHN HALL
1780	JOHN HAYWARD
1781	JOHN HARDEN
1782	HUMPHRY JONES
1783	HENRY COTHERY, JNR.
1784	HENRY COTHERY, JNR.
1785	EDWARD CRAWSHAW
1786	ROBERT PARK
1787	JOHN MOTT
1788	ROBERT CLARKE
1789	JOHN PEARSON
1790	JOHN ROBERTS
1791	JOHN PATRICK
1792	THOMAS DRUCE
1793	THOMAS WILLSON
1794	CHARLES IBBITSON
1795	THOMAS HARRIS
1796	EDWARD CAMPPEN
1797	JOHN JENNINGS
1798	JONATHAN PEGRAM
1799	JOSEPH KAY
1800	- SCAMBLER
1801	JOSHUA PRING
1802	{ JOHN LOMAX
	WILLIAM REW
1803	HENRY NEWTON
1804	JOHN JOBLING
1805	ROBERT CLARK
1806	THOMAS LEWIS
1807	JOHN JONES
1808	TIMOTHY STANSFELD
1809	WILLIAM HOLEBROOK
1810	JAMES HOLT
1811	JOHN GRAVE
1812	JOSHUA PETERS
1813	HENRY GRAY
1814	JOSHUA CRANK

1815	JOHN NIXON
1816	MARSHALL SPINK
1817	JOHN HOLMES
1818	STEPHEN BUTLER
1819	WILLIAM WATERHOUSE
1820	GEORGE SEX
1821	FRANCIS JOLIT
1822	JOSHUA PEARSON
1823	DAVID SADLER
1824	THOMAS GILBERT
1825	JOHN JONES
1826	GEORGE SEXTON
1827	THOMAS WESTON
1828	JOHN TANNER
1829	JAMES BISHOP
1830	JOSIAS STANSFELD
1831	WILLIAM PEPPERCORNE
1832	JOHN BADDELEY
1833	HENRY SCAMBLER
1834	BENJAMIN ROBINSON
1835	SIR CHAPMAN MARSHALL (Lord Mayor 1839)
1836	EDWARD EYTON
1837	RICHARD DIXON
1838	WILL1AM PARDY
1839	DANIEL E. SPINK
1840	CHARLES DRUCE
1841	WILLIAM URWICK
1842	JAMES POWELL
1843	HENRY GRAY
1844	{ WILLIAM S SMITH JOHN TANNER
1845	GEORGE W. SHURY
1846	HENRY VUKRESS
1847	THOMAS STEWART
1848	EDWARD SEX
1849	GEORGE PARDY
1850	{ GEORGE RADLEY JOHN TANNER
1851	GEORGE TANNER
1852	GEORGE GILES
1853	SIR THOMAS SCAMBLER OWDEN- (Lord Mayor 1877)
1854	WILLIAM J. CHAPLIN
1855	JAMES RICHARDSON
1856	JOHN NEWTON
1857	LEEDS PAINE
1858	BENJAMIN WORTHY HORNE
1859	ISAAC JOLLIFFE
1860	JOHN MONGER
1861	HENRY WOODS
1862	DAVID BRANDON
1863	SIR H. MUGGERIDGE
1864	R.M. PHILLIPPS
1865	CHARLES DRUCE
1866	CHARLES CLARIDGE DRUCE
1867	JAMES HEENAN
1868	JOHN SHORT
1869	WILLIAM PARDY
1870	JOHN BOYES
1871	EDWARD H.SANDERSON
1872	GEORGE C. GRAVES
1873	WILLIAM H. URWICK
1874	HENRY RYDON
1875	WILLIAM LOVEJOY
1876	GEORGE H. BECKFORD
1877	THOMAS MITTON
1878	WILLIAM NATHAN
1879	JAMES DEAL
1880	TRAVERS BARTON WIRE
1881	THOMAS S. RICHARDSON
1882	HENRY GIBBON
1883	ROBERT CLARKE
1884	JOHN GIBSON
1885	WILLIAM H. HEENAN
1886	HORACE J. RYDON
1887	WILLIAM E. S. SANDERSON
1888	BEN. DOLAMORE
1889	JOHN P C. GRAVES
1890	HENRY H. LAVINGTON
1891	{ JOSHUA . S. LAVINGTON - WILLIAM H. URWICK
1892	HENRY C. ROBERTS
1893	SAMUEL D. NIX
1894	CLARENCE G.BECKFORD
1895	HARRY F. PARDY
1896	WILLIAM J.LAVINGTON
1897	JOSEPH D. MATHEWS
1898	GEORGE WALTER
1899	HENRY W. BALL
1900	THOMAS A.WOODBRIDGE
1901	GEORGE GABB
1902	SIR WALTER H. HARRIS
1903	CHARLES B. BRADEN

1904	JOHN COLLINSON
1905	WILLIAM B. GIBBS
1906	ALFRED H. BAYNES
1907	HENRY H.MONTAGUE-SMITH
1908	JAMES H. L. BISHOP
1909	FREDERICK W. BISHOP
1910	HARRY F. PARDY
1911	WILLIAM J. LAVINGTON
1912	SIR HARRY S FOSTER
1913	JAMES W. WALTER
1914	ALAN RICHARDSON
1915	SIR CHARLES J0HNSTON (Lord Mayor 1914)
1916	JOHN . T. GARDNER
1917	JOHN R. COOPER
1918	THOMAS W. HALL
1919	THOMAS W. HALL
1920	WALTER D. CRONIN
1921	ALFRED BRICE BEATON
1922	EDWIN FOX
1923	EDWIN FOX
1924	ALFRED S. RUSTON
1925	WALTER J. RUEGG
1926	JAMES S. BUCKINGHAM
1927	HENRY E. MATHEWS
1928	HENRY E. MATHEWS
1929	GEORGE L. WALTER
1930	LT.-COL.C. H. L. BASKERVILLE
1931	ROBERT S. PATERSON
1932	ERNEST M. COLLINSON
1933	EVELYN GWYDYR JONES
1934	ARTHUR L. RYDON
1935	EDWARD J. LUSBY
1936	SYDNEY J. WALTER
1937	JOHN E. GARDNER
1938	WILLIAM E. BIBRA
1939	ARTHUR E. SAVILL
1940	FRANCIS DRUCE *(killed in air attack)*
1941	RALTON G. HAMMOND
1942	FRANCIS J. CAUNTER
1943	CECIL R. WYLDE
1944	JOHN A. CAMPBELL JOHNSTONE
1945	W. AUSTIN BALLS
1946 } 1947	GRP. CAPT. C. S. RICHARDSON
1948	L. E. HALL *(died in office)*
1948	GEORGE L. WALTER
1949	CECIL W. HALL
1950	H. L. GARDNER
1951	H. H. LAVINGTON
1952	H. BURGESS BALLS
1953	M. J. B. WHITBY
1954	S. H. BISHOP
1955 } 1956	B. S. TATHAM
1957	MAJOR B. N. GIBBS
1958	F. C. D. WOOD
1959 } 1960	G.R. APPLEYARD
1961	F. W. PORRITT
1962	RONALD A. WYLDE
1963	THE REV E. G. TURNER
1964	HORACE A. MELLERY-PRATT
1965	NORMAN L. HALL CBE
1966	ERIC W. RICE
1967	ERIC W. RICE
1968	MICHAEL McDONALD
1969	DANIEL MAHONEY
1970	RICHARD G.TANNER-SMTIH
1971	ARTHUR J. EVANS D.F.C.
1972	JOHN G. WYLDE
1973	COL JOHN A. HAIRE
1974	DERRICK ANDERSON
1975	DR IVOR R. HAIRE
1976	DR IVOR R. HAIRE
1977	DEREK BALLS
1978	SIR RONALD WATES
1979	JOHN DE SAVARY
1980	HIS HON.GEOFFREY D. LOVEGROVE
1981	GEORGE IRELAND RUSSELL
1982	GEOFFREY B. C. HUGHES
1983	HENRY J. LAVINGTON
1984	J. SYDNEY PARK
1985	CHRISTIAN J. WHITBY
1986	JOHN F. WEBSTER
1987	STEPHEN DRUCE
1988	JOHN N. BARTLETT
1989	DONALD C. ROBERTSON
1990	ANTONY J. D. MATHEWS
1991	MICHAEL VASS

1992	SIR MALCOLM H. CHAPLIN CBE
1993	HOWARD E. HARRISON
1994	MICHAEL E. WATES
1995	ROGER G. AMES
1996	ADRIAN R. HOUSE
1997	CHRISTIAN H. G. BRANN
1998	ANTHONY C. LORKIN
1999	DR RICHARD B. GLOVER
2000	GUY M. SAYER CBE
2001	ANTHONY G. FISHER

APPENDIX III

CLERKS SINCE 1785

Charles Druce (1)	1785 – 1835
Charles Druce (2)	1835 – 1857
Alexander D. Druce	1857 – 1897
John A. Druce	1897 – 1910
Francis Druce	1910 – 1926
John C. Druce	1926 – 1947
John H. Bentley	1947 – 1980
John Edwardes Jones	1980 – 2000
Douglas E. Bulger	2000 –

APPENDIX IV

SELECT BIBLIOGRAPHY

Archer, Ian W., *The Pursuit of Stability: Social Relations in Elizabethan London,* 1991.

Borer, Mary C., *The British Hotel through the Ages,* 1972.

Bossy, John, *Christianity in the West: 1400-1700,* 1985.

Calendar of Letter-Books preserved among the Archives of the Corporation of the City of London, 1275-1498, 11 volumes, 1899-1912.

Calendar of Plea and Memoranda Rolls preserved among the Archives of the City of London, 1323-1482, 6 volumes, 1926-61.

Carlin, Martha, *Medieval Southwark,* 1996.

Duffy, Eamon, *The Stripping of the Altars: Traditional Religion in England c. 1400-c. 1580,* 1992.

Doolittle, I. G., *The City of London and its Livery Companies,* 1982.

Everitt, Alan, 'The English Urban Inn, 1560-1760' in Alan Everitt, ed., *Perpectives in English Urban Histoiy,* 1973.

Fidler, K. *Stories of Old Inns,* 1973.

Fisher, F. J., 'The Development of London as a Centre of Conspicuous Consumption in the Sixteenth and Seventeenth Centuries', *Royal Historical Society Transactions,* 4th Series, xxx (1948), 37-50.

Galloway, David, ed., *The Elizabethan Theatre: Papers given at the International Confereuce on Elizabethan Theatre held at the University Of Waterloo, Ontario, in July, 1968,* 1969.

Gibson, Sarah, Excavations at Innholders' Hall, 29-30 College Street', Archive Report for the Department of Urban Archaeology, Museum of London, 1990.

Hammond, P. W., *Food and Feast in Medieval England,* 1993.

Harper, C. G., *The Old Inns of Old England,* 2 volumes, 1906.

Harrison, William, *The Description of England,* ed., George Edden, 1968.

Heal, Felicity, *Hospitality in Early Modern England,* 1990.

History of the Worshipful Company of Innholders of the City of London, 1922.

Hollaender, A. E. J. And William Kellaway, eds., *Studies in London Histoty Presented to Philip Edmund Jones,* 1969.

Hutton, Ronald, *The Rise and Fall of Merry England: the Ritual Year, 1400-1700,* 1994.
Jones, P. E. And R. Smith, *A Guide to the Records in the Corporation of London Records Office and the Guildhall Library Muniment Room,* 1951.

Jusserand, J. J., *English Wayfaring Life in the Middle Ages,* 1950.

Kahl, William F., *The Development of the London Livery Companies,* Baker Library, Harvard Graduate School of Business Administration, 1960.

Kellett, J. R., 'The Breakdown of Guild Incorporation and Control over the Handicraft and Retail Trade in London', *Economic History Review,* 2nd Series, X, no. 3, (1958), 381-94.

Kramer, Stella, *The English Craft Guilds: Studies in their Progress and Decline,* 1927.

Levin, Jennifer, *The Charter Controversy in the City of London, 1660-1688, and its Consequences,* 1969.

Liber Albus:The White Book of the City of London, ed., H. T. Riley, 1861.

Manley, J. M., *Some New Light on Chaucer,* 1926.

Memorials of London aud London Life in the XII XIV and XV Centuries, ed., H. T. Riley, 1868.

Miller, John, *The Glorious Revolution,* 1983.

Munby, Julian, 'Zacharias's: A Fourteenth Century Oxford New Inn and the Origins of the Medieval Urban Inn', *Oxoniensa,* 57, 1992.

Norman, Philip, 'The Tabard Inn, Southwark, The Queen's Head, William Rutter, and St. Margaret's Church', *Surrey Archaeological Society Collections,* XIII (1897), 28-38.

Pantin, W. A., 'Medieval Inns' in E. M. Jope, ed., *Studies in Building History: Essays in Recognition of the Work of B. H. St. J O'Neil,* pp.166-91, 1961.

Parkes, Joan, *Travel in England in the Seventeenth Century,* 1925.

Pearl, Valerie, Change and Stability in Seventeenth Century London, *London Journal* 5 (!979), 3-34.

*London at the Outbreak of the Puritan Revolution: City Government and National Politics, 1625-1643,*1961.

Porter, Roy, *London: A Social History,* 1996.

Rappaport, Steve., *Worlds within Worlds: Structures of Life in Sixteenth Century London,* 1989.
Reddaway, T. F., 'The Livery Companies of Tudor London', *History,* 21(1966), 287-99.

Report of the Royal Commission on the City of London Livery Companies, 1884,

Report of the Royal Commission on Municipal Corporations (England and Wales): London and Southwark; London Companies, 1837.

Rosevere, Henry, *The Financial Revolution 1660-1760,* 1991.

Schofield, John, *The Building of London from the Conquest to the Great Fire,* 1984

Sheppard, Francis, *London: A History,* 1998.

Stenton, F.M. *Norman London with a Translation of William Fitzstephen's 'Description',* 1934.

Swan, Carolyn Taylor, ed., *The Old French Prose Legend of St Julian the Hospitaller,* 1977.

Taylor, Derek, *Fortune, Fame and Folly: British Hotels and Catering from 1878 to 1978,* 1977.
The Golden Age of British Hotels, 1974.

Taylor, J. R. *Reform Your City Guilds,* 1872.

Thomson, David, *England in the Nineteenth Century,* rev. Ed., D. Beales, 1978.

Thrupp, Sylvia L. *The Merchant Class of Medieval London,* 1948.

Unwin, George, *The Guilds and Companies of London,* 4th rev. Ed. 1963.
Industrial Organisation in the Sixteenth and Seventeenth Centuries, 1904.

Warner, Oliver, *The History of the Innholders.* 1962

White, Arthur, *Palaces of the People: A Social History of Commercial Hospitality,* 1968.

* * *

APPENDIX V

RETAIL PRICE INDEX 1300 – 2000

Year	£ Value	Significant Events
1300	**£1.00**	
1400	**£1.00**	
1500	£1.00	
1550	£1.50	
1600	**£3.50**	
1670	£5.50	The Hall rebuilt after the Great Fire
1700	**£5.75**	
1750	£5.25	
1800 – 1815	**£17.00**	The Napoleonic Wars
1850	£8.50	
1900	**£7.50**	
1914 – 1919	£14.25	World War I
1939 – 1946	£16.50	World War II
1950	£20.50	
1960	£30.50	
1970	£45.50	
1980	£167.25	
1990	£316.50	The Hall redeveloped
2000	**£425.75**	

PRICE LEVEL

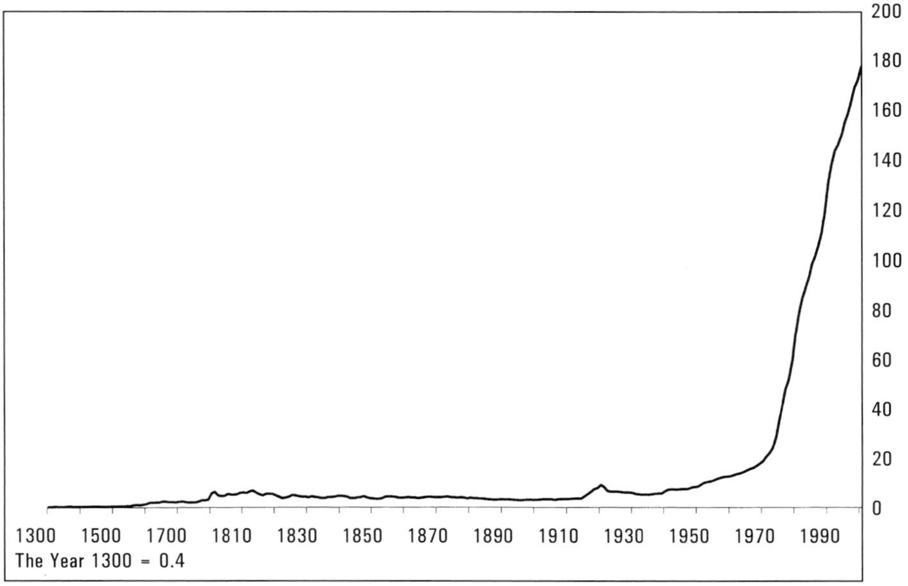

APPENDIX VI

LONDON LIVERY COMPANIES IN ORDER OF PRECEDENCE.

Dates given are those of the earliest clear evidence of a Company's formation, ordinances or charter. Most Companies will have been in existence prior to this date, in some form, in many cases for centuries.

1.	Mercers	1394
2.	Grocers	1345
3.	Drapers	1364
4.	Fishmongers	1272
5.	Goldsmiths	1327
6.{	Merchant Taylors}	1327
	Skinners	
7.		
8.	Haberdashers	1371
9.	Salters	1394
10.	Ironmongers	1463
11.	Vintners	1364
12.	Clothworkers	1528
13.	Dyers	1471
14.	Brewers	1437
15.	Leathersellers	1444
16.	Pewterers	1348
17.	Barbers	1308
18.	Cutlers	1344
19.	Bakers	1486
20.	Wax Chandlers	1371
21.	Tallow Chandlers	1462
22.	Armourers & Brasiers	1453
23.	Girdlers	1327
24.	Butchers	1605
25.	Saddlers	1362
26.	Carpenters	1362
27.	Cordwainers	1272
28.	Painter-Stainers	1268
29.	Curriers	1415
30.	Masons	1677
31.	Plumbers	1365
32.	**Innholders**	**1514**
33.	Founders	1365
34.	Poulters	1368
35.	Cooks	1482
36.	Coopers	1501
37.	Tylers & Bricklayers	1416
38.	Bowyers	1371
39.	Fletchers	1371
40.	Blacksmiths	1325
41.	Joiners and Ceilers	1571
42.	Weavers	1155
43.	Woolmen	1522
44.	Scriveners	1373
45.	Fruiterers	1605
46.	Plaisterers	1501
47.	Stationers & Newspapermakers	1403
48.	Broderers	1561
49.	Upholders	1626
50.	Musicians	1350
51.	Turners	1604
52.	Basketmakers	1569
53.	Glaziers and Painters of Glass	1637
54.	Horners	1638
55.	Farriers	1674
56.	Paviors	1479
57.	Loriners	1261
58.	Apothecaries	1617
59.	Shipwrights	1387
60.	Spectacle Makers	1629
61.	Clockmakers	1631
62.	Glovers	1349
63.	Feltmakers	1604
64.	Framework Knitters	1657
65.	Needlemakers	1656
66.	Gardeners	1605
67.	Tin Plate Workers	1670
68.	Wheelwrights	1670
69.	Distillers	1638
70.	Pattenmakers	1670
71.	Glass Sellers	1664
72.	Coachmakers	1677

73.	Gunmakers	1637
74.	Gold & Silver Wyre Drawers	1693
75.	Makers of Playing Cards	1628
76.	Fan Makers	1709
77.	Carmen	1517
78.	Master Mariners	1926
79.	Solicitors	1944
80.	Farmers	1952
81.	Air Pilots & Navigators	1929
82.	Tobacco Pipe Makers	1619
83.	Furniture Makers	1963
84.	Scientific Instrument Makers	1955
85.	Chartered Surveyors	1976
86.	Chartered Accountants	1977
87.	Chartered Secretaries	1977
88.	Builders' Merchants	1961
89.	Launderers	1960
90.	Marketors	1977
91.	Actuaries	1979
92.	Insurers	1979
93.	Arbitrators	1981
94.	Engineers	1983
95.	Fuellers	1984
96.	Lightmongers	1979
97.	Environmental Cleaners	1972
98.	Chartered Architects	1985
99.	Constructors	1976
100.	Information Technologists	1992
101.	World Traders	2000
102.	Water Conservators	2000
103.	Firefighters	2001

Information obtained from ***The Livery Companies of the City of London*** produced by the Corporation of London Public Relations Office. First published March 1997; second Edition published December 2001

Companies without Livery:
Parish Clerks
Watermen & Lightermen
Hackney Carriage Drivers
Management Consultants
Tax Advisers

INDEX

Page numbers in *italic* refer to illustrations and captions

C

G

H

S. PAULES CH
THAMESIS
The Eell Schipes
The Bear Gardne